ZELZELAH

ZELZELAH
A woman before her time

MARIAM BEHNAM

MOTIVATE
PUBLISHING

Dedicated to the fond memory
of my late husband Abdullah Pakravan

Published by Motivate Publishing

PO Box 2331, Dubai, UAE
Tel: (04) 824060, Fax: (04) 824436

PO Box 43072, Abu Dhabi, UAE
Tel: (02) 311666, Fax: (02) 311888

London House, 26/40 Kensington High Street, London W8 4PF
Tel: (071) 938 2222, Fax: (071) 937 7293

First published 1994

ISBN 1 873544 52 9

Printed by Emirates Printing Press, UAE

British Library Cataloguing-in-Publication Data.
A catalogue record for this book is available
from the British Library.

CONTENTS

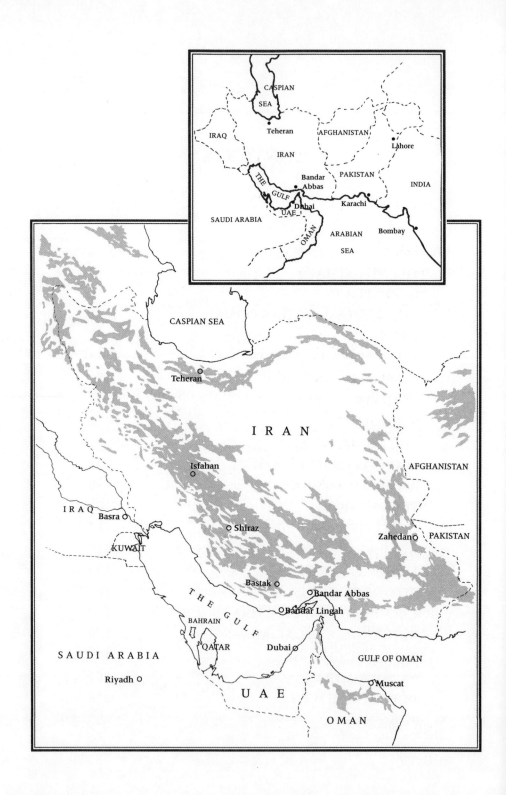

PREFACE

When I was a child, my long-suffering grandmother scolded me with the words: "May your grandchildren torment you as you torment me." It must have been the worst thing she could think of and, like most of the things she wished of me — things like conformity, obedience, demure and ladylike behaviour — it was not to be. But then she lived, quite simply, in a different world. I remember it like one remembers a restless night full of unfulfilled dreams.

Life is so full of surprises that sometimes they even surprise you when you relive them through the retelling. My grandchildren have been great ones for prompting memories. "Were you naughty?" one would ask. Well, perhaps a little but of course I never thought of it like that. "What games did you play?" another would interject, and before there was time to answer, a third would pipe up: "Did you ride in a *doroshkah*? What sort of school did you go to?" The questions tumbled out of these young minds faster than I could answer.

Friends from time to time have also inundated me with questions. How did you get out of Iran? What impact did the Revolution have on you? Did you shock everyone by fighting so publicly for social reforms in your day? As a champion of women's causes, did you ever fear for your life? How does such a restless spirit as you now cope with retirement?

Questions, always questions. The more I was asked, the more I remembered, until one day I found myself talking to a tape-recorder. Then the memories unrolled like a carpet and I became fascinated by the rich textures and the interlocking patterns that have been my life.

At the end of my 'magic carpet ride' was this book. It is

simply a record of my life. Being the second and therefore rather unwanted daughter of a conservative, aristocratic family, fate left me two options: I could sit patiently behind closed doors and let things take their course, or I could roll up my sleeves and fight my way out of the stifling environment so characteristic of southern Iran in the early 1920s.

I opted for the latter. Again and again I broke barriers. Through childhood into student life; from local politics to a career as a diplomat and through nightmares of riots, civil violence and destruction, war and revolution I fought against prejudice, and in so doing achieved what was rightfully mine: a richly fulfilled life.

My motto, and my advice to my children and young friends has always been: "Don't sit behind closed doors — give your best to whatever you do." This has served me well. As I watch with delight I can see my children and grandchildren, nieces and nephews take up that same challenge. Life's pattern continues to unfold.

Living in a wonderful place like Dubai has given me the peace of mind to write my autobiography. The environment is conducive to reminiscing and thinking creatively. Though Dubai today is a modern and fully-developed state which can compete with any advanced land in the world, the old charm, the familiar people, culture and traditional sentiments recall bygone days.

I have been singularly lucky in life: the devotion and support of friends and family have sustained me through some critical moments. This book was written in part to say thank you. Forgive me, dear friends, if I have not mentioned you, or if my memory has served me less than perfectly; that trickster, old age, has been knocking at my door for some time now.

But above all, this book is for my most persistent questionners — my beloved children and grandchildren. Let these memories of the past help you understand the present and shape the future.

MB
Dubai, 1994

CHAPTER 1

THE PILGRIMAGE

The door was firmly closed. I sat, a modest figure, draped in black, and waited. The year was 1991, the hour still quite early, around 8.30, a beautiful spring morning. It was that peaceful time of day when I loved a leisurely cup of tea in the fresh air and shade of my garden. I could almost smell the oleanders and taste the tea now. I fidgeted and sighed deeply, wishing I was there at this precise moment, instead of sitting on a hard wooden chair in an impersonal and increasingly crowded room. In the old days...

Eight-thirty became nine and still not a sign of activity from inside. It was going to be hot, judging by the cloudless blue sky, a typical April day in Dubai. I adjusted my *abaya* for the umpteenth time. It was irritating me, and its blackness seemed to soak up the heat. I felt stifled, my impatience and frustration increasing with the passing minutes. What could be so very difficult about a visa? Part of me wanted to turn around and go; I never was very good at waiting. Another part of me wanted to grasp the handle and open the door myself. In the old days, the Consul-General himself would have been there to greet me. We would have passed a pleasant few minutes while whatever business took me there was being attended to. But those days were past, swept away with the changing times, and I was annoyed with myself for even thinking about them.

So I waited. Doubt and uncertainty kept re-appearing, little cracks in the stone wall of my resolve: "Why am I putting myself through this? What will my family and friends say? Why should I need a visa to get back into Iran? Iran! What will happen if I am recognised?" I had asked myself these questions and so many more in the days and nights since I had made up my mind to visit the homeland engraved in my memory. There were no easy answers to any of them.

Nine-thirty became ten, and then the door opened and I was ushered into a room.

"Mariam Behnam. Who is this person? The name sounds familiar." A man's voice echoed loudly in the next room and my heart pounded.

"Excuse me *khanom*," a polite young man said to me, "would you wait outside a little longer? Your papers are not quite ready." He smiled apologetically and, sensing my unease, suggtested: "Why don't you go home and return at noon?"

"No, no, it's all right," I said nervously, "I'll wait."

I stood and shuffled back to my chair. I felt close to snapping; not a pleasant sensation, nor one I had experienced more than once or twice before. I recalled momentarily how I used to supervise officials not much different to these, and entertain their superiors up to the highest level with not a flicker of nerves. Chiding myself for being such an old woman, I suddenly thought: "But I am an old woman." It was just that I had never felt like it before.

Ten-thirty became eleven. The heat intensified. Life flowed in front of me and I sat still – a black statue not daring to think or hope. All I could do was wait.

At last the door opened once more. It was the pleasant young man. In a daze I accepted my passport. In it was the precious visa. My journey home was ready to start.

Twelve years had passed since I had set foot on Iranian soil – a score of years since my fearful flight from a land I had served tirelessly and loved deeply. It was a long time … too long. Too long to be separated from your roots, the very things that give your life meaning and purpose, and the people you share them with. As surely as life goes on, some things are never left behind, and now in my adopted home, the faces and laughter of my childhood and younger years filled my dreams, beckoning me. In the middle of the night I would awake in confusion – had I not fled in fear for my life? How could I then go back, and knowing the answer to this, why was my otherwise practical, pragmatic mind tormenting me with the very idea?

It troubled me for months, and knowing what my family would say if I shared my worries with them, I didn't. But I must have known in my heart of hearts there could only be one way of dealing with my unresolved questions, and during Ramadan, the holy month of fasting, I made my decision. I would go back to Iran, whatever the risk.

"You're mad, Mariam," said my friends. "You must be joking, Mama," my daughter Shirin exclaimed – it was April Fools Day when I announced my plans. But they could tell by the look in my eye that my mind was made up, and knowing me all too well, consoled themselves with sighs, tuts, a few tears – and then got down to helping me with my preparations.

One week later I climbed the steps to the airplane for the short hop over the Gulf from Dubai to Iran. My heart was in my throat as the plane roared down the runway and took off into the cloudless blue sky. Below on the sparkling turquoise waters of the Gulf the little wooden dhows that plied back and forth between these same two countries mingled with tankers and container ships. As we descended, Iran's mountainous coast came into view. Then we were down. When the doors opened again, we were in Bandar Abbas, and I smelled again the sweet scent of the *bad-e-Nowrooz,* the breeze of the New Year. It was the smell of home! There was no turning back, but even had I been given that choice, I would never have taken it. I had waited too long for this. Something told me every thing would be all right.

Nobody knew I was coming until I was almost there. An hour before takeoff, Shirin phoned her cousins in Bandar Abbas. "Khala Ziba," she said, "please go and collect Mama – she is on her way." Amid tears and laughter they did just that, then whisked me away from the airport, and I was back with the family I loved dearly.

I did not know what to expect: Bandar Abbas had changed – it looked bigger and so crowded, almost unrecognisable with so many buildings and new construction. It was heartening to read signs like 'Open University' and 'Medical College'. I promised myself the opportunity to explore later: For the moment, with no definite plans, I was content – and perhaps prudent too – to stay at home with my dear ones around me. "Mama, be careful," they advised, "we won't venture out. There could be a snake sneaking somewhere. If people come to know you are in Iran after all these years ..."

All these years: My mind was crowded with memories of the many happy and productive years that I had spent in Bandar Abbas with my husband, Pakravan. Now this 'once looked down upon' town held little for me. Somehow I had to leave its dusty confines. I knew I had to travel somehow to Bastak, the home of my ancestors, and to Bandar Lingah, where I was born. But doors started to open. Mohammad Shahini, an old family friend, came to the rescue. The passage of time had done nothing to dampen his sense of humour. "Madam," he said, bowing low, "your chauffeur. Your command is my pleasure!" And so the journey began.

Up the coast we drove, to Bandar Lingah, a once bustling and important port in the days of thriving sea trade with other Gulf ports, India and Africa, but now lonely and deathly silent – a little town sleeping through the long hot days of Ramadan to awaken after sunset. As I stood by the dome-shaped water reservoir built by my grandfather, known as *berkah-e-Abbas*, memories of my youth flooded in. Tears blurred my vision when I saw the ruin of one of our former homes, a desolate pile of rubble denying my happy recollections of childhood.

North of Bandar Lingah in the hills lies the town of Bastak, once ruled by the Khans, the Bani Abbasis, descendants of the Khalifat of Baghdad, who migrated there in the Eighth Century. It is a centre where, for hundreds of years, men of letters, thinkers, artists, philosophers and religious leaders had come to teach and learn. It was the birthplace of my ancestors and yet in all my travels it was a place I had never visited. It drew me like a magnet.

In Bastak I particularly wanted to view the *mazar* of one of my most famous and revered ancestors, Haji Mulla Ahmed Arshi, who had lived and taught four centuries ago. By my visit to the town and to this tomb, I had hoped to gain a meaningful link with the past.

The new road from Lingah was clear and we made good time, arriving at sunset. The long shadows were casting their warm glowing shapes when I walked up the steps towards the elaborately painted tomb adjacent to the beautiful mosque, Jame Masjid, a landmark in Bastak. Devotees travelled regularly to pray at the beautiful tomb; a crowd of them now surrounded me. I paused before stepping through the old, intricately carved wooden door, inlaid with turquoise which gave off a bright blue glow. Inside it was cool and dark. A green satin cloth covered a simple grave where the remains of the great man lay. I bowed in reverence. I felt light-headed from my day-long fast, but intensely alert and I was awed by the thought that I was part of a long line stretching back 12 generations and more.

The sudden bang of the cannon and the *muezzin's* call of *"Allah-o-Akbar"* – God is Great – announced it was time for prayers and *Iftar*, the end of the day's fast. Dates appeared mysteriously. There appeared to be no one around taking care of the tomb. I looked at my friend Mahmood Bastaki, my gracious host on this trip, and then at the faces of other fellow pilgrims, and saw the same thoughts reflected. We ate the dates thankfully.

As I stepped out into the soft, purplish dusk I turned to say *"Fiamanallah"* – with God's protection. I paused again and a sudden, mischievously irreverent thought which I couldn't suppress crossed my mind. It was as though a door opened and my past swept through, and I could hear my sharp-tongued grandmother, whom we called Monkhali, 'the mother of uncle' lecturing me after another of my numerous pranks: "Zelzelah Bibi, you will have our ancestors turning in their graves!"

It made me wonder, standing there at the tomb of my revered ancestor, whether my whole life had kept these same ancestors in perpetual motion. I took heart in another one of Monkhali's sayings, one which I have lived by. "Never under-value yourself," she would tell me. I'm sure that, although I might have shocked the ancestors, they would have admired me, albeit perhaps grudgingly, for what I achieved, despite the fact that I am 'only a woman'.

It is perhaps sad but true that many men simply do not understand the strength and power that women are capable of wielding. Muslim society has since time immemorial been a patriarchal one and the Muslim religion, while teaching that women are equally important, has condoned and encouraged this way of life, for it is practical. It ensures that men will look after the safety of the woman and her family.

For all that my family was thoroughly traditional, it was the women who were the dominant forces in our huge household. Little wonder then that I grew up with a belief in the strength of will of the female character. All the influential women in my life – my great-grandmother, my grandmother and my mother – wielded a power even over the men that seemed to me to be limitless, even though it was all behind closed doors.

My destiny was to be the first woman of our family to open those doors. Since daring to walk out of the first one, many doors have been opened and closed on me. The experiences – some good, some bad and some incredibly painful – have ultimately enriched my life.

I was born in 1921 – not so long ago really, but in other respects in a different age. Nobody is sure of my exact date of birth for such things were not always recorded in those days; though, if the child was considered an important addition to the family, a note would be made on the back of one of the pages of the Holy Quran. Being the second child, and even worse a female, I certainly wasn't considered important enough for such a record. However, all who were around at the time remember the year of my birth as the year of the terrible earthquake in Bandar Lingah. Because of this I was known as 'Zelzelah Bibi' – Little Miss Earthquake – and wasn't called by my given name Mariam until I was five or six years old.

Truthfully though, I have to say there was another reason this name seemed appropriate and that was because I was always the one to cause a commotion and upheaval in our family. If there were loud noises in the house or anything was broken, I was usually blamed. "Where is Mariam? She must be

around. That Zelzelah Bibi! She will destroy everything!"
During my childhood, they even tried to blame me for the
death of my baby brother and for natural disasters. I came out
looking so much worse, because my older sister, Fatma, true to
her name, was a good and noble child. She had an important
position in our family for she was the eldest daughter and, as
such, was treated as a sacred being, for there was a belief that
the first child, if named Fatma, would be the saviour of her
parents in the life hereafter.

"Why can't you be like your sister?" people would chide me.
I hated it when they used to compare us. It was true – we were
poles apart. Fatma was soft-spoken and gentle; she respected
her elders and obeyed them absolutely and unconditionally,
which I found difficult to do. On reflection, I can understand
how in some ways I must have seemed as bad and destructive
as that earthquake. Nowadays we would probably dismiss such
behaviour, saying "Oh, she's just a little girl looking for
attention."

But things were different then to what they are today; it was
a difficult world in which to be an individual, especially an
individual woman. I realise now that I was lucky to have had
that added impetus of having to prove to my family and the
world that I was someone to take note of. Without it, I could
never have accomplished all that I did.

CHAPTER 2

EARLY YEARS IN LINGAH

I grew up in a large and wealthy household in the most important port in Iran at that time – Bandar Lingah. It is a town deep in the south of Iran, but because of its position the townspeople have always had closer ties and felt more akin to the Arabs of the Gulf region than their own compatriots in central and northern 'Persia' as it was once known. The only languages commonly heard in Lingah in those days were the local Farsi dialects of Bastaki and Awazi, and Arabic.

The port area bustled with trade, ships constantly arriving and departing for the various sheikhdoms, kingdoms and sultanates in the Gulf region and India, Africa and even Europe. Huge *booms* belonging to a few wealthy families used to sail out of the port several times a year filled with aromatic and medicinal herbs, tobacco, goatskins and shells and return with holds full of sacks and boxes of rice and tea, shoes, sandals, textiles and building materials, and often with slaves. Ocean-going steamships of the British India Company also visited the port several times a week. These were large iron ships of about 3,000 tonnes and carried cargo and passengers. Being such a prosperous place, Bandar Lingah attracted foreign merchants and traders, and several countries set up consulates. In fact, Iran's first airport was built in Lingah.

Well I remember the day, sometime in the 1920s, when the first aeroplane flew overhead like a huge and ungainly bird. Everyone was awed and a little frightened by the prospect of something unknown and ominous. We rushed to the rooftop. "Come down immediately!" the elders cried out. "It might fall on your heads!" They brooded over this air-borne intrusion, shaking their heads and quoting from classical Persian poets who had predicted "a time would arrive when man will be seen flying in the sky..." "What next?" they asked each other.

Lingah was an active little town, with plenty to entertain foreigners and citizens alike – theatres, stadiums, clubs. Cricket, football, hockey and tennis were popular then as they are now, though for a girl there was no opportunity to take part in or watch anything of this kind. I remember as a child watching my father dash in and out of the house, clad in white, and carrying a tennis racket or a cricket bat. The people were not just commercially ambitious, but forged ahead culturally and educationally as well. Some of the first elementary and high schools in Iran were founded in Lingah and boys were sent to study law, medicine, engineering and business at universities in India, Paris and London. Many of the most important families in Lingah during the early '20s are among the best-known families living all around the Gulf region and spread around the world today.

Though Lingah was our home, my family originally came from Bastak, a town a little way inland and up in the mountains. Known as Bastakis, we spoke a dialect of our own. Over the centuries Bastak has been considered a special haven for scholars and *sufis*. Being situated up in the mountains it was the perfect place to live in peace and pursue knowledge. In fact for a while it was even known as Darul Aman, a house of security.

There are conflicting theories on how, when and where the people who originally settled in Bastak came from. Generally it is thought that most came from Baghdad and some from Madina and Taif. However, there is a belief that a few came from Afghanistan, a theory possibly borne out by the fair complexions, delicate, attractive features and green eyes of some Bastaki families.

The word *bast* means 'closed' or 'to take shelter', so it is very likely that the people who came to the Gulf were having problems in their country of origin and obviously found the hilly, closed-in areas around Bastak to their liking. It is said that many first went to the Gulf states but were not comfortable in the hot, arid desert region, so they travelled on until they found a place with a more moderate climate.

Wherever our ancient roots lie, there have been many noted religious leaders in our family. The most important man in my time was Great-uncle Sheikh Abdul Rahman Mohammad Yousuf, who was a Sultan-Al-Olema, a title granted after he completed his studies at Al Azhar University, the oldest in Cairo and the greatest institute of Islamic learning in the world. He was considered the authority on all religious and scholarly matters.

The Sheikh was indeed quite an exceptional man, spending his life studying and teaching. His library in Lingah was considered one of the most magnificent in Iran. He always believed that there was little difference between a teacher and a student. "There is always something more to be learned," he would say.

As Sultan-Al-Olema, he was a community leader; he constructed several *berkahs* and other civic amenities and set up theosophical schools and hostels in Lingah, Bastak, Saudi Arabia and Dubai. In those days, and in a society where social responsibilities were long established as customs, rather than law, wealthy families undertook to improve the community by building berkahs, guest-houses and schools at their expense for the benefit of all. Anyone who wished to study could therefore do so, free of charge.

It seems that scholarship runs in the family; Great-uncle Sheikh's son, Sheikh Mohammad Ali, took over from him and is the present Sultan-Al-Olema. He has turned our old house in Lingah into a theosophical school. His extensively researched book in Arabic on the history of Lingah was published in two volumes in Dubai, and his Centre for Islamic Studies opened in Dubai in 1993.

Between them, these two remarkable men have written several books, in Arabic and Farsi, which are part of the regular curriculum in many theosophical institutions throughout the Islamic world.

My family is also connected through marriage with the Bani Abbasi family, the famous Khans, who ruled over vast areas of the region for centuries and whose magnificent palaces are still standing in Bastak. Descendants of this family are the handsome and cultured Mostafa Bin Abdul Latifs, who now live mainly in Bahrain and Dubai.

As children – especially daughters – of a wealthy family, our whole way of life was aristocratic and conservative in the extreme. I was taught from an early age to understand the concept of traditionalism. However, as I grew older I also began to understand that traditions, though valuable as guidelines, can impose a stifling influence on growth, development and especially individuality.

My great-grandfather was the head of our household, but he died while I was quite young so the most important man that I remember well was his second son, Great-uncle Farooq. We were all, in fact, known as the Farooq family. I remember him as a tall and impressive figure with a thunderous voice. He always wore boots with iron heels so that he made a great deal of noise when he walked. Any important domestic problems or disputes were always taken to him, for he was a wise, just man and once he had made his decision it was considered final and there was no higher appeal. Everyone was a little frightened of Great-uncle Farooq.

Not only was he an important man in our family but he was a towering personality in the entire Gulf region, and was widely known for his contribution to the development of trade in the whole area. He was one of the first of the Bastakis to move to Dubai where he built a great fort-like house and so laid the foundations of the Bastakia Mohalla which is one of the oldest residential areas in Dubai, just on the edge of the Creek. A few of the picturesque windtowers that stood like sentinels above the houses throughout the district still can be seen.

Great-uncle Farooq was respected as a man of fierce integrity; this combined with a sound and intelligent mind produced a brilliant businessman. He was also an adept horseman and his association with the late Agha Khan, the spiritual leader of the Ismailis, was based on their mutual passion for horses as well as their love for Persian literature.

His first wife was a daughter of the Fikree family but she died young, leaving three sons. He then married Fatma, the niece of the Sheikh Sultan-Al-Olema. This great-aunt, Haji Fatma, whom we called Zinkhali, was also an uncommon person, for she was a scholar in her own right and the kindest and most loving lady I have ever known. Her door was open to anybody whether young or old, rich or poor; she received everyone in the same softly-spoken way, giving support and strength to all. Her petite frame and fine, delicate features belied the energy that she possessed. She was always smiling. I was often calmed by her tranquillity that could never be ruffled.

Even when Great-uncle Farooq was away for long periods of time, she always received him on his return with dignity and a smile. She bore him two sons, Mohammad Amin who married my older sister Fatma, and Mohammad Akil.

In those days members of our family only married within the family and never outsiders. Occasionally though such a marriage did take place. One such was that of Father's brother, *Ami* Abdul Rahman. A notorious playboy in his youth, he caught a glimpse of a beautiful woman through the porthole of a ship in which he was travelling, and declared he would marry no other but this wondrous beauty from Saudi Arabia.

The family were not pleased and made every effort to dissuade him. Finally Great-uncle Farooq was consulted. He mulled over the situation, then pronounced: "The family is not giving a daughter away to outsiders but bringing a daughter in from outside." This was permissible and so in the end Uncle Abdul Rahman married the lovely Zohra, who indeed made a welcome addition to the family for she was very cultured and spoke several languages. For me, however, it later proved to be a fateful connection, though not a particularly happy one.

Zinkhali needed all the strength and courage she could muster to be married to a man such as Great-uncle Farooq, for during their marriage he actually wed three other women from well-known families. One of these wives was from the ruling Al Qasimi family of Sharjah. He also married a daughter of Sheikh Mostafa bin Abdul Latif, one of the community leaders and philanthropists from Bastak, and by this marriage had a daughter.

However, the woman with whom he spent the last two decades of his life was a Tunisian. They lived in Arcachon near Bordeaux but they travelled constantly between Paris and London until the Second World War. Their only child, a daughter named Faiqa, proved to be quite an exceptional woman for she became the first Arab Ambassadress and has represented

Tunisia in such places as Senegal and England and at the United Nations in New York.

Throughout Great-uncle's life an office was maintained in Rue Lafayette in Paris. At least once a year he visited the Gulf, but always on his own. It was not until 1982 that Faiqa, fulfilling a long-cherished dream to visit the land that her father had told her so much about, came to Dubai. I was thrilled to finally meet her for throughout my growing years (we were of a similar age) I was inspired by the stories I had heard of her. I was also secretly envious of the opportunities she had had, for she was well-educated and fortunate enough to have lived without the restrictions that so hindered me. But life has a funny way of colouring our perceptions – it seems she also had been looking forward to meeting me, for she had been told so many stories about my exploits.

As for Great-uncle Farooq, he seemed to disappear from our lives, especially during the upheaval in Europe through the Second World War. We were living in Karachi at the time, and his mother and sister, Monkhali Gappi and Monkhali Kingely, would wander around the house sighing and wondering where he was. Monkhali Gappi spent a great deal of time on her prayer mat praying loudly for his safe return. The whole family was desperate to know of his whereabouts and so one day, on hearing about a particularly good *faqir* who could foretell the future, we decided to pay him a visit.

This remarkable and extremely religious man lived on a small and barren island; how he managed to even survive was incredible and awe-inspiring. We approached him and asked the question that was preying on everyone's mind: Would we see Great-uncle Farooq again? The gaunt-looking holy man sat silent and still. When, after what seemed like an eternity, he finally spoke it was barely a whisper.

"He will appear in disguise and stay only a while before he leaves on a long journey," said the *faqir*. This of course was enough for us. We were overjoyed and went home to wait for his return.

Months passed, and then one night Mabmoodi, one of our *gholooms*, came running upstairs to say that an exhausted traveller was asking to stay the night. "He is most unkempt in appearance, has piercing eyes and a long beard. It is strange for he speaks Bastaki and seems to know about the members of the family. He is asking many personal questions. He says he only wants a small space in the *majlis* to sleep. Is it safe *Bibi* to let him in?"

"Why not?" Monkhali answered. "Feed the stranger, look after him and we will find out who he is in the morning."

Next day pandemonium broke loose, for the 'stranger' of course turned out to be Great-uncle Farooq. He was sick – doctors had given him six months to live – and had taken many risks and employed every method of travel to reach his home and family in order to spend his last days with us and to organise his affairs.

To us he seemed a changed man, no longer the stern and aloof disciplinarian of our younger years, for until his death a few months later he was always cheerful and very loving. He played chess and draughts with his children and grandchildren, he renewed contacts with old friends and he loved to hear me read classical Persian poetry. I was continually astounded by his remarkable mind for he often recited verse after verse from memory. It made it all the sadder when Great-uncle Farooq departed on his final journey.

If Great-uncle was the head of our extended family, it was my grandmother, Monkhali Kingely, tiny but strong-willed, strict but loving, who looked after the actual day-to-day running of the household. Her life was a bit of a tangled web, held together by the glue of her own forceful personality. My mother, Hafsa Abbas, was Monkhali's only child; she might have had more children except that she left my grandfather, Haji Abbas, when he married another woman. Although polygamy was quite legal, and men often had three or four wives, my grandmother refused to share his affections with another. The only daughter among four sons, Monkhali was very special to her parents, who tried to no avail to change her mind. She had a strong personality, and was used to getting her own way and being treated as a cherished individual. We never knew our grandfather until many years later.

Monkhali was more of a parent to my three sisters, my brother and myself, than our own father and mother. Perhaps we were the other children she herself never had. She was certainly qualified by blood for the job – as well as being our grandmother, she was our great-aunt because my father, Abdul Wahid, was her nephew.

Father was often away from home, either travelling or studying, so that it was around my mother that our life seemed to revolve. She was lovely but aloof and was always treated with special care and deference. To us, the children, she seemed incredibly dazzling. I was not surprised to see people, when they came to visit her, kiss her hand and call her *maleka*. Magnificent but unapproachable though she was, in the insular world in which I lived, she was the most precious person I knew.

The earliest memories I have of my mother are of her being beautifully dressed in colourful, gold-embroidered *thobes* waiting for my father to come home. Her love and adoration for him encompassed her entire existence. We children weren't really part of their world at all.

Father was a few years younger than my mother and their marriage had been arranged by her family, but it had been done quite hastily to prevent my mother being married to a man of her father's choice.

The rift between Monkhali and her husband Haji Abbas had been very deep and although mother never met her father during her childhood he still felt he had the right to make the decision of who she would marry. Consequently he promised her to his nephew.

When my mother reached marriageable age, a ship was sent to Lingah to take her and her chaperones to Haji Abbas's house in Bombay. The news spread like wildfire and a sense of tragedy filled the town. The audacity of the man!

The situation had to be dealt with sharply and wisely. Monkhali and her family could not bear the thought of their precious child being taken from them, so they married her to my father, who just so happened to be the first eligible cousin available. The ship and Haji Abbas's representatives had to return to Bombay bearing shocking news: "She is already married to her cousin Abdul Wahid." Haji Abbas was so angry he disinherited his daughter then and there. Besides, he had plenty of other children by the wives he had married over the years.

For Monkhali this was a double triumph – she had managed to hold on to what was most precious to her and, at the same time, show that in this instance her family had been able to exert more influence than the equally wealthy and powerful Abbas family.

Mother did eventually meet her father many years later, during her last fateful pregnancy. They were reconciled and Haji Abbas vowed he would change his will and acknowledge her as his daughter with a rightful claim to a part of his legendary wealth. My mother, having all the material things she desired, was not concerned with his wealth but was delighted that the separation had ended. On her bedside table she had always had a photo of him, dressed in an impressive gold embroidered *aba* with a gold *khanjar* at his waist. It was taken with his entourage on one of his visits to the House of Commons in London, events which were written up at length in the local papers in the 1930s.

Looking back with the more experienced eyes of an adult I don't really know if my parents' marriage could be thought of as a happy one, for father was away a great deal and often all mother had to comfort her and remind her of the great love of her life was a new baby. In all she bore eight children, though only five of us survived through infancy – Fatma, myself, Ahmed Noor, Bibiya and Badria. Mother would sing lullabies to her latest newborn as she sat in her private chamber that remained decorated throughout her life as a *hijla* or bridal room. She never wanted it changed, for I don't believe she ever lost the feeling of being a new bride waiting anxiously for her husband.

In those days a bridal room, and a bridal dress, took almost a year to prepare. Firstly, the walls and ceiling of the room were completely covered with gold brocade, then a number of mirrors of different shapes and sizes were mounted and finally numerous coloured glass baubles were hung from the ceiling. An elaborate, crystal chandelier was the main lighting in the room and, with the addition of assorted delicate but glittering gold and silver ornaments on the shelves, the whole room had an exotic sparkle and glow. This sight was meant only for the eyes of the newly-married couple.

The only furniture in this splendid room was a massive bed and huge mirrored cupboards, although there were many colourful gold embroidered cushions called *mokhadas* scattered around and arranged against the walls. A curtain of gauze netting was hung over the bed, so that it seemed to become a secret alcove within this whole intensely private area.

A simpler room was attached to this glamorous chamber where mother fed her babies and it was here that we were summoned when she wanted to see us. On those rare occasions sometimes we would be lucky enough to glimpse the splendour and glitter of the *hijla*. To me it looked like the legendary cave of Ali Baba.

One of the delights of our home life was listening to mother sing. She had a lovely voice and sang devotional songs and sometimes even popular Indian tunes with Persian verses. My appreciation and attachment to Amir Khusrau's *ghazals* and *qawwalis* stem from those days. Khusrau was the 13th century genius who made a happy blending of Arab, Persian and Central Asian music with traditional classical music, laying the foundation of the composite culture which has been handed down to us. Mother used to recite Persian verses from the *Masnavi* of Moulana Rumi in Khusrau's Darbari style – to the delight of her selective audience. She had a love for music and played the harmonium well. Often I would sneak into the room to try it out, and in time was able to teach myself how to play reasonably well.

I loved music and as a pastime it gave me real pleasure. It is my sister Bibiya though, who really inherited our mother's talent and, had she been trained, I'm sure she would have become a brilliant vocalist. However, at that time, such an idea would have mortified our family. They weren't entirely against music for we did own gramophones but the only songs allowed to be sung were those of a devotional nature. Any other songs were considered frivolous and any natural musical talent was certainly not encouraged.

Life in our large household was restrictive in so many ways, stifling to an active, inquisitive child. Our paternal family all lived under the same roof, though in Bandar Lingah we actually had two houses with several outhouses attached. The house surrounded a courtyard garden shaded by almond, *lowz,* Bombay *berr,* date palm and lemon trees. Aromatic shrubs and jasmin flowers which we picked and threaded into bouquets for our hair grew round about. The house where my great-grandparents lived was the original family home; it was known as *khoone zeer* or lower house and was more than two centuries old. The newer, larger, fort-like house where I grew up was known as *khoone bara* or upper house; huge and elegant, it had 60 rooms and five windtowers. The windtower is an attractive and useful addition to a building, for in the years before electricity, it helped to keep the house cool. It is a structure about 15 metres high and looks like a conventional tower but is open on all four sides, so that a breeze from any direction will be caught and directed downwards to the room below. Most normal-sized houses had one or two windtowers and, without them, life during the summer would have been almost unbearable.

We also maintained large houses in Bombay, Bahrain, Dubai, Karachi and Paris. Renting a house was out of the question and because the family usually spent at least a year at a time away from home base when we did travel, it was necessary to have a house in all the places we visited.

Our family business was selling and distributing commodities such as textiles, building materials and particularly pearls on a wholesale basis. Towards the end of the '20s and the early '30s, pearl fishing in the Gulf was one of the most important industries, and Lingah rivalled even Bahrain for the quantity and quality of the pearls found. In fact, one type of mother-of-pearl shell sold in Europe by one of the leading merchants was known in Germany as the Lingah shell.

The pearls were normally graded and traded in Bombay where Europeans, especially the French, went to buy them. Being important pearl merchants, my maternal grandfather, Haji Abbas, as well as my father and uncles visited Paris often and spent a great deal of time (and money) in the cosmopolitan capital of France. From what I gather, some of them, particularly the young men, were prominent participants in *'la belle epoque'*, living it up abroad in a society without the traditions and restrictions imposed by our own. They truly led two distinctly different lives.

But, of course, the womenfolk never accompanied the men to such far away and alien places. We seldom left the four high walls of our home, though we accompanied the men around the Gulf region and to India, when they had business there, for their work could take at least a year at a time. Even when we did travel, there was no real feeling of coming out from behind those walls, for wherever we went, it was as a household – servants, retainers, and even the *mullah* and a *muezzin* always came with us.

I remember travelling aboard ships, usually steamers of the British India Company, where half the ship was reserved just for our party. The first-class cabins would be taken by the men and any newly-wed couples, while the women, with their personal maids and other attendants, plus the children would be made comfortable in the second-class area. The male retainers would have the deck.

Besides this, our party also took up a great deal of the freight area for, along with crates full of furnishings, cooking utensils and personal effects, were goats and gunny bags full of rice and other grains. We always took our own food, concerned I think that what would be available in foreign lands would be unclean and not prepared in the Islamic way.

Although we travelled in great style and on a grand scale, all the same restrictions and routines applied. The only exception to this was when we travelled during the stormy, monsoon times and almost everybody would be too seasick to care what happened. I was one of the lucky few who did not suffer from seasickness, and would take advantage of the situation and, unless I was actually chained to my groaning nanny's bed, I could roam whenever and wherever I liked for nobody had the strength to reprimand me. Those days at sea in the Gulf and Indian Ocean were the only times I ever knew any real freedom as a child; other than on those trips, I was constantly guarded and spent most of my time indoors.

It seemed there was seldom excitement in Bandar Lingah, but when there was, it was frightening. I remember only too well the terror of a devastating fire in the neighbourhood. Several houses were burned down. "Our house will be next!" the women screamed in panic. With no fire brigade or running water, people rushed to the sea, *berkahs* and wells with whatever they could hold together to carry water to fight the flames. Black smoke blotted out the sun for days. It was terrifying. All the women could do was run up and down watching the frantic activity in the streets all around them and shout orders, pray and shout at the children as if they actually expected us to sit still and wait.

Nobody ever let me forget about the bad earthquake which accompanied my entrance into the world, but as I had not experienced any tremors, I wondered what it felt like. Some months after the big fire, a terrible earthquake shook Lingah and the area around it. I have since been through earthquakes in Lahore and Bandar Abbas, but this one in particular is stamped in my memory. I was about six years old. Sand storms and torrential rain, punctuated with severe tremors that continued for three days, made it difficult either to stay indoors or run outdoors. "Keep quiet and pray," the women admonished the children. "It is God's curse! Human beings are not obeying Allah enough – this is to be expected." We ran for one of the great stone doorways, the safest place to be during a tremor.

I remember locust plagues during the summer, but we had our own way of dealing with these. When they swarmed into the town eating everything they landed on, servants and children were sent out to catch them. What fun and excitement. All of us ran with a cloth bag in our hands, chasing these welcome and at the same time unwanted visitors: while farmers feared for their crops, naughty children loved the sudden break in their dull day-to-day routine. We then got our revenge for we roasted them fresh and ate them – they were quite delicious!

Because life indoors during the earliest years of my life could be tedious, my happiest memories are of summertime in Bandar Lingah, when the hot, dry weather forced us outside onto the flat roof of our house. During this season, our family lived on the upper floors; the windtower rooms were wonderful cool havens, but at night when it was too hot even in these rooms, we slept out under the stars. I loved those hot summer nights for it meant our routine changed. It was exciting just to be outside, though of course under constant supervision. I remember those delightful nights well.

Nearing sunset, *gholooms* loaded with *koozas*, Monkhali's *qalyoon*, a type of water pipe that she loved to smoke, lanterns, fans, food, cutlery, crockery, rugs and prayer mats, would climb the steep ladder-like stairs to the rooftop. They would then put bedding and carpets on the large *sablas* which were raised platforms with coverings like tents to protect us from insects and reptiles. Especially during the hot, dry summers there would be plenty of these, as even the most cautious snake would be attracted to the water in our jugs and urns. After sunset we would all eagerly and excitedly clamber up out into the open. To be outside and to see the large assembled group that made up our family was a rare and interesting experience for usually each family group stayed in its own rooms and its members lived their own lives. Out in the open it was not always easy to maintain this segregation, especially as eavesdropping on the conversations and goings-on of neighbours was a favourite pastime of summer nights. Many a good story was told after an especially clear night.

Fortunately our house, unlike many in the town, was not joined to others and our roof was even large enough to be sectioned off for couples and different families, so it meant we had some chance of privacy. Everybody, though, seemed to get caught up in the air of gaiety and I remember it as a happy time.

What with the barefooted *gholooms* continually climbing up and down the stairs, carrying and moving things, the elders sitting smoking their hubble-bubble pipes or drinking endless cups of coffee as they talked, and we children running to and fro excitedly and being constantly reprimanded, the scene was colourful and vibrant. The air was full of the noise of chattering children, murmuring adults, laughter, and sometimes even the thin scratchy sound of our prestigious and rather wonderful 'His Master's Voice' gramophone as its large needle, revolving disc and enormous horn magically produced music that enthralled us. I can still picture it to this day and still almost feel that brimming, tingling thrill of being part of all that activity.

The sky, the moon and the stars seemed so clear and bright. Being out on such a night has a profound effect on people and even the strictest disciplinarians in our household seemed to soften. I loved it when Monkhali, the least romantic of people, would tell us stories about the stars, especially the two known to us as Moshtari and Zohra – *Romeo and Juliet* in different guise.

These two, she said, spent every night of the year apart except during March, when finally they were able to meet for a while. "They were once human beings and had fallen in love on earth from the moment they caught a glimpse of each other while on neighbouring roofs on just such a summer's eve as tonight," she would say.

"Both came from good families who, unfortunately, were enemies, so the two knew it would be impossible for them ever to marry. Every night from across the rooftops, they would look longingly at each other. Moshtari felt he would die if he could not at least tell Zohra how much he loved her so, through an old woman of the town, he decided to send her a message.

"Unhappily he chose an evil messenger for she was a spy for Zohra's family and immediately told them of Moshtari's passion. The family were incensed and the issue became one of honour. It was unheard of even to think of marrying a daughter to an outsider, let alone to such a family.

"Zohra was not told of the developments but that night she was closely watched. She tried not to look towards Moshtari, but her own feelings of love were too great and, as the moon rose high in the sky and lit the night with its silvery glow, she raised her normally lowered eyes and stole a glance in the direction of the neighbouring roof.

"Moshtari had been waiting anxiously for just such a look, which was so full of yearning but, unfortunately, so also were Zohra's family. They needed no further proof of the love between the two. In a rage Zohra's father and brothers rushed to the neighbouring house and up on to the roof. In despair Zohra ran to try and warn her lover but in doing so, she missed her footing and fell headlong from the roof. Moshtari saw her fall and leapt after her and so they were finally joined in death."

Such were the fanciful and idyllic nights of summer, full of stories and sweet aromas. Winter, by contrast, was cold and we had to abandon the upper area of the house, especially the windtower rooms. Boards were fitted into the windtowers to prevent draughts and we all migrated to the bottom, windowless but warmer areas – back down to earth and the duller, more confining routines.

CHAPTER 3

KANEEZES AND GHOLOOMS

We needed a large home quite simply because of the great number of people who made up our household — not just family but also a legion of servants and slaves, *kaneezes* and *gholooms*. They played an important role in our lives for it was a time when the amenities and labour-saving devices we now take so much for granted hadn't even entered our wildest dreams; everything had to be done by hand then.

My early recollections are of the big, strong *gholooms* carrying water from *berkahs* or from the kitchen well to be filtered for drinking. Household tasks aside, cows and goats had to be milked, then butter or yoghurt made from the milk: we had one set of slaves whose job this was, while another group tended our palm trees and vegetables.

A special team worked from dawn to dusk looking after what seemed to me to be a constant stream of visitors in the *majlis*, ranging from foreigners, local dignitaries and merchants to poor men, as well as farmers bringing produce from our lands. Lavish hospitality is an important part of our cultural heritage and the servants were kept busy carrying food and a water jug and bowl called *aftaba lagan* for washing hands after a meal; preparing *qalyoon* for smoking, and of course the ubiquitous and never-ending cups of tea and coffee for anyone, whether he was an important sheikh or a poor peasant.

Feeding everybody was a massive task because of the number of people living in the house, not to mention the visitors we entertained. A great deal of our food came from our own land, for we grew fruit, especially dates, and vegetables. We also kept hens, goats and sheep. Rice, which was one of our staple foods, was imported — by the boatload, it seemed.

Mangoes and other exotic fruit came from India by the crate. Nothing arrived at our house came in small quantities!

The cooking was done by another group of specially-trained servants, closely supervised by my grandmother and great-grandmother. The kitchen was in a building quite a distance from the main house; I have vivid memories of the splendid procession of giant, dark-skinned *gholooms*. carrying huge trays piled high with mouth-watering meals.

The young girls of the household were never allowed to go outside and especially to the kitchen because it was near the *majlis*. Besides, it was considered beneath *bibis* to visit the kitchen area. That at least was the thinking then, and the result was that none of us ever learned to cook, a problem I have to this day.

As children, we all had our own special nanny and escort who looked after us, doing everything for us and accompanying us everywhere – even, when we eventually got there, to school. When we weren't keeping our 'minders' fully occupied steering us out of harm's way or out from under the feet of the grown-ups – often the same thing – they would be busy with such jobs as preparing snacks, or burning incense to keep our clothes and rooms smelling sweet, or lighting the hundreds of lanterns, candles and chandeliers. They were pleasant and educated, and in many ways were often the most important people in our lives. We were very attached to them.

Mostly our slaves came from Habasha and other parts of Africa. They were usually brought into our household in exchange for goods; as members of the household they would often adopt our name and accompany the women wherever we went. In such an entourage, slaves were treated with courtesy in deference to the family they served. A person would no more have thought of tipping a *gholoom* than he would have thought of accepting it. Slaves married and had their own families within the family circle. As the ensuing years brought changes in customs and patterns of social behaviour, slaves led more and more independent lives. Many, however, chose to remain attached to their families all their lives.

Once when I was quite young a little girl of about five was left on our doorstep with a note pinned to her bonnet: she was being given to us in exchange for a trade debt. In those days little or no account was generally taken of the feelings or emotions of *zar-kharids*, or how cruel it was to separate small children from their parents. My family, however, did not like this sort of arrangement. Grandfather tried to find this poor child's parents, but learned that they had already sailed away with their master so, although he would gladly have foregone his claims, he couldn't do anything else but bring her into our house.

The little girl's large, dark eyes clearly showed how terrified she felt. I remember my sisters and I, barely years older than this little one, sympathising with a child in such a situation. We named her Hasina, meaning 'beauty', and despite her childhood trauma she responded to our love and affection, growing into a happy and charming person.

Another story about our slaves has the enchantment of a fairy tale. Many years ago a woman named Saleha and her baby daughter, Zuleika, were given to one of my Great-uncles, Ahmad Arshi. He had many servants of his own so he passed them on to his father-in-law, Mohammad Mahmood in Dubai. They were treated well in this household; the story goes that if Saleha did not have enough milk or was too busy, the baby was even suckled by the mistress who had a baby of her own. Little Zuleika grew into a beautiful girl. She could read and write, and excelled in the fine art of embroidery.

As she blossomed into maturity, however, Mohammad Mahmood was concerned that, with a house full of *gholooms*, life would be difficult for her. With great sadness he took her and her mother to a slave dealer, who supplied rich and noble families in Saudi Arabia. The agent, Bin Ghorab, assured him he would find them an excellent home.

Because Saleha and Zuleika were personable, educated and well-mannered, Bin Ghorab decided that they would bring him much honour if he presented them as a gift to the Royal Court. But once aboard the ship that was to take them to Saudi Arabia, he tried to seduce Zuleika. She fended him off, and when Saleha tried to protect her daughter, Bin Ghorab beat her savagely. Fortunately for the two distraught women, the captain of the ship took them under his protection and, when they reached Riyadh, Saleha, being a strong-minded character, lodged a complaint. This was a most unusual procedure as slaves were considered the property of their owners and suffered any ill-treatment as an 'occupational hazard' which onlookers were most likely to put down to their being lazy.

However, because of the nature of the assault, the bravery of Saleha and the beauty and charm of Zuleika, the story was much talked about and they were given a great deal of sympathy. The story of the brave mother and beautiful daughter, who at any rate were on their way to the Royal Court, soon reached the ears of Malik Saud (then King of Saudi Arabia). They were brought to the court where they became part of the king's massive household.

The two soon got into the routine of the place. Then one day while Zuleika, always the image of modesty, was pouring water for Malik Saud to wash his hands after a meal, he saw for himself how beautiful she was. She soon became his favourite; later he married her and she was renamed Maleka Turkiya. Over the years, she has stayed in contact with our family, remembering the kindness shown her and her family, even sending a private plane to take members of our family to the memorable wedding in Riyadh of her eldest son. Since the death of Malik Saud, she spends her time between her chalet in Switzerland and her palace in Riyadh.

Although I would say most servants and slaves were treated well and kindly, in our young minds there were only two types of people – lords and ladies, and those who served them. Special names were reserved for the servants – for the women, Jameela or Hasina (beauty), Morwareed (pearl), Shireen (sweet); the men were often known as Yaqoot (a precious stone) or Mubarak (lucky). This was one distinction between the served and the servers.

Another was the style of dressing. During the stifling heat of summer, I envied the maids in their light cotton clothes, for we had to wear silks and heavy brocades, all embroidered with gold. On top of this we were laden with various golden ornaments. If ever a cotton dress was worn, it had to be of the highest quality and trimmed with lots of lace, frills and pleats. Those were the days when simplicity was frowned upon: anything, no matter whether it was clothes, jewellery, furniture, crockery or cutlery, was only considered valuable if the workmanship was complicated and intricate.

Personally, I didn't care for gold but loved the pretty glass bangles and light trinkets that the maids always wore, I used to collect these, keeping them in a box just so I could look at them from time to time. This earned me the name of 'Mariam Kaling', the junk collector. Strictly speaking *kaling* means 'seashell' but it is used to describe anything that is useless or worthless. Of course I was never allowed to wear my pretty *kaling* for I was a lady, so for a child, being a lady could be something of a burden!

One day during the festival of Eid, I was wearing an extremely heavy, ornate golden necklace. I hated it, for it made me feel hot and uncomfortable. While sitting by a window on the second floor of our home I noticed a beggar outside. He was skinny and old, and looked as if he hadn't eaten in days. "May God help you; please help me!" he cried piteously.

I felt sad to see the poor man and suddenly I had an idea about how I could not only help him but myself too. Quickly I unfastened the necklace which was such a nuisance to me and threw it down to the beggar. I was happy and he was over-joyed – though I remember thinking at the time that his thanks were delivered in rather a hurried fashion. He promised his eternal gratitude, predicted that I would live forever in Paradise, then rushed off faster than I would have thought possible, a moment earlier, on those old, skinny legs.

I may have earned a place in Paradise with that gesture but my own family were not at all pleased with me. "There is no hope for Mariam," they said, "an iron hand must be used in her upbringing."

CHAPTER 4

DAILY LIFE

Discipline was the keystone of our life. As an adult I can understand why discipline is necessary in one's life, but as a child with a restless and inquisitive nature, I found it difficult growing up in such a strict and orderly household, where unquestioning obedience was expected and demanded and harsh punishments were meted out for minor offences. Worse than this, though, were the restrictions we had to endure because we were of the fairer sex. Our world was defined by the four high walls of our home; we never expected to go beyond them throughout our lives, for even when we married, it was into our own family. It was quite customary to remain in our own family home from birth to death.

I grew up in the same household with my great-grandparents, my maternal grandmother, my great-uncles and their wives, various cousins and sundry other relations, and, of course, my own parents, sisters and brother. It was – and still is – a large and complex family, further complicated by the tradition of inter-marrying.

My mother lived in the home of her mother, which was the home of her mother. While this style of living ensures the security of women, it entails its own set of problems, especially if the women are strong-willed and used to having their own way, as was the case in our household. Arguments, therefore, not surprisingly, occurred frequently.

The main protagonists in these battles of will were my grandmother, Monkhali Kingely, and my great-grandmother, Monkhali Gappi. Their differences of opinion covered just about everything, from recipes to the way we were brought up. Their clashes were sharp, for these two ladies were noted for their quick wit and biting remarks. But worse, most of the household would end up being dragged, willingly or otherwise, into these 'battles of the Grannies'and the tension would be felt for weeks.

As a girl, the life I led was a narrow, restricted existence, stifling to my curious spirit. Although in Islam women are considered to be as important as men, the upbringing of girls in a Muslim society is quite different from that of boys. From a reasonably early age, boys are allowed a certain amount of freedom but, because the honour of a family rests with its women, girls are well-guarded.

The monotonous daily routine was meant to subdue and suppress our spirit, for we girls were being moulded to fit the traditional role of a lady. This meant being demure, refined, graceful and, above all, completely obedient.

Our day began before dawn when we were woken for *fajr*, the first of the five daily prayer rituals. The *muezzin* would call in his powerful and compelling tone, and bleary-eyed we would assemble in our special 'women only' prayer room. After prayers we rushed back to bed to salvage what sleep we could from the remaining hours before daylight.

As Muslims, hygiene was of paramount importance to us, especially prior to praying. There were several bathrooms in the house and attached to each were *rakhtkans*, special rooms for changing clothes. In the bathroom we clumped about in *kabkabs* or bath slippers. These were usually wooden but some were silver-plated and my mother even had gold-plated ones.

Our bathrooms, as might be expected, were primitive by today's standards, being usually windowless rooms with often only enough space for the huge *samovar* and the basins in which we performed our ablutions. The water in the *samovar* was heated by a small, coal fire underneath it and, because the rooms were without ventilation, there was often the danger of being overcome by fumes. However, as we were watched and escorted every minute, no real harm could ever befall us.

Lavatories were never situated in the bathrooms and there were not that many inside the house, because of the strong stench they caused. Pouring kerosene into the toilet was the normal method of removing smells but, being a privileged family, we were able to buy Dettol and other sanitary solutions from visiting ships.

When at last it was time to rise, our personal *kaneez* helped us dress. Day dresses would then replace our night clothes. We wore *kandooras* and *nimtas*. What with the glitter of our heavily embroidered and gold-braided clothes and the constant jingling of our gold necklaces, bracelets, earrings and even anklet chains, we must have created quite a spectacle.

When we were small, our heads were always covered with a gold-embroidered *bokhnak*, a cap or large bonnet; this was replaced by a veil or scarf and a long, outer cloak as we grew older. Our veils were also heavily embroidered with gold.

Our hair, which was always kept long, was styl ed into *chelgees* or forty plaits. There was one special person, a *mashata*, who looked after everybody's hair. She tidied it every day and washed, combed and plaited it once a week. It took a long time to wash and comb and, because we had no such things as shampoo and conditioner, all sorts of herbal devices were used. These strange, red mud-like mixtures often tangled our hair quite badly, making it agonising to comb – the pulling and tugging exhausted both the victim and the 'torturer'! Often combs were broken in the process. However, the mixtures were nourishing and they helped us grow the beautiful, thick, long hair we all desired.

Our day began again with breakfast. The breakfast table was also often adorned with home made jam and honey, *bilalit*, eggs, beans, *halwa*, *rangina* and home-produced butter, yoghurt and doogh – and the ubiquitous dates. Breakfast, or any meal for that matter, always included dates – natural, dried, in some prepared dish or as a thick honey-like juice eaten with bread. Delicious and nutritious, dates have a religious significance and are usually eaten to end a Muslim fast. Apparently when Hazrat Mariam (Holy Mary) gave birth to Essa (Jesus), Allah told her to eat dates to give her strength.

Another popular breakfast item, eaten with bread, was a dark paste called *mawa*. This usually consisted of sardines, herbs and special spices. *Mawa* can be preserved for years without ever needing cold storage and, in fact, people often placed jars of it in the sun. Because it was an excellent source of nutrition and could be crushed to a powder form, men often took it with them on long journeys. It must have also provided some kind of a yardstick on civilisation: a *gholoom*, who travelled to Paris with Great-uncle Farooq was not impressed with the glamorous French capital for, as far as he was concerned, it was "an awful place; you can't find anything here, not even *mawa*". I don't imagine you can find it in Paris even now, but in the Gulf region it is as popular as ever today.

We ate a great variety of different breads with names such as *ru'gag, dartasha, balatawa, litak, falazi, rikhta, motubbak, khamiri,* and *koloocha*. The differences were in the size, content and flavour, and a great deal of expertise was needed to prepare them. These forms of home-made bread are found only in the Gulf area. The most common bread that we ate though, was *tanoori* or *tandoori* nan and it was mass produced in a huge kiln, which stood outside in the courtyard.

After this first meal of the day we were taken to our school rooms. Our family, with its background of scholarship, placed a lot of emphasis on education and the pursuit of knowledge and lived by the *hadis paighombar*, sayings of the Prophet (Peace Be Upon HIm) which exhorts all to "acquire knowledge from the cradle to the grave. Acquire knowledge even if you have to go to China." In fact, there was no member of the household, boy, girl or even slave who was illiterate. Everybody was taught at least to read and usually to write as well. Schooling though, especially for girls, took place in the home and teachers were brought in.

Naturally all these special tutors were women with one exception – a very old man with a flowing white beard who taught us the Quran. He was a *mullah*, a respected religious man and a *Hafiz-e-Quran*, which meant he had memorised the entire Quran. We disliked him intensely, as he used to pinch us when we got things wrong, leaving big, blue bruises.

By the time I was five, I had learnt to read the Quran, though without any comprehension of it. However, I believed the effort was worthwhile because the attention which I always craved was, for a short while, diverted from my more favoured elder sister towards me. Besides the Quran we studied the famous literature of Persia and here again I was often able to capture everyone's attention for I learned to recite literary pieces. I loved nothing better than the sound of my own voice and used it to impress and delight my elders with renditions of these wonderful works of art, usually verses from *Moulood-e-Noori,* a history of the Prophet's life, by Syed Noor Bakhsh Shirazi. And they must have enjoyed the show, or at least have been able to put on a good act themselves, because I can remember seeing heads and bodies sway and eyes moisten in response to my recitation. Their reactions gave me a thrilling sense of power – but I did not understand a word of what I was saying.

As young ladies we were taught embroidery and fine needlework; if it was heard that a woman was a particularly skilful needleworker or had created new patterns, she was brought to our house, so we could learn from her. Of the different types of embroidery that we learned, my favourite was called *kumduzi.* A *kum* is a large, wooden frame, which, when covered by animal skin is used as a musical instrument, a drum-like tambourine. With the skin removed, material can be stretched across it and it becomes an embroidery frame. A crochet needle was used to pull the thread through the cloth, then sequins and beads could also be worked into the pattern. It was normally an uninspiring activity but I enjoyed it, especially when I could create new patterns – it was an outlet for my vivid imagination and drawing skills.

We also learned another handicraft skill, called *badela bafi,* which is unique to the Gulf region including Lingah and Bandar Abbas. This involves braiding gold and silver wires with coloured thread and then weaving the braids on a special stand. The results, when skilfully done, are works of art.

The morning's work was considered done when the second call to prayer, *zohr,* was heard. Lunch followed our prayers. The food we ate was always good, wholesome and fresh but unvarying. For lunch we always had fish and rice; occasionally chicken and goat meat. Though there were a number of different ways of cooking and presenting the food it was certainly a monotonous diet and another indication of our

regulated household. It was not that we did not have variety at
our disposal. On the contrary, our store-rooms were full of fruit,
sweets and chocolates, home-made and at times brought in from
foreign countries. However, we children were only allowed very
small portions of these delicacies for they were kept for
presenting to neighbours, important people of the town and a
never-ending flow of guests. Tantalised and frustrated by the
thought of this hoard of goodies in the house, it was no
wonder that my eight-year-old mind resorted to little devious
ploys to procure the forbidden goods.

I remember one incident involving mangoes, a fruit I
particularly enjoyed but was never allowed enough of despite the
fact that the store-room was crammed with crateloads of them.
Zinkhali Farooq, my great-aunt, used to keep a basketful of them
hanging from the ceiling. The idea of keeping them high up was
to catch the cool breeze and I suppose also to keep them out of
reach of sticky little fingers.

I stood gazing at them and craved for just one. They were
the big, delicious Alphanso mangoes from Bombay. It wasn't
long before I hatched a plan: all I needed was an accomplice
and the right time. The room was normally closed, but
sometimes Zinkhali chose to pray there. I knew that was the
time to put my plan into action, for once she began her
prayers, she could not be interrupted or stop to tell us off.
Quickly my cousin, her son, bent down and I climbed on his
back and was able to reach the basket. Zinkhali, helpless on
her prayer mat, began to call *"Allah-o-Akbar"* loudly and
frantically as a signal for the other adults to come to her
rescue. We had just enough time to fill my skirt and his long
thobe with the ill-gotten fruit and get away. We also managed
to eat most of our fruit before we were caught, and being
beaten with the hubble-bubble stick didn't seem to hurt as
much on a full stomach!

After lunch the custom was to rest until *asr*, the third prayer
time, while the late afternoon and early evening was usually
spent doing needlework. The womenfolk loved beautiful
things and placed a lot of importance on having a pleasant
environment, so there was always a need for new and even
more intricately designed *pushtis*, wall hangings, table-cloths,

bedspreads and curtains. We also loved to embroider the cuffs of our sleeves and borders of our trousers, so we never had time to be idle.

Where we lived in Bandar Lingah we seldom saw greenery but I created my own designs of flowers, birds, leaves and trees – far more exotic than anything known there. I would draw these wonderful shapes on paper and then cut them out, so they could be pinned to the material and copied by drawing around them with a pencil. Evidently the results did not go unnoticed, for white poplin and satin started to arrive, even from outside our household, with a note attached asking for 'Mariam Bibi' to draw a certain design or wondering whether 'Mariam Bibi' could select the right-coloured embroidery thread. It was a gift that gave me a lot of satisfaction, and even better it showed me that I was needed and appreciated.

When the sun disappeared below the horizon, the *maghreb* call to prayer was announced from every minaret of every mosque throughout the town and for the fourth time of the day we prayed.

We always had a light meal or supper after which the elders would gather to talk. It was a very relaxing interval in our daily routine. Every evening my Great-grandfather, Haji Mohammed Aqil, would walk the few miles from his house to join the gathering. 'Haji' was added to the name of those who had performed Haj – pilgrimage to Mecca. At that time such an undertaking was a hazardous affair and was usually performed only by the wealthy.

Great-grandfather always brought sweets and a special fruit called 'Bombay *ber*' as a treat for the children. The fruit was delicious and he had the only tree in Lingah, a plant he had brought from Bombay. Locally it was known as *konar* and small varieties of it grew wild in the area, but the big *konar*, which looks and tastes like an almond, were normally found only in India. It really was a treat for the youngsters to have something special like this.

One evening I thought I had the perfect plan to get more than my share. It seemed to me that when a hand was stretched out, one sweet and one *ber* was put in it, so after taking my portion, I went back behind the rest of the clamouring, outstretched palms and put my hand out again. I liked thinking up ways to outwit others and even more I loved boasting about my clever schemes later. However, this plan was not destined to work for I made the mistake of standing behind my elder and more virtuous sister, who I always called Dada Fatma and who did not have an adventurous bone in her body. She squealed on me: "No, no, no," she warned, "this is *khongoy's* hand again so don't put anything in it." Not only did I not get the fruit, but I was punished for two days. "Let that be a lesson to you," I was told sternly.

During this evening period, the elders often played chess, draughts, backgammon or cards – games to stimulate the intellect. Chess is a traditional Persian game but the other popular amusements had been brought back from foreign countries by the men. I enjoyed watching them play for I appreciated the craft and cleverness needed for such pursuits though, being a child, I was never allowed to participate.

Sometimes we read, but our own Persian literature was difficult and demanding. It needed close study so usually we continued with our embroidery and listened to the talk of our elders. Children were never included in conversations and nobody ever answered our questions, no matter how intelligent or foolish they were. Instead, we played children's games with our cousins and any visiting children, much as our parents and grand-parents had before us, games like *chash benaki* (hide-and-seek) and a form of blind man's bluff where the blind-folded 'victim' was asked to guess "*Aspe ma che rang?*" – what colour is my horse. We played *yakol chakol* with pebbles, seashells and marbles, and when we were older, ball-and-bat games a little like baseball and tennis.

Before we were old enough to sew or read, we were allowed to play with our favourite toys, which were usually raggedy, home-made dolls or balls. Being from a privileged family we possessed marvellous toys, for we were often sent gifts from abroad, but these were always packed and put away for some time in the future "for special occasions", or even worse "for your dear little brothers and sisters".

We used to catch glimpses of beautiful dolls, delicate and ingeniously-made clockwork toys, and brightly-coloured trinkets from Paris and India before they were locked away and displayed in a special glass cupboard. I remember going and touching the cupboard or lying down next to it to feel the closeness of those beautiful things to which I never had access – and never understood why.

Isha was our final prayer for the day and when this was performed we went to bed. Even the preparation for bed was a difficult ritual, for all the hooks and buttons on our clothes had to be undone. Our jewellery had to be removed; taking out heavy gold earrings was often a painful experience. It was wonderful to be relieved of all the weight and a great relief to get into bed. However, even here we were never alone for servants and slaves always slept with us. Neither were we allowed to find peace, for either Grandmother or our nannies would tell us terrible stories about *jinns*, the evil spirits, *Iblis*, the devil and *galazangi*, horrible-looking pitch black men with horns. We were told that all of these awful creatures would do dreadful things to bad children.

We often heard of the word *zar*, which seemed to be attributed to the workers. "Don't tread on their toes, don't hurt their feelings: they will transfer their *zar* to you or they will curse you." To children, it was quite scary.

African in origin, *zar* was a form of exorcism. Some scholars believed that it could be an act of release from pressure of work by the African slaves, or used as a group weapon against oppression, not unlike voodoo. As a child I snuck a look at a session and got the fright of my young life. Attracted by the sound of drums, I peeped through a door and watched as labourers gathered around their ring leader, known as Baba, chanting while others shook, swayed, howled and shouted in frenzy, tearing their hair and shaking their heads. This went on for hours, until the *zar* was driven away from their bodies and they collapsed with exhaustion.

Everyone pussy-footed around the Zar people, so as not to hurt their feelings for fear of being threatened. Later on, in Bandar Abbas and the Gulf region, I heard about such acts being performed among the local traditional musical groups and labourers in general, but at the time I glimpsed a session, I had many a sleepless night.

Most of our staff were gentle and pleasant. I especially remember, Zamzam, Monkhali's special attendant and a great story-teller. Her tales were funny and interesting but half-way through she would doze off and no matter what we did to wake her up she wouldn't respond.

For all the years of my childhood, I believed the sinister tales of the elders, and that the world was flat and was balanced on the two horns of a bull, and that between this world and the next was a bridge as thin as a hair that you had to walk across when you died. If you had been good the bridge would become broad and your journey across would be safe. However, if you had been bad you would find it impossible to balance on the thread-like bridge and you would fall into hell below and be eaten by wild animals.

The day of judgement was a horrifying picture! The idea was to scare us into good behaviour but all it did was give us nightmares, especially me who was always being told how bad I was:

"Why aren't you like other girls in this house and community?"

"Why don't you behave in a lady-like way?"

"Sit down quietly, cover your head modestly."

"You must learn to obey."

Accusations, orders, instructions and demands – was I really that naughty and different? It was true that I hated restrictions and wanted to feel free, so it's no wonder that when I had the chance I would sneak off to play marbles and climb trees with my boy cousins, which was, of course, absolutely forbidden for girls. A beating with the hubble-bubble stick was the usual punishment; this was no laughing matter but, even though I knew the consequences, I persisted with my pranks.

I hated the practice of everything being put away for the future. I could see overflowing store-rooms of wonderful delicacies that I craved to eat but of course was forbidden to, for it was always "for later" or for "someone more important".

I wanted to know why we had to wear clothes and shoes that were at least a size too big. I was told that it was so we would "grow into them", but I didn't want to have to grow into them: I wanted them to fit now and be comfortable. I wanted things to be different, so rebellion soon became second nature to me. The grown-ups' way of thinking seemed so confusing.

There was only one person in that whole household on whom I could rely to love me unconditionally and to whom I always went when I was sad, angry, hurt, or if I just needed to be held and hugged. That was Jameela, a *kaneez*.

Jameela was huge and black, noisy and colourful, always cheerful, and to me, incredibly beautiful. As was usual with our slaves, Jameela was African. She had been with my family for years and I don't remember a time without her. She was married to one of our male slaves and had children of her own but I believed I was the most important person in her life. I was her *bibi*, her Miss.

She was my nanny so she had to be with me all the time and, instead of being frustrated and angry with my antics, she encouraged my sense of adventure and used to laugh even as she scolded me. At times when I used to threaten to throw myself off the roof or go on a hunger strike, instead of becoming panic-stricken she would laugh and know that I was having fun. She understood why I got up to such escapades and my need to feel free.

She often snuck food out for me, although she would have been severely punished had she been caught, but it upset her to see me looking pale and faint. To her it was cruel to expect a small child of six or seven years to survive for long periods without food or water during the long, hot days of summer, especially in Ramadan.

Huge and comforting, she would protect me when I ran to her and, as far as she was concerned, it was never "my *bibi's* fault". She was the only one who truly ever accepted me as I was and delighted in the spirit that she saw in me.

It was not a pleasant experience growing up in a world where it was considered wrong to show affection to or praise a child but Jameela allowed me to see the other side of life – she showed me that love and compassion can help develop a person's character to its full potential.

CHAPTER 5

TRIAL AND ABSOLUTION

Manhoos – I first heard the word whispered around our household the day my baby brother died. He was only a year old and I knew I should have felt sad that our family had lost the longed-for and well-loved boy but it was hard when, for that whole day, we were given a day off from *maktab*. Besides he had only been a baby and I hardly knew him. He had been in the constant care of my mother and was always surrounded by a retinue of servants and even had a foreign nanny.

It had become almost customary to blame 'Mariam Bibi' for most things that went wrong in our household, and usually with good reason, but I was shocked when I discovered I was the one being called '*manhoos*'. According to all the old superstitious women in our household, I was to blame for my brother's death: no child born after me could live because I was a person of ill omen.

"*Daghosh bokoni* – burn her," I heard an old woman I did not know tell my grandmother. "A burning stick must be held at the nape of her neck to drive out the evil in her. Only then will the curse be lifted." A wave of fear swept over me.

Later I discovered that this old woman was one of those who were known as 'mobile intermediaries', women who had a strange but necessary place in our society. Because ladies of reputable households seldom left their homes, there was a need for such people to facilitate contact between families and the town outside.

These women were usually old and, it seemed to me, ugly and often had frightening reputations. They were normally used as advisers or sometimes as matchmakers (though not for our family). Often in the case of illness they were called in and they always seemed to know the most awful cures for the strangest ailments. Some were good and wise but others were mischievous and put peculiar ideas into simple heads and helped spread superstitious beliefs. They wielded great influence. I knew the accusations they made against me would be taken seriously, and what compounded my fear was that there was nobody I could turn to for help.

My father, although he never bothered much with his children, would have put a stop to this nonsense, for he was an educated man and certainly did not believe in old wives' tales, but he was away on a trip and not expected back for a few months. My mother was still in mourning for her infant, so could not be disturbed, though I'm sure she would have been horrified if she had known what was being planned.

For once in my life I tried to be quiet and melt into the background, avoiding the attention I normally constantly sought. My apprehension and feeling of helplessness only intensified as I realised that people were watching me warily and the look in their eyes was not kind.

One day after a study session they caught me. I was held so tightly I could not move or even cry out. They dragged me to the hearth – the old familiar hearth, where a fire was always burning to light the hubble-bubble and to keep the *manqals* and the little teapots that sat on them hot so that tobacco and tea were always ready to be served. Suddenly it no longer seemed a pleasant and cosy place but a place of evil and cruelty.

I was terrified. The nasty, acrid odour of something burning filled my nostrils. It was a piece of black cloth. My grandmother ordered a servant to hold my hair out of the way and then, before I knew what was happening, the old woman whipped the cloth out of the flames and pressed it hard against my bare skin right at the top of my spinal cord. The pain was intense. I screamed at the top of my voice, jerked violently from the grip of the adults and ran for my life.

The skin on my neck was seared and the pain was excruciating. Somehow I found Jameela and collapsed in her arms. She washed and dressed the wound as best she could but it was days before anything resembling a normal atmosphere returned to our house, weeks before my neck healed, and a lot longer before my young mind could once again place any trust in adults.

Fortunately my mother did eventually give birth to another boy. He was named Ahmed Noor, and what rejoicing there was. I was seven when he was born, and lived in a state of apprehension for many years, believing that if my younger brother died, this time I would be burned to death. I prayed for his well-being day and night. After my brother, two more girls were born, lifting the 'curse' of *manhoos* from me.

This experience, though, left a mark that was not just physical. I became more rebellious, defiant and questioning of the ways of the elders. Harmony in a household as large as ours was always precarious, and my actions and attitudes certainly did not promote a peaceful atmosphere.

One of the views of the elders that frustrated me more than anything was that a child or an unmarried girl should never learn the 'facts of life'. Details of marriage, birth and death were all hidden from us. I wanted to know about everything, but at a very young age I discovered that questions would never be satisfactorily answered so, if I heard the elders discussing these deliciously forbidden subjects, I would become the non-existent, quiet child they all wished me to be and soak up what information and knowledge I could. Of course it was never long before one of the elders looked over her shoulder and saw me sitting there and would whisper, "A little fly is around", or "Beware of clouds". Consequently much of what I learned from these conversations was only half-baked knowledge mixed up with a good dose of superstition: for instance, I believed that the 'evil eye' and *jinns* caused sickness and other problems.

Ladies of leisure who had little else to do but laze around, beautify themselves and think about their own problems usually did have a lot of domestic problems – perhaps real, perhaps imaginary; probably a little of both – and were often 'ill'. If the social environment could be blamed for such ailments, it also provided the antidote in the form of.gipsy women, locally known as *sharshan*, who when called in arrived with flattering tongues wagging and lumpy sacks bulging. They were always able to offer mysterious stones and other strange remedies to cure such 'ailments' as lack of affection from a husband, interference from in-laws, and the like. Jacks of all trades, they turned their hands to fortune-telling using a *raml*, which was a set of stones of different shapes and sizes.

More sinister – and potentially lethal – was a rather strange and gruesome operation, known as *hijamat*, which was meant to purify the blood and relieve pressure in a person – a form of blood-letting, carried out annually. When we heard the gipsy women out on the streets shouting "*Hijamat! Hijamat!*" we knew the time had come. A servant would be sent out to fetch one of the gipsies and all the older women would gather and ready themselves for the operation. The gipsy carried her equipment, which consisted of a horn-like object and a sharp knife, in a goatskin bag called a *mashk*, a common sort of bag generally used for carrying water, milk or yoghurt.

I would watch wide-eyed and horrified as the gipsy began her work. Firstly, she made a deep incision at some point on the body, normally somewhere along the spinal cord. She then placed the horn-like object on this point and sucked hard on the mouth of the horn until dark, gurgling blood gushed out. Fortunately only the elders seemed to need this treatment but they all said how wonderful and rejuvenated they felt afterwards.

It was enough for us children that we had to force down a weekly dose of castor oil – for what purpose I'm not sure. I learned much later in life that the same treatment was administered practically the world over in the 1920s, was universally hated and that to avoid it, others, like me, often hid. Once, however, the strategy backfired badly when I chose a huge vase to hide behind. I resisted vigorously when they tried to drag me out; the vase toppled over and smashed. Apparently it was a very valuable piece and in the confusion that followed, I escaped up a tree. When they finally caught me, I was severely punished – and I still got my dose of the hated castor oil!

Truthfully, even now with the knowledge that castor oil genuinely can produce some beneficial effects, I don't believe the regular doses did us much good, for throughout our growing years, we were all quite pale, thin children. People noticed and used to remark about it. Monkhali always replied by saying, "Ah! But you should see them when they are in Bombay. There they flourish and have pink cheeks. It's just this terrible climate." The only flaw in her logict was that this miraculous change in fact did not occur in Bombay and, when people there passed similar comments on how wan we looked, she would say, "Ah! But you should see them in Lingah; there they are happy and look so well. It's just the awful climate here."

Fascinated as I was by the mysteries of life, as I grew a little older it was discovered strangely enough that Zelzelah Bibi had the 'healing touch'. Imagine: from being branded a *manhoos*, now it became common for the elders to summon me and ask: "Mariam, press my head. *Dastut soboken* – your hand is light."

Soon, I was even being asked to help ease the pains of women in childbirth – despite the fact that a child was normally never even allowed to pass the room of a woman in labour. Only about eight at the time, I would hold the struggling woman's hand and read *suras* or verses from the Quran, especially *sura-e-Mariam*, the story of the revered mother of the prophet Essa (Jesus). I was mystified how in some way my presence seemed to help, but it did, and in a complete turn-around I began to be considered more and more 'lucky-footed'.

My artistic bent was also earning me unexpected rewards. I had always been fascinated by the elaborate make-up worn by brides, and at a young age took to beautifying my dolls in this style. As I grew, I must have run out of dolls, or perhaps just became more ambitious, because it wasn't long before I was practicing on the faces of children in our household – always willing models. This too did not go unnoticed, and it wasn't long before I was being asked to help with the make-up of real brides. This was remarkable because again unmarried girls were usually forbidden to go near those who were about to enter the blessed state of matrimony although the bride might not be that much older – usually between 14 and 16.

Normally a *mashata* did the bridal make-up but girls from families who could not afford such a specially-trained woman were brought to our house where I was given the task of doing up her face and helping her dress, assisted by her close family members. Because I was so small, being barely nine, I would have to sit on two or three cushions just to reach the girl's face. It was a complicated process and could take up to three or four hours to complete and it was quite an experience for the bride for, as an unmarried girl, she was only allowed to wear *surma*, a mascara of Mughal origin.

During the make-up process and the actual wedding ceremony, the bride had to sit as still as if she were carved out of stone. The one thing she was most definitely not allowed to do was smile. Years ago the wedding ceremonies could last for weeks and the poor bride was turned into a 'statue' but nowadays the 'torture' usually only lasts a few days!

The first step of the make-up process was threading, which meant that all excess hair was removed using powder and a cotton thread pulled over the face. It was a painful method but it usually gave the bride's skin an extra glow. After this, intricate designs were drawn upon her face and sequins were stuck on her cheeks and over her eyebrows with a special herbal glue called *behdoona*, made from fruit seeds and harmless to the skin. It was also used to arrange kiss curls around her face. The rest of her hair was always done in the same special style – parted in the middle and two plaits or several small plaits were made. The ends of these plaits were worked into a number of smaller, thinner plaits and special golden ornaments known as *tee-zulf* decorated the tips.

To complete the facial make-up black beauty marks were made on the face and *surma* was used for the eyes to make them look large. Lastly, rouge – or, in its absence, some moistened red tissue paper – was applied to give a healthy look to the cheeks, and lipstick put on to redden the girl's lips.

Fabulous designs were drawn on the bride's hands and feet with henna. This was an important tradition and henna is used on any joyous occasion, but the most exciting henna sessions are witnessed during a wedding when it is applied to the accompaniment of music and dancing.

After the bride's face, hands and feet are done, elaborate, heavy, gold jewellery had to be donned. Each piece had a special name and significance: the *angoshtar*, rings for each finger; *fitakh*, the ring for the large toe; *khalkhal*, the great gold anklet band and *meel* and *champli* for the ankles; *doorgoosh*, the earring; *katchacha-va-mahak*, the elegant coined cap with a pendant hanging from it that is designed to sit on the forehead; a nose button and round ring attached to the nostril are known as *patri* and *poozi* (holes were pierced in the nose and ear lobes of girls very early in life but no ornaments were used on the nose before marriage); *jollowi* and *shekhap* is the band that is stretched across the bride's chin and pinned to her cap. Bangles known as *chombor* and *morasokh* decorate the wrists. Finally several necklaces of different length and design known as *dalal*, *setani*, *morsia*, *mansoori*, *mortasha*, and *gardanband*, are placed around her neck. These necklaces are joined on to a *kandar* or wooden rod to make one incredibly heavy ornament designed to sit on the neck like a yoke.

The entire set from head to toe had to be worn together but only wealthy families could afford all of them. Other families often had to borrow each piece. Fortunately, this skilful art of dressing a bride has not died out and traditional brides in the Gulf region are still made-up by *mashatas*.

To be given as a child such responsibilities and importance on the one hand, and then to be continually reprimanded for being precocious and rebellious on the other, created in me a seething mass of conflicting emotions, which, of course, spilled over into words and actions. It was, therefore, the general opinion of the household that I was not normal and something was seriously wrong with me.

Monkhali decided that a doctor should be consulted. It just so happened that at that time an English doctor, who was based in Muscat, was visiting Lingah.

"The girl is not contented and constantly does things that are against our traditions," the doctor was told. He examined me thoroughly, all the while asking questions which I was uninhibited in answering.

Finally he made his diagnosis: I remember the words to this day. "The only thing wrong with the child is that she was born a few decades before her time."

Monkhali's diagnosis was that the man had clearly taken leave of his senses and she pronounced his opinion worthless.

CHAPTER 6

PASSING OF AN ERA

Mother and Monkhali had many visitors, though I'm not sure if they were actual friends, for we never reciprocated many of these visits, mainly because women of such aristocratic background seldom visited anyone, unless it was a lady of similar breeding.

One very good friend of mother's was Saleha Mondegar, and we did exchange visits with her for she was then the newest and most beloved wife of our uncle the Sheikh Sultan-Al-Olema. I remember Aunty Saleha as a graceful and lovely young woman who wore a *batoola*, the black mask favoured by some women of the Gulf, Bandar Abbas and Lingeh region. These masks come in different shapes and sizes; Saleha wore a tiny one, decorated with gold coins and tassels. She filled the room with her gaiety when she visited, and the fragrance of her perfume lingered in the house long after she had gone.

Much later, our two families became even more interwoven when my youngest sister, Badria, married the youngest son of the Sheikh and Saleha, and my other sister Bibiya married the Sheikh's grandson.

Mother and Saleha, being of equal importance, met often, but there were other ladies Mother only visited once a year, despite the fact that they might live only a short walking distance away. However, such an exchange between local dignitaries was considered a special honour and once a year was felt to be quite sufficient.

These visits were very grand affairs and were never conducted without a large entourage of at least 40 women which included Mother's close friends, a few attendants and children.

I remember the occasions when we entertained important lady dignitaries of the town. Elaborate preparations were made for the day-long ceremonial visit – dresses were sewn; lots of gold jewellery was selected; mountains of food was cooked; everything that did not move was polished until it shone and all the movable items were also cleaned until they too gleamed. I'm sure with the amount of work and fuss involved, most people were thankful they were only honoured once or twice a year!

Because trips outside our own house were rare, we children all looked forward to going visiting. We had to be prepared well beforehand to make sure we looked proper and acted correctly. As a very young child (or for that matter even when I grew older), I found it difficult to remain demure for any length of time, especially on such exciting occasions, so Jameela was always given very strict orders to keep me under control. It was a hard task, though I was usually quite good during the grand procession from our house to the one we were visiting, for I loved being outside and I especially enjoyed the feeling of being part of an important parade. I always held my head high and felt like a princess. All other traffic was stopped until we passed – not that any vehicles plied the sandy, bumpy roads. Hawkers with their donkeys loaded with radishes, carrots and other produce, and men walking to the mosque would be about the only other traffic on the road. Even they had a habit of disappearing when they saw a procession of ladies coming towards them. To me it appeared as though men ran way from women rather than the other way round.

The houses we visited were always wonderfully grand and inside everything glittered. One in particular has stuck in my memory, a truly grand house with sparkling chandeliers overhead and walls completely covered by mirrors. Ornate six-door cupboards and magnificent vases full of artificial flowers from India and China were the main pieces of furniture and decoration in the room for we never sat at tables or on chairs but rested on beautifully embroidered quilts and against gold-tasseled *mokhadas*. The spicey and sweet aromas of *ud* and *bokhoor* hung heavily in the air and to add to the splendour the

hostess was always bedecked in glittering attire. On display
were several 'Omani' chests. Actually they came from Surat in
India – we called them *Sandooqe Surati*. Regal and impressive,
they were also known as dowry chests and were made of teak
and rosewood, generously engraved with copper and brass
decorations. Some also had drawers.

This kind of chest was common because they were actually
used to store her trousseau. It would be started by her mother
and grandmother when she was as young as five. Elaborately
embroidered *kandooras* and *nimtas*, intricately designed cloaks
would be packed away; they would even put in triangular
gold-embroidered henna bands with long tassles to wrap
around the feet and hands after henna had been applied. Tray
covers (mostly in green as this was considered a lucky colour)
and hand-embroidered curtains, embroidered purses for *surma*
and Quran covers were also part of this trousseau. Of course it
would take years to complete as everything was done by hand,
but still everything was usually ready several years before the
girl actually got married. Today, I would give anything to
possess one of those grand *sandooqes*. The ones I see in antique
shops bear only a slight resemblance to the original chests.

With so much to see, hear and smell, I couldn't help but be
fidgety and restless during the rather boring welcoming
reception. I was usually too excited to contemplate food
though there was a wonderful *fala* or brunch consisting of
numerous home-made sweets, tinned fruit and beans. Being so
young and full of energy, I was impatient as the women sat
around and nibbled on these wonderful goodies and drank cup
after cup of tea, coffee or lemonade. However, I was usually
still under strict supervision, and only my eyes would roam
around.

The room in which we were entertained was windowless
but had a number of doors opening into a corridor and a
courtyard. Every traditional house had a *mosanni* in the centre
of the courtyard where huge palm and wild almond trees
shaded the greenery beneath and made a cool garden.

As I sat quietly I would watch with fascination as servants
appeared as if by magic through one of the many doors
carrying yet more coffee or sweets.

After a while the delicious smells of lunch would begin to waft into the large room and despite the earlier brunch my stomach would start to rumble and my mouth to water as I watched the hostess and her family begin to supervise the preparations for the meal.

Firstly, the *sofra* – an incredibly long piece of material spread in the middle of the room – was laid out. There was seating room for hundreds of guests. Ornaments and artificial flowers were then placed on the *sofra*.

Finally, the moment we children had all been waiting for would arrive. Whole goats stuffed with chickens, rice and eggs would be brought in and served on huge, round, silver trays, accompanied by dozens of other dishes. The hostess would then politely ask us to approach the *sofra* and eat. Dignity and manners were of utmost importance; the children were held back from all the delicious food so as not to seem greedy or rude. Several more times the lady repeated her invitation then finally she left the room, closing the doors firmly behind her.

This was a particularly Arabic custom and was designed to let guests feel free to eat. On one occasion when I was very eager to taste all the exotic dishes, it worried me that the hostess might change her mind and come back and our 'good manners' would prevent us from eating what we liked, so I quickly ran and locked all the doors from the inside.

"Now we can eat and jump and sing in peace!" I was pleased with myself for my quick thinking but the look on Monkhali's face told me I was in trouble yet again!

The part of the visit I really enjoyed was after lunch, when we were finally allowed to use up some of our suppressed energy for, while the women reclined on their cushions and relaxed, we were taken outside. This particular house had a large enclosed garden full of assorted imported trees and even bourgainvillea attached to the main living area. I was able to romp and roam as I liked, though the whole time Jameela watched me like a hawk.

One year while enjoying myself outside I lost an earring. Because I was having such a good time I didn't realise what had happened but when I went back inside my mother noticed the missing earring and quickly removed the one I still had on.

She ordered us not to mention the incident, for, as a guest, it was considered bad manners to mention such a thing, despite the fact that the earring was gold and studded with pearls.

The next year when we were strolling through the same garden on our annual visit Jameela suddenly screamed as though bitten by a snake. However, it was excitement not pain that made her yell, for she had found my lost earring, although it was now covered in mud and almost unrecognisable!

"Allah be praised, *male halal rahe door nachit* – rightful belongings do not go far," was the general verdict of this adventure.

When it was finally time to leave, we were all exhausted; unaccustomed to such excitement, young children were often carried home in the arms of nannies after the final ceremony which included being dabbed on the wrists and behind the ears with a fragant *attar*, an oily perfume, and having our clothes and hair sprinkled with rose water and scented with the smoke of *ud* and *bukhoor*. These sumptuous and stately visits were a wonderful break from our rather humdrum routine.

Although all of us adored our mother and craved her affection, none of us could compete with our brother, for he was the pride and joy of her life. Ahmed Noor was thoroughly pampered. After he completed the first chapter of the Quran, his *tahamada* was celebrated for a week by the whole town with great pomp and ceremony. It was grander indeed than most weddings.

Ahmed, who was only about five or six at the time, was dressed in a gold brocade outfit and mounted on a horse to be taken for his ceremonial bath in the town square, and there was a huge procession with attendants carrying henna – rituals normally only associated with weddings. The container for the henna was carved in the shape of a ship (inside the container there were candles, mirrors, glass and silver baubles and artificial flowers) and carried by a *gholoom*. Behind him were others with trays of sweets. Accompanying the procession were by dancers, flautists, drummers and others playing an instrument known as a *nihangboon*, made out of a goat's stomach. that looks and sounds like the Scottish bagpipes.

The procession, which included small children chanting in chorus, was a spectacular sight as it wound through the streets of the town; *noql,* specially prepared round sweets, and coins were strewn at random. Finally there was a huge feast where not only the rich and privileged ate, but the poor were also fed for the entire week of celebrations.

Less joyous – at least for Ahmed – was the ceremony and celebration of his circumcision when he was six or seven. In considerable pain after the operation, which was done by the local *hajam,* he nevertheless recovered quickly, encouraged no doubt by the thought that now he was a man. Gifts, food and sympathy were showered on him, and the celebration lasted three days with singing, dancing and feasting.

I couldn't really understand why, just because he was a boy, he should be given such preferential treatment. It seemed unfair – even silly – to ignore his sisters, who were hard-working and more intelligent. Nobody seemed to care that he was quite a slow learner. However, we had to accept the fact that mother doted on her only son.

During one of these wonderful celebrations held in honour of Ahmed, Mother was heard to say: "I must have all my ambitions for him fulfilled in my lifetime, for I may not see his wedding ceremony." She was blessed with a strong intuitive sense, something I seem to have inherited from her; sadly this hunch was correct and not long after, she fell ill.

One morning when we got up, she was sitting, staring blankly and unable to speak. Family and friends gathered around. Nobody could guess what was wrong. Everybody blamed the 'evil eye', so the famous uncle, Sultan-Al-Olema, was summoned. Being the absolute final authority on all religious matters, he was the only hope for getting rid of such a dire curse. He sat my mother on a cushion, drew a circle around her, and began to chant religious *ayats* and *suras,* verses from the Quran.

After a while, when Mother's condition had not changed, the Sheikh called in the resident English doctor and local homeopathic *hakims.* Fortunately Father, who spoke English and French fluently, was with us at the time and could communicate easily with the medical team. Mother's condition was judged serious enough to summon two doctors from Muscat, who were flown in. Their opinions confirmed the worries of the others, so it was decided that she be moved to Karachi as soon as possible.

"But how?" The big question loomed in everyone's mind. Travelling in those days was a major undertaking, especially for families like ours which seemed to thrive on complications. For one thing, it was a must for the immediate family to travel together with all the trappings: Mother, Grandmother, Great-grandmother, all the children, their nannies, Father, two doctors and one *mubasher*, a sort of adviser and overall manager.

Travelling by ship involved several days so a 20-seater plane was chartered from Muscat. I recall it was a military plane normally used to ferry army personnel about, and was hired through the good offices of His Majesty, the Sultan himself. Of course it was our first experience of flying, and as far as I was concerned at the time, I hoped it would also be my last! It was exciting but extremely frightening. Father sat in the cockpit, and the rest of us squeezed into the passenger hold, some attendants sitting on the floor. Everyone prayed loudly. The plane shook and rattled mercilessly and the noise was painful to the ears. Above it, I heard one remark so clearly I can hear it still – "Mariam is, thank God, frozen in her seat so there will be peace." The flight seemed to last forever; the buzzing in my ears certainly accompanied me for several days.

The rest of the retinue with countless crates, heavy iron trunks, bedding, several carpets and carton loads of heaven knows what were to be sent by ship later on. This was most unusual for us, for although family houses in Bombay, Karachi and Bahrain were always staffed and ready to receive travelling family members and visitors, arrangements were not considered adequate unless personal staff created familiar surroundings. But this time it was an emergency and we had to wait for the rest to arrive. It was a relief that at least Jameela and Zamzam were with us.

The doctors in Karachi finally discovered that Mother had had a stroke. They advised her to lose weight and not have any more children. Her treatment seemed to consist of plenty of peace and quiet, and for this our rambling house in Karachi with its lawns, trees and flowers was ideal.

During our couple of years' stay in Karachi while Mother was recuperating the big *zelzelah* shook Quetta (now part of Pakistan), almost destroying the entire city. Newspapers and people talked of nothing but this destructive earthquake for months, as the helpless and homeless poured into Karachi and other towns. It also gave Monkhali added ammunition when she was angry at me: "Mariam, God help us, everywhere you go there is a *zelzelah*!"

Mother responded well to treatment during her year's convalescence, but again became pregnant. Although they knew full well the implications, the family viewed abortion as sacrilegious, so my mother had no choice but to go through with the pregnancy.

Around the time Mother was due, an influenza epidemic swept through the town and nearly everybody in the household was sick. It was a strange and unnatural time. In fact, with nurses everywhere, the house looked like a hospital .

I had also been sick and confined to bed but I knew something terrible had happened. I heard my grandmother calling *"Allah! Allah! Madad!"* as she asked God for help and strength. Quietly I crept out of bed and made my way towards the sound. I found my mother covered with a white sheet and my grandmother sitting alone, praying. When my grandmother saw me she told me to go back to sleep and that my mother was all right. I knew she was shielding me from the truth, and I went back to bed feeling forlorn and helpless.

In the morning I learned that Mother had died in the night; her baby had died the day before during childbirth.

Although Mother had been remote from us, I still felt torn by her death. I ached to hear her lovely, singing voice again, and to feel her regal presence. She was about 38 when she died; the year was 1934. Our family had lost something very special and precious.

Monkhali was heartbroken. She took all five of us into her tiny, loving arms and held us tightly. We were now all she had to live for.

CHAPTER 7

YEARS IN BOMBAY

After Mother's death, our household seemed to disintegrate. We spent the rest of our growing years mainly in Bombay and later Karachi and seldom stayed in Lingah. Mother's magnificent marble tomb is in Karachi and Monkhali wanted to live and eventually die there, so she could be buried as near as possible to her beloved daughter.

It was very odd but even in death there was still a sense of something very special about Mother. We were not the only ones to feel this; apparently residents of the area used to pray at her shrine, for they believed that because she died young and in childbirth without having all her dreams fulfilled, she was especially chosen by Allah.

Father, who had never shown a great deal of interest in us, now had even less to keep him home, so it was not long before he joined an Ango-Iranian oil company in Abadan, Iran and his periods of absence became longer. Eventually he remarried and his sense of responsibility for us seemed virtually to disappear.

An ambitious man, he always seemed to need more money and although he had inherited some wealth from his parents, on one of his infrequent visits he laid claim to Mother's jewellery and possessions too. Legally he was not entitled to what Mother owned, for it had been given to her by her family when she got married.

Mother had been wealthy in her own right; her jewellery in particular formed a rare and magnificent collection of gold, diamonds, rubies, sapphires and big, beautiful pearls. Mention "Hafsa Abbas's jewellery" and people would nod knowingly. Besides this, there were valuable household items such as silver cutlery, trays, crockery, sewing kits, vases and chandeliers. Some of the pieces had been in Monkhali's family for years but Father insisted that he needed the money to buy more land.

Monkhali was well-off, for she had been left an equal share of her father's wealth. This was unusual for, according to Islamic law, the daughter inherits considerably less than the son. The reason for this is quite logical as a boy will eventually have the responsibility of a family while a girl's wealth is hers alone and she is not obliged to use it to care for others. However, Monkhali's wealth was at all times controlled by her brothers and she only received monthly allowances.

Because Father contributed only small amounts towards our maintenance, and infrequently, Monkhali found it hard to stretch her means to cover the expense of keeping five growing children. She felt the constant strain of her responsibilities, and consequently our living standards were considerably lowered.

But Father thought his need was greater than ours and he knew one sure way of getting more money out of our family. He told Monkhali simply: "Then I will take the children with me."

The idea of parting with Mother's collection was heart-breaking for Monkhali, as she had protected it with her life and had planned to hand it down to us. But losing us would have hurt her more. She had no choice but to hand it over, though along with the jewels and valuables, she cursed him: "Behnam *khair nabenesh* – you will gain nothing. You are doomed."

With the money he got for the jewellery, he bought land and built cinemas and apartments in Abadan, but he was misguided; perhaps the 'curse' had some effect. The people who worked for him and were constantly around him soon began to gain everything and he always ended up short of funds. Had he been less a philosopher and more a businessman, things might have worked out better for him.

With Father gone, and Monkhali left with the awesome responsibility of rearing the five of us, we came more directly under the protection of Monkhali's brothers, particularly Uncle Haji Ahmad Arshi who had his own responsibilities and was often away. However, Monkhali's legal adviser Mohammad Mohammad Sharif, a close relative and a kind man, became our father figure and was very protective towards us. His daughter Fatma Gul and I got on famously. She too was high-spirited – in fact, she taught me how to ride a bicycle, which was pretty scandalous for girls in those days!

For some years after Mother's death, we lived in Bombay. Being one of the main centres for pearl trading, Bombay was naturally an important place for pearl merchants, so it was like a second home to us. We had stayed there often and for reasonably long periods during the earlier, happier years when Mother was alive and when pearl trading was our family's main business.

My grandfather Haji Abbas was one of the most successful and wealthiest pearl merchants, a man of great faith and strong moral convictions, which gave him an incredible strength of character and ensured that he was the one who was always in control of any situation. We never met him until after Mother's death. Ironically, it fell to Monkhali, Grandfather's estranged wife, to prepare us for this important occasion. I clearly remember her instructions: "Only speak if you are spoken to; kiss his hands; bow to him; sit with your hands clasped together and look demure."

Three senior *kaneezes* accompanied us, including Jameela, and we travelled quite a distance from Kethwadi, where we lived, in *ghora garis* – horse-drawn buggies. It was exciting to be coming face to face with such a legendary character. Although old, he was still a strong and able man; at the age of 84 he fathered a child by Haji Aisha, a wife with whom he was reunited after he returned to Bombay from Paris.

My memory of my grandfather was that of a regal figure sitting erect in an ornate, gilt chair. He was as splendid as I had always imagined him to be. Awed by his reputation, it was difficult to regard him as a real human being, for in our minds he was a larger-than-life figure – someone out of a story book. However, when he wept with us over the loss of our mother, his daughter, we began to warm to him. This eased the tension we had felt in his presence and I soon forgot all the 'behaviour lessons'. I was the most talkative, and consequently Grandfather turned to me for coherent information. He repeatedly asked Fatma and me, "Who is the elder of you two?" I replied, "I am Mariam, the second daughter." He acknowledged with a knowing smile – sending a message to me. He seemed to understand my plight in a blink. It is one of my fondest memories of him.

I was also dazzled by the beautiful woman who stood behind Grandfather's chair. Her name was Nazmia; she was his last wife, a young lady of Turkish origin whom Grandfather had met in Paris. Nazmia had been brought up in the court of Sultan Abdul Hamid of Turkey, a companion to the daughters of the Sultan. When the Sultan was exiled by Kemal Ataturk, founder of modern Turkey, the whole court including Nazmia settled in Paris. This was an expensive undertaking and, especially as the traditional source of income had been so rudely taken away from him, the Sultan realised that he had to take drastic measures, so he decided to sell the royal jewels. At the time my grandfather, recently and tragically widowed, was also living in Paris and ended up not only buying the jewels but marrying Nazmia. After this marriage, Grandfather then supported the Sultan's whole family for years. Later his son, my favourite Uncle Yousuf, married Nazmia's equally beautiful younger sister, Sabahat.

During this period in Bombay we also met Aunty Mahra for the first time. A daughter of Haji Abbas, her grandfather was Sheikh Mohammad bin Khalifa who ruled in Lingah for a number of years in the 1890s until a rift with one of the powerful Khans of Bastak prompted him to return to Sharjah. Aunty Mahra had married an Abbas cousin and settled in Bombay. Years later, her children settled in Dubai, where they still live, near their relatives, the ruling Al Qasimis of Sharjah.

At the time we met him, Grandfather was very sick; his special physician, a German doctor, travelled with him wherever he went. Apparently he had suffered a series of strokes, one of which had impaired his vision. It was said that the physician managed to restore his eyesight by sitting him on the beach outside one of his palatial houses in Bombay and letting the strong waves splash his temples. Sadly he died of a stroke not long after our meeting. He was then in his late 80s.

The paternal side of our family was also involved in the pearl industry. Great-uncle Farooq in particular had been a well-known and respected trader and dealer, which is why he spent so much of his time in Paris.

There has always been a mystical quality about pearls; it is a well-deserved reputation. A pearl doesn't sparkle and glitter in the ostentatious manner of a diamond but has an elegant, elusive beauty that intrigues rather than overwhelms.

Even the actual trading of these gems was spiced with a great deal of mystery. The pearl merchants, dressed in their gleaming white *dishdashas*, would sit huddled together with Indian brokers around a special red material that was spread out on the carpet. A similar red cloth was spread over their heads like a canopy. A handful of pearls was strewn onto the material and the men graded, negotiated and conducted the whole business with coded hand gestures in almost complete silence. The need for secrecy concerning the price was considered paramount. Often the only sound that could be heard was the soft chirring of the pearls as they rolled around the material.

When the men finally finished their business and picked up their scales, we children used to try and sneak in to grab the very tiny pearls that had been left behind. These normally would only be used by the women to sew on to cuffs and collars. I loved these pretty little things and kept them in a bottle and later threaded them as a necklace for my doll. One can only speculate on the value, by today's standards, of the Gulf pearls my doll was wearing around her neck.

Like most of our family houses, the Bombay place in what was then Kethwadi Main Road was huge. Here too we lived with a number of uncles, aunts, grandparents and cousins all in our own separate areas. An integral part of the household were *dhobis* and *darzis*, the men who worked as launderers and tailors. The entire building with ten families shared the services of the *dhobis* who used to astound me with their remarkable ability to take away hundreds of pieces of soiled clothing and, without making a single note – they were illiterate – return garments to their owners. The *darzi* moved among the closed balconies on each floor of the house, stitching clothes all year round. The sound of the little manual Singer sewing machine constantly rang through the house. When I peeked, I saw a little man permanently bent over his machine.

The entire first floor of our house was taken up by a kitchen and a *majlis*, where the men congregated for prayers and conducted their business. There was also a magnificent library located here, as well as rooms kept ready for visitors and guests, most of whom seemed to me to be from Dubai, Bastak and Lingeh. People just walked in, trailed by a porter with their baggage, which in those days was bulky and heavy. There was never any question about whether anyone would stay, and how long or short their visit was to be did not cause any problem or concern: guests were considered blessings from Allah. Well I remember the verse inscribed in the imposing stone archway at the entrance to the compound: *"Goshadah bad bedowlat hamishah in dargah, Behage. Ashado An La Ellaha Ellalah"* – "May this hospitable door be always open, in the name of Allah, the Almighty."

Upstairs, each section of the extended family had their own suite. There were also two similar houses on either side of the main building. One of these belonged to Sheikh Mostafa, another successful merchant and philanthropist who was related to us – one of his daughters was married to Great-uncle Farooq and two others, at different times, had married my grandfather, Haji Abbas. The other house belonged to Grandfather's elder brother Haji Mohammad Abdulla Abbas.

The houses were all within walking distance and the men saw a lot of one another but, as women and children, we lived well-hidden behind our own walls and seldom met those from the neighbouring houses, even though we were closely related.

Despite being in another country, life was no different from what it had been in our home country, which meant that it was regulated by the same routines and we suffered the same restrictions. We were not, for instance, permitted to roam freely in the large landscaped garden, which was part of the beauty and charm of the house. In Bombay's tropical climate, all manner of exotic fruit grew – forbidden fruit, as usual. The mangoes, guavas, boras, bananas, jamuns, papayas, custard apple, chickoos and coconuts were so tempting. As usual it was only the men who could roam freely through the garden and play tennis. I remember sneaking out to climb the tall trees. I had a ball, but the repercussions were not as pleasant. There were many nights, therefore, when I went to bed wishing that I would wake up as a boy.

The only time we were allowed any freedom was when we holidayed in Poona, a beautiful place up in the hills not far from Bombay. Ahmad Abbas had bought a sprawling bungalow there which was called 'God's Gift' and each family used it in turn. It was a wonderful summer resort and it was always with feelings of relief that we left the sweltering streets of Bombay behind to travel to the cool, clear air of Poona. Here no high walls surrounded us, only the hills looking for all the world like beautiful scenic portraits that could be admired and even explored. The whole place had a relaxed air about it. Many wealthy and aristocratic families stayed there during the summer months so it was a time when we met and socialised with other people on a more casual basis.

After the carefree time spent in Poona it was doubly difficult to return to the restrictive and often tense atmosphere of the house in Bombay. With so many different families living in the one house, there were numerous petty problems often caused by jealousies and personality clashes, fuelled by gossiping servants.

The problems would usually begin in the women's section and they would take their grievances to the men, who would then have great arguments among themselves until the peacemakers, invariably the grandfathers and grandmothers, could calm everybody down.

Baugappi and Momba (my father's parents) could often ease a tense situation just by being there, for they were kind and gentle people. Devoted to each other, they were well-respected by all the family. It was wonderful to see them together, for they shared everything. They prayed together, read the Quran together – even ate off the same plate. I loved being in their company. They were kind to me and seemed to enjoy listening to me read paragraphs from religious texts and traditional Persian literature such as *Gulistan va Boostan-e-Saadi, Meraj Hazrate Rasul,* and *Moulood-e-Noori.* Afterwards I would sit and listen as they discussed what I had read to them. My understanding and appreciation of these works now is in part due to what I learnt during those discussions.

Our studies could not be neglected while we were in Bombay, so local teachers were brought in. It was here that we began to learn English and Urdu, as well as learn Indian styles of sewing and embroidery. Unfortunately, our old tutor, the terrible *mullah,* Ismail, had also been brought to instruct us in the Quran. It was believed that although the Indians had good religious teachers, their pronunciation was not as good as a native Arabic or Farsi-speaker. Our bruises multiplied!

Staying within our own households even applied to our schooling for, though there were a number of children in the house and we all had the same teachers, we did our lessons separately and our teachers moved from floor to floor and household to household.

Because of the restrictions and the fact that we had rather abruptly become almost like orphans, this period was not a particularly happy one for us. Monkhali was always worried and so stricter than ever and, although we were well cared for, we often felt quite lonely.

Nor was Bombay a particularly healthy place to live in the mid-1930s, suffering as it did outbreaks of serious epidemics such as typhoid and diphtheria. There were no sure cures for such illnesses in those days, and when two of my young cousins died from typhoid, the women decided the house was unlucky and wanted to move out. Although the men were known as the policy-makers and the rulers in the outside world, within the four walls of the house, it was the women who wielded authority, so it wasn't long before the house was sold and the families moved en masse to Karachi.

CHAPTER 8

SCHOOLDAYS

In the late 1930s, exciting news was coming from Iran – Reza Shah Pahlavi had abolished the *purdah* system under a sweeping reform popularly known as *kashfe-hijab*. In one stroke he ordered women to discard the veil and men to adopt practical western-style clothing. We heard all about it from our home in Karachi. It was like a new, spring-scented breeze blowing through out lives. News has never been so sweet, nor caused such pandemonium. While there were those like me who rejoiced, the reaction of some women – incredible though it seemed to me as a teenager then, and incredible though it seems to me still – was to commit suicide; others simply fled Iran. Those who stayed yet were uncomfortable with the new dictum adopted overcoats with huge scarfs and hats, gloves and stockings winter and summer to cover as much of themselves as possible. The tailors must have had a heyday. For years after, we revelled in hearing about and discussing those traumatic and fun-filled times, when women were forced to venture out.

But as usual, I was out of step at the time with everyone else in our house. We were living in Garden East with Great-uncle Arshi, another of Monkhali's brothers. The reaction of the elders to these crackling voices on the radio was to thank God that we were not in Iran and that none of our women would have to endure such a disgrace. To be obliged by law to walk about without *chadors* seemed to signal the end of the world!

"A woman's greatest desire is to stay within the walls of her own home, caring for her own family," they said. "How can we possibly attend public functions without our veils? We have rarely been exposed to the public eye even with veils. The indignity of it all!" I saw to my sadness that many women were genuinely happy with their lot. My sister Fatma, for example, was content with our way of life, but I felt differently – I was restless, I had ambitions and more than anything I wanted to feel free.

After the initial disappointment of not being in Iran and still stuck with wearing my *chador* and *chadernomaz*, I began to feel excited when I realised what effect these profound and dramatic changes might have for me and all those other women who I had always believed lived in an unjust world.

I wanted change too and I began to make demands!

The first major change I wanted to bring about concerned my schooling. I desperately wanted to go to a public school, to sit on a bench with other children, to learn history, geography, science, art and music – all the things we didn't learn at home. It was true we had an excellent grounding in the Quran. We read and learned from our traditional Persian literature, and we even knew a great deal of English, but, for me, this wasn't enough. I wanted to know more about everything. I wanted to live according to the principle: "*Ze gahvare ta goor danish bejooy* – acquire knowledge from the cradle to the grave."

The arguments began. Although Monkhali was a very intelligent woman with a lot of foresight, was extremely well-read and kept her own bookshelf of classics such as *Kimeya-e-Saadat, Tafseer-e-Quran, Diwan-e-Hafiz, Shah Nama Firdausi* and the *Rubayat-e-Khayyam*, she was too committed to tradition and, possibly, too stubborn to understand my way of thinking. She threatened me with dire punishments – and carried out her threats. She predicted terrible things would occur to me in later life, but, having inherited her stubbornness, I refused to give in. "May your children harass you one day as you have done me!" was one of her favourite curses. It was probably the worst thing she could think of for anybody to have to endure, and in a way, her prediction proved correct. I was reminded of her words when my own children were growing up, one of my daughters in particular flying when other children ran, and even now I have to smile when I see familiar old patterns emerging through my grandchildren.

But back in those days, escaping the stifling mould of

tradition seemed like a matter of life or death to me. It fell to Great-uncle Farooq, who was on one of his rare visits from Paris, to tip the scales in my favour. Monkhali explained the problem.

"It is so difficult to control this Mariam. She wants to go to school. What for? She says to learn English, get degrees. Why? Does she want to become employed somewhere? How can this be? We employ people, our men have never worked for salaries. How can we let a woman go out and be exposed to the ugliness of life? We can provide all the teachers she needs right here in our home but she wants to go to school!"

Great-uncle Farooq, for all his loud and frightening ways, was an intelligent, caring man with a good sense of humour and, when he stared at me with his clear, piercing eyes, I stood unflinching and stared right back. It was a bold and rude thing to do but, if I hadn't, I would never have seen the twinkle in his eye or understood this softer side of him. I pleaded and argued and quoted the Quran and entreated, "Great-uncle, your own clever daughter, Faiqa, goes to school. Why can't I?"

He was a little taken aback by this argument and then he smiled and confided that he and Faiqa had often laughed about my escapades. "If Faiqa were here, I know I would have two of you pleading with me to agree to your latest scheme," he said, and gave his consent.

Arrangements were made for Fatma and me to go to school. I was ecstatic. We were about 15 years old at the time – the age many girls finish their school life – but I didn't care. My real education had begun!

The school chosen for us was Jufel Hurst High School. It was run by two old spinsters known as the D'Abro sisters. There was a third sister but she was mad and was locked up in the attic. Occasionally we heard screams and yells and sometimes if we were lucky would catch a glimpse of her face, when she escaped and got out onto the landing. She had a nightmarish grin and her face was framed with wild, bushy hair. The memory still makes my hair stand on end.

I often think we must have appeared weird and strange to the rest of the school with our style of dress, customs and lack of worldly knowledge. We always travelled to school in two horse-drawn buggies, which were covered at the front to separate us from the driver. In addition Jameela and a gholoom, Mahmood, always accompanied us. Mahmood stood by the gate and Jameela sat at the back of the classroom. We had never been left alone before, even for an instant, so it would have been a strange and frightening experience to be put amongst strangers without at least one personal retainer.

Our *janamaz* or prayer mat and a container of water were carried with us everywhere and at prayer time, no matter how busy we were, or what we were doing – even during exams – Jameela would spread out the *janamaz*, prepare the water for our ablutions and we would pray. Naturally everyone watched us in fascination because, for them, religion was personal and confined to the home. This made me feel embarrassed, so I would hide behind Jameela's substantial bulk. However, because of the sensitive situation we were in, we carefully abided by the rules of home. I had my wish and I was at school, so I did not want to be removed. Later a separate prayer room was provided, which made things a lot better for us and other Muslim students.

I hated our cumbersome, ugly clothes. Underneath the calf-length dresses we wore white trousers trimmed with a variety of lace and pleats. Over these trousers we put on stockings to conform to the school uniform. We kept our heads covered with several veils and a *chador* was worn over everything. It was especially embarrassing when we joined in gymnastics. With every few jumps, our stockings would come down and everybody would laugh. I loved sport but hated being a laughing stock so something had to go.

Every morning when I got to school, I took off all the extra uncomfortable clothes and changed into more normal ones. For this I had to bribe Jameela with lots of sweet words. She was the easy one. It was Dada Fatma who worried me the most for she did not like physical activity, so there was always the threat that when we argued at home she would report me to Monkhali, but she must have realised how much it meant to me for she never did tell.

However, it was not just a matter of religion, or the way we dressed, or even the fact that we were always escorted everywhere like two princesses; our whole attitude was different. For example, if we were asked to bring a 'dish' to school for a special occasion, from our house would come a huge pot of rice and meat *biryani,* and numerous other things – enough to feed a battalion! Consequently we were thought of as being exotic and treated in a special way – we never actually knew what 'normal' meant.

On the whole, I loved school. I worked hard and achieved good results. But more than anything I wanted to join in every extra-curricular activity available. School picnics, concerts, sports: "Why can't I participate?" I would ask. The answer was always the same: "It was not done in our family."

Some things, however, I managed by subterfuge. I took music classes under the pretext of going to Arabic lessons and I even managed classical Indian dancing for a while, which was quite an act of rebellion, for dancing was something entirely forbidden in our family. In fact, we were always told we must walk straight and never sway our hips as it was not ladylike.

At one time Monkhali relented a little and let me learn the violin for she wanted us to be accomplished and considered ladies. Unfortunately, one day she heard that people were saying that the Behnam girl was learning to play the *chung,* a primitive street musical instrument, and her worry about what other people thought won out over her ambitions for us. She immediately broke the violin to pieces and refused to speak any more about something that was causing people to talk about us.

The very worst thing I ever did in everybody's eyes was to have my hair cut. A woman with short hair was considered undignified and if somebody said, "*Sorot bachenen* – may your hair be cut", it really meant "May you be ridiculed and humiliated". The most horrible name to be called was '*domboreeda* ' or monkey with a cut tail.

I didn't care. I found my long, knee length hair a nuisance. Every day I had to go through the ordeal of having it plaited; mercifully it was only two plaits and not the 40 of our early childhood, but it was still a tedious ritual. I envied girls I saw with short, manageable hair.

Every month I began to cut an inch or so from my long,

thick locks. Monkhali was in the habit of measuring it with her hand, and couldn't understand why it was getting shorter and shorter. "Remember the fever I had last year?" I would tell her. "My hair hasn't grown since then." Or I would say that I hadn't been out in the sun lately, or some similar nonsense that appealed to her superstitious side.

This went on for some months. Monkhali, though suspicious, seemed to accept my excuses, but I continued to long to be free of that heavy, dragging hair. Finally I couldn't bear it any more. I went to a beauty salon and told them I wanted the lot off.

In those days girls were meant to get permission to have their hair cut but I had Jameela with me, so the hairdresser supposed that it was all right. Clip, clip... my head felt light and the hairdresser had enough hair to weave a rug!

Suddenly the realisation of what I had done hit me like the south-east monsoon, all cold and clammy. I dreaded the thought of going home and showing the family my new hairstyle. As it was a cold, rainy day, I wrapped my head up in a scarf, put on my *chador* and, shivering more from fright than from the cold, prepared to meet my fate.

"Why have you got a scarf wrapped around your head?" Monkhali wanted to know.

"I have a headache and I think I'm getting the flu," I replied and quickly disappeared.

I scrubbed my eyes and nose and forced out fake sneezes and coughs but this deception only lasted two days. Monkhali was definitely suspicious.

A couple of nights later after I had gone to bed she came into my room and discovered that the sleeping head on the pillow had shockingly short hair! She woke me up and I got a sound thrashing, though it didn't hurt as much as she had hoped because by this time I'd learned the trick of cracking the hubble-bubble stick, which made it a less painful form of punishment. Anyway I felt the achievement was worth any punishment, for I was the very first girl in our whole, huge family ever to have had her hair cut that short.

Going to school brought me into contact with people outside my family circle, and I began to realise how different other people's lives and upbringing could be from my own. I had been brought up by the grannies with their rigid codes of conduct, restrictions and deprivations, and while my background had a certain novelty value, it made it difficult for me to fit into 'normal' society.

Nevertheless, I desperately wanted to make friends, so I decided I needed to join a club called the Ladies Progressive Club of Karachi. It offered cultural, sporting and educational activities and I knew I could learn so much there. The club had been founded by the Ashraf girls, daughters of the wealthy Ashraf brothers, who had set up business originally in Bahrain but had been so successful that eventually they had stores trading in all the countries throughout the Gulf. Around the 1940s they were living in Karachi.

After much pleading with my family I was finally allowed to join the club but, to my embarrassment, I found I was too different to fit in. Teenagers can be cruel and demanding for, being unsure of themselves, they develop a rigid and often unspoken code. Everyone must look, act and speak in the same way and those who don't are ridiculed mercilessly.

It was a devastating experience to discover how different and definitely 'wrong' I was. Everything about me seemed to be wrong. My clothes were out of date; I held a badminton racquet awkwardly; even my voice which I had always believed to be powerful and appealing, made everyone laugh when I tried to sing modern Urdu and English songs.

Being different was just not acceptable and I was not accepted. Particularly hurtful was the way Ruqaya Ashraf laughed at me and made me the butt of her jokes. Humiliated, I left the club.

The experience made me even more determined to show that I could be as good as anybody so, in secret, I learned how to play badminton, I memorised the words of the modern songs and the way to sing them, and I insisted on wearing fashionable clothes. Within six months I rejoined the club; no longer a misfit, I was now accepted. In fact, Ruqaya and I became quite close.

My friendship with Ruqaya (who went on to become a professor at Bombay University, the mother of a doctor, a writer, and a university lecturer) and the other Ashraf girls has lasted through the years. Their large, happy family gave me affection in abundance. I often compared this kind, generous family with my own and wondered why I couldn't have grown up in a more congenial and harmonious atmosphere. I was envious of the way the Ashraf children were so obviously loved and respected. Although I knew I shouldn't need a demonstration of Monkhali's affection after all she had done for us, being young and insecure, it was what I dearly wanted. So I used to make up stories at home in order to get away, to join my friends at their homes and enjoy for awhile some of the warmth and friendliness that seemed to be lacking in my own family life.

Another lady who was a great influence at that time was Lady Nusrat Haroon. 'Aunty' Haroon had been a close friend of my mother's. She was an Iranian from Shiraz and had married Sir Abdullah Haroon, a prominent citizen with an impressive personality. At the time of the creation of Pakistan, Lady Haroon and her whole family worked tirelessly towards achieving that goal. A dynamic person, she held the strong belief that, except for being physically weaker, women were often superior to men as she felt they had more common sense, more tolerance and usually a more agile mind. She used to say that "to educate a man is to educate an individual but to educate a woman is to educate a family."

I admired her for being what she was, and hoped that one day I could be like her. Because of my contact with her, I began to develop a social consciousness and to direct my energies positively toward becoming a useful member of society.

I became a Girl Guide and a National Guard volunteer and it was Aunty Haroon who encouraged me to make my first public speech. I can't remember what my topic was, but I do remember the experience was nerve-wracking. However, once I got over the stage fright, it gave me a great deal of pleasure for I found I actually enjoyed conveying messages to an audience of women and girls who were striving towards the same goals as myself.

Because I was with somebody as socially important as Lady Haroon, I was allowed to participate in such activities, yet I was still not allowed to go on school outings even with Jameela and Mahmood in attendance. I was tired of the tired-out excuse – "Girls of our family just don't do things like that." More than anything I wanted to do these things, so I was continually scheming and plotting to get Monkhali to change her mind. One of my school friends helped think up a particularly good but rather mad plan. The whole scheme relied on the co-operation of the girl's father, who was a doctor. Fortunately he was a kind man with a good sense of humour and a great deal of common sense. When we put our plan to him, he agreed to help. Crazy or not, the scheme worked, thanks to him. This is the way it went.

One day after returning from school, I confronted Monkhali about going on a school outing. She of course absolutely refused permission. At that point I fell down, moaned and acted at being unconscious. There was a terrible uproar; Monkhali was frantic. Water was poured over me, I stiffened and held my breath.

"My God!" Monkhali cried. "This poor motherless child has been entrusted to me. What shall I do?"

Things went exactly according to plan. Dr Joshi was summoned and he asked what had caused the collapse. Monkhali told him it occurred after she had forbidden me to go on a school outing.

"Ah!" said Dr Joshi knowingly. "There is your problem. The child has a weak heart and you must not suppress her too much. If you do not agree to things that are reasonable and logical, this is likely to be the result. There should be no problem with her going on a school excursion. My own daughter will be there. No harm can come to her."

Hearing all this and the general negative reaction I began to whimper, "Oh Mama! I am coming to you!"

"Oh no!" cried poor Monkhali. "The child is seeing a vision. Ya Allah! You get well and we will let you do what you want."

I tried not to make my recovery too miraculous else Monkhali smelt a rat, and I was able to use my 'weak heart' problem time and again. Deceitful though it may have been to devise such methods, I had to resort to any ploy I could to try and gain the freedom and independence which I felt seemed to be reserved for others.

The whole concept of independence particularly was a completely unheard-of idea in our family, even in the early 1940s. Elsewhere in the world women and young girls were working in factories, nursing soldiers, and often being put in situations where they just had to be able to cope by themselves because of the terrible World War that was devastating so many countries, and threatening to change the whole face of the world.

Monkhali, however, had always lived within four walls with the ideal security of family and wealth, and for her the outside world was a place ladies did not inhabit. So it was difficult for her to understand why anyone should ever want such a strange thing as 'independence'.

CHAPTER 9

CHILDHOOD'S END

As I grew up, I became more headstrong and made life increasingly difficult for my little old grandmother, trying her best to make me march to a tune I could not hear. Sometimes she believed there was a demon inside me, but irrepressible youth is what it really was. I had all the confidence, courage and arrogance of the young. I believed my way was the best and only way.

Nothing pleased me more than to show how clever I was. Sometimes this backfired and more than once I found myself in tricky situations where I suppose confidence, arrogance, common sense and luck in equal proportions carried me through.

In other instances, quick thinking genuinely did save the day. One rather delicate problem that I was able to resolve involved a 'misunderstanding' between one of our great-aunties and the Customs Department. The auntie had lost her husband of 30 years to a younger woman. Heartbroken, the dear, childless lady packed all her gold jewellery, which weighed 20 kilos or more, and made plans to join her family in Karachi.

In those days, no customs tax had to be paid on jewellery that was worn and, with all our travels between India and Iran, I can remember being literally weighed down by our own ancestral gold (which we always declared) around my neck, my arms, on my fingers and ankles. God knows the value of what we were wearing! However, this simple-hearted lady had so much she could not possibly wear it all, so a gunny bag of rice was 'honoured' with a few pieces; each pair of shoes received a few earrings; her gold brocaded dresses had more pieces sewn into the cuffs and even each pot and pan became a gold carrier.

On arriving in Karachi she didn't declare even one little ring. The Customs officials confiscated the lot and wanted to impose a huge fine. It was a calamity and when word went round, pandemonium broke out in our household. The poor lady had no home, no husband and now no money. It seemed an impossible situation.

In desperation, the family turned to me: "Mariam, Mariam, may Allah reward you, may he fulfil all your dreams and wishes! Please go to the Customs as you are familiar with the outside world. Please do something for our dear one."

By making a few enquiries, I found out that the Customs officer in charge was elderly, literate and particularly interested in the Persian classics. He received me cordially, and after briefly explaining the situation to him, we enjoyed a discussion of the verses of Hafiz, Saadi and Omar Khayyam. The gentleman's attitude began to soften as we talked. He admitted that it was possible a mistake had been made, so an antique expert was called in, who confirmed that all the gold and gem stones were at least 40 years old. Considering the lady's background and age, it was reasonable then to assume that the huge amount of valuable jewellery could indeed be her personal belongings.

I quoted a couplet from Omar Khayyam: "*Oo bad konado to bad mokafat dehi, pas farq miyane to va oo cheest begoo*? — He makes a mistake and you in turn treat him badly. What then is the difference between you and him?" The situation was saved, and everybody's belief in my shrewdness (including my own) grew to staggering proportions.

At times though I could be frustrated by those who always wanted me to help them. My sister, Fatma, often annoyed me the most. We were such different people. She was immaculately tidy and fastidious and when we went visiting she always took her own cutlery and would not use any other. She even had her dishes washed between courses. Worst of all though, she never shared anything. In fact, if I so much as touched any of her things, she would throw them away, saying she did not want them any more. So if ever I wanted something of hers, I would deliberately use them and she would curse me, "*Jahanamot!* — to hell with you! — Keep it now; I don't want it." The ploy always worked, although she was often advised by Monkhali, "Tear it, burn it, but don't give it to her!"

All this fuss irritated me. During the day we were always fighting but at night in our huge bed, which was the only thing we did share, things were different. Every morning around 2 or 3am, Fatma would very softly and sweetly wake me up by whispering, "*Khongoy, khongoy.*" When I dragged myself out of my sleep she would say, "*Khongoy*, please get up, there is a funny noise under our bed. I think there is a thief."

Our bed was huge – a step was needed to climb up into it – and a whole legion of thieves could have hidden under it, but it was only her terrible fear of darkness that could make her actually believe they were there.

However, she wasn't the only paranoid one. The whole household seemed to be infected. At this time there were no men living inside the house as Great-uncle Arshi and his son Mohammed Akil lived in an annexe. All the women in the house, even Monkhali, felt insecure.

During the day there was the constant talk of us all being robbed and murdered in our beds, so it was not surprising that at night those fears became more real and terrifying. I enjoyed teasing everybody and always laughed at their fears for I knew that the house was well-guarded and no incident had ever occurred to make them think such a thing could happen.

I also became increasingly tired of being woken up for such silly reasons, so I started to hatch a plan to teach them all a lesson and have a bit of fun myself. The opportunity came one night when Monkhali told us all to go to bed early. I knew this meant that she wanted to open all her precious trunks, for she constantly worried about the safety of her belongings. Whenever we travelled everything seemed to accompany us. Consequently we had trunk upon trunk full of coins, old books, silk, satin and jewels, which were always kept in her own room, so she could keep her eagle eye on them.

Hardly any of these valuable things were ever used or presented to anybody but Monkhali seemed to love just possessing them. She was the archetypal hoarder. Her greatest pleasure was gloating over her goods in private. She didn't trust anybody and believed that everybody was trying to get hold of her property by witchcraft or other means.

This particular night I stuffed some pillows into my side of the bed, so Dada Fatma would not notice that I had gone, then very quietly I got out of bed, took a sheet and crept across the darkened corridor to Monkhali's room. Her door was ajar.

I watched in fascination as she began to open all her boxes and trunks and take out each valuable item one at a time and look at it. Sitting in the dim yellow light cast by a single lamp, she was soon surrounded by swathes of beautiful material, piles of gold coins, heaps of ancient manuscripts and a fortune in precious stones.

The time was right! Quickly I draped the sheet over myself and with a stick in my hand I pranced into the room. Monkhali shrieked and in the half-darkness tried to push everything back into the trunks, all the while cursing and jabbering in a wild concoction of Arabic and Farsi for, in her terror, it seems she had forgotten her own Bastaki dialect

I leapt, whirled and hissed; in her state, Monkhali must have thought a whole troop of 'whirling dervishes' had attacked her. The noise she made was incredible and soon everybody came running.

"Get Mariam," they all screamed. "Where is she?"

They raced to my room and found Fatma lying stiff and scarcely breathing out of fright and to the others it must have seemed I was in the same state for I, too, was silent.

"Mariam! Mariam! *Jahanamot Mordostesh*! (Oh hell! Are you dead?) Tonight when I need you, you are dead! May Allah punish you." Monkhali called and threatened me.

In the meantime my great-grandmother had woken up and as she was not scared of anything, she took the most handy weapon, a stick, and began to chase the apparition around the room.

I rushed out, ran into my own room and managed to get under the bed but Great-grandmother thrust the stick after me. As she pushed, I pulled and as this crazy tug of war went on the others were all screaming for me to wake up.

By this time the men had been called. Normally Great-uncle Arshi and his son would never come to the women's quarters without prior notice, but in an emergency like this there were no second thoughts.

Because it was dark, nobody could see what was happening and everybody was too frightened to come close. Fortunately for me no one had thought of turning the lights on. When Great-grandmother finally retreated, I managed to slip into bed before the men arrived and pretended I had just woken up.

"What's happening?" I asked, yawning and blinking my eyes.

"My God, after all this commotion which you somehow managed to sleep through, you have the nerve to ask what is happening?" Monkhali was trembling and almost incoherent.

Great-uncle Arshi immediately had his suspicions. He nodded his head. "Mariam, come outside I want to talk to you," he said. "All right, tell me all about it," he demanded when we were alone. "I know you are the culprit."

I had to explain everything and why I had done it. When I finished Great-uncle Arshi chuckled but he also pointed out that Monkhali could have had a heart attack and I would have been responsible, which made me realise that I wasn't as clever or funny as I had thought. But he was wonderful and later, it became a great family joke – even Monkhali used to join in the laughter. The best result of all was that from then on the other women seldom disturbed my sleep.

Despite her rigidness in so many things, Monkhali was nothing if not a good sport. This gradually dawned on me as I grew up and saw her joining in the fun even though she was often the target of the joke. She loved the get-togethers that were our principal form of entertainment.

However, years later we did receive a visit from a real thief and it was my room on the third floor of the house we were living in that he tried to burgle. I had come home very late from a wedding and, after removing my jewellery, had put it in the cupboard, ready to give to Monkhali in the morning to place in the iron safe.

During the night I was awakened by a noise and found myself staring into the face of a little black man. He wore red pants and had covered his body in oil to prevent people getting a good grip on him. Although I was frightened he looked even more so and made a dash for the window. I scrambled out of bed and rushed out of the room screaming, *"Dozd! Dozd! —* thief! thief!" The family's reaction was not what I had hoped it would be: They all locked their doors and crept under the covers. I realised then I would have to do something about the situation myself. Quickly I ran to the bathroom, grabbed an iron stool and raced back into my bedroom.

By this time the thief was trying to escape by climbing down the drain pipes. I leaned out of the window and crashed the stool over his head, knocking him down to the first floor balcony, where he was then captured. It later transpired that this same thief the night before had burgled a house, removing 20 bangles from a lady's hand while she watched, petrified and helpless, only shouting the alarm after he had escaped. Brave by impulse, I crawled back into my bed shaking like a leaf.

Although we were happy living with Great-uncle Arshi, the house wasn't large enough for everyone, even though our household had been considerably reduced. Only six servants remained, including Jameela. It was therefore decided we would move in with father's brother, Uncle Abdul Rahman. He lived in a big two-storey place and his family only used the top floor, so we were able to have the lower section of the house.

Uncle Abdul Rahman was the one who had married Zohra, the beautiful 'outsider' from Saudi Arabia. From the moment we moved in, this family had a profound influence on me. My aunt was beautiful and clever and my uncle was a carefree, happy-go-lucky sort of man. He often quoted Omar Khayyam who believed in the breadth rather than the length of life. After the stifling atmosphere of Monkhali's household where everything was reserved for some distant time in the future, I found this concept exciting and heady stuff indeed.

The whole family seemed to like and respect my intellect, as I did theirs. Often Aunty Zohra's mother used to say, "We have given your family a daughter and someday we hope to get a daughter in return." Always she looked at me. Soon my aunt and uncle began to talk endlessly about Aunty Zohra's brother, Zakaria, and I began to show interest. Monkhali was horrified.

"It is said that he is married to a lady in Johannesburg and has a daughter and has apparently left them," she told me. "It's a complete mismatch — he doesn't work, he is not well educated, he's not even from our social background. He is not a relative and not even a *khodmooni*."

This, however, pleased me, for I had always declared that I would not marry a relation, which was a revolutionary concept at that time.

What I knew of Zakaria's family was good. His father, Sayed Siddique, was a travelling religious leader and because of this the whole family often travelled to South Africa, India and Saudi Arabia. He taught the Quran and Islamic literature to the children of well-known families. Besides this he was a *sayyed*, a direct descendant of the Prophet, and so not only was he a learned man but a respected one also. The girls of the family, who were as cultured as they were beautiful, had all married well. *Sitti* Nafisa was the wife of the grandfather of the present ruler of Oman, His Majesty Sultan Qaboos ibn Said; her son, HH Shabib bin Taimur, was born just a couple of years before my own son. *Sitti* Zainab married into the Ali Reza family, one of the most distinguished and internationally reputed Saudi merchant families whose roots can be traced to the Lingah area. And then of course, there was Aunty Zohra who was married to my uncle.

"He is Aunty Zohra's brother," I protested to Monkhali.

"That is not good enough." Monkhali wanted no more talk about it. To get away from the 'bad influence', we moved back to Great-uncle Arshi's house and severed all relations with Uncle Abdul Rahman and Zakaria's family. I was even taken out of school and put under 'house-arrest' by my own family. Given my nature, this had an adverse effect, so my attitude became more defiant.

During all this time – more than three years – Zakaria and I had never met or spoken a single word to each other, though we had been able to exchange whimsical notes that didn't really mean much. Marriage in those days was a gamble, for neither the man nor the woman really knew what the other even looked like, let alone what sort of character each had. It was all word of mouth and exaggeration, and the suppression of certain not-so-flattering details was normal. Girls especially had no say in their future and, certainly where a marriage was concerned, the matter was settled by the family, though boys at least had the chance to refuse.

At 18, marriage to me meant freedom from the restrictions of my home life. Also, as a wife, I would be viewed differently by the world. I would no longer be just a young girl so I believed life would be less restrictive and I made up my mind to marry Zakaria, although there were two other names suggested. I believed, too, that once Zakaria and I were wed, we could both continue our education and help and encourage each other to grow into mature and responsible members of our community. Deep down I was an insecure, inexperienced teenager. I craved for someone to understand me; love me for myself and show me the outside world. He had travelled a great deal and I felt he was the ideal choice.

My dream was blissful and I wanted it to come true. Soon people began to link our names and my family after two years of opposition finally agreed to the marriage. I felt excited and on top of the world but Monkhali had terrible misgivings. I was soon to find out that she had been right all along. My marriage from the very first day was a failure. We were from different worlds and had married for the wrong reasons.

We lived with his family in Bombay. They were kind and wonderful to me, especially Zakaria's sister Zubaida and her husband Dr Mohammad Abdullah Abedin, a gem of a friend and always great support. I needed all the love and understanding that these two kind and wise people gave in abundance, for I had lost confidence in myself and felt I was to blame for the situation I now found myself in. I had believed my judgement was sounder than Monkhali's.

When Zakaria told me that my family and I were haughty and arrogant, and that he had only married me to prove that the impossible could be achieved, I knew my marriage had very little hope of survival. Within three months he left for

South Africa, supposedly to look for work, but really to leave Bombay behind. All I could do was nurse the secret hope that he would return soon to take me back with him.

I was crushed. I missed my home and Monkhali desperately for it was the first time I had ever been parted from my family. Ignorant of my problems, yet concerned for me, Monkhali made an excuse to visit Bombay. By then my health had suffered. I looked a ghost of my old self. Monkhali was shocked by my state of affairs and insisted that I go back to Karachi with her and wait for Zakaria to return. Later we heard that he had remarried, and I never saw him until a decade later.

I returned to Karachi a very different person from the happy, confident but naïve and innocent bride I had been when I left. My dreams were shattered, my spirit in tatters and I was to become a mother.

Monkhali was wonderful. She nursed me and always kept me close to her. One night she woke me up and she was smiling. "Mariam," she said. "I have just dreamt that I saw a huge bird descending from the sky. On one wing was written *solh* or peace, and on the other was the name 'Essa'."

Not long after that, in the autmn of 1944, my son was born. We named him Essa. Then in the spring of 1945, the end of the Second World War brought the peace we had all been praying for.

CHAPTER 10

SHORT-LIVED FREEDOM

Suddenly – or so it seemed – I was a mother, though still young and inexperienced. I loved Essa but was not prepared for such a responsibility, especially under the conditions. Having lived all my life in a large household with an extended family group, I expected others to look after the day-to-day problems of bringing up my baby. Fortunately for my sweet little son, Dada Fatma by this time was married and had also just given birth to a boy, so the two children were brought up together in the same house, and his Aunties Bibiya and Badria doted on him. Monkhali adored him: "He is a gift of the Almighty," she used to say.

Meanwhile I tried to patch up my life. The break-up of my marriage was a considerable blow to my self-esteem. It was especially bitter as I had gone ahead with the marriage despite the disapproval and warnings of my family. I hadn't considered their reasons convincing enough, because I thought I knew better. Now, however, I felt like a door had closed off a part of my life. The roles were reversed on Mariam the clever one, the problem-solver, the consoler, and the one who laughed at everybody's fears: now I was the object of pity, the one with the seemingly insoluble problem. Even worse was the discovery that I was fallible and could make irreparable mistakes.

I felt a range of conflicting emotions. Zakaria had disappeared completely, yet in our son I was left with a lifetime of responsibility and even worse a constant tangible reminder of that brief unhappy time. This made me angry and at the same time worried about how I would cope. I could no longer just think about my own life, for my son's welfare became more important than my own. Bitterness and unhappiness changed my whole character for many months. I moped and wept and refused to leave the house, partly because I hated people pitying me, but more because I was frightened of the future.

However, I was young and managed to pull through this dreadful and difficult time with the help of family and friends: people like the Fikrees in Karachi were wonderful to me. This marvellous family, with its branches spread around the Gulf region, has been associated with my own family for generations. They gave me love and warmth and theirs was the only house I could bear to visit. There were many days when I would take Essa and spend hours there just sitting, playing with the young children. The strength of this whole family's friendship eased some of my pain and with their encouragement I slowly began to repair my badly shattered confidence.

What I lacked was a sense of purpose, so when long-time family friend A K Brohi, a prominent lawyer in Karachi, encouraged me to continue my studies, I found it just the shot in the arm that I so badly needed.

Monkhali had first approached Mr Brohi to see if my short-lived marriage could be dissolved. It took us a long time to contemplate such a step, because this was not the done thing. A wife was expected to wait, and endure patiently – for years if necessary – for a miracle to bring her husband back. In fact whenever she was asked about Essa's father, Monkhali told people that "We received a letter just yesterday" or "He's in Africa and Mariam will join him there soon". These were of course all 'face savers' and in truth I was embarrassed by the position I was in.

For some time I had waited (though not particularly patiently) for some word, some indication from my husband, but nothing ever came. Through Uncle Abe and Aunty Zohra I learnt he had remarried and was taken up with his fast growing new family (he had five children in a very short span). It did not seem fair to me that my life should be at a standstill for the sake of respectability and that I should be forced to live all the while in the obviously false hope that he would one day return. Besides, after having been so humiliated, my pride would have kept me from meekly accepting to remain his wife if, in fact, he ever did come back.

It was therefore with a great sense of relief that we put the case into Mr Brohi's hands. Monkhali, with her well-developed sense of propriety, especially hoped that the whole thing could be handled discreetly. Nevertheless it took seven long, tiresome years and many letters and unanswered summonses, before he was able to get me the legal release which I now knew was an inevitability. It was admitting defeat and it hurt.

I was a difficult person to console in defeat but Mr Brohi was a patient and persevering man, who obviously did not want to see the cheerful young girl he had known turn into a bitter woman. He knew I had always shown a keen interest in learning, so from his own extensive library he lent me books and encouraged me to discuss them with him. He was a very well-read and erudite man, so discussions with him were always enlightening. Slowly I began to regain my taste for learning and, with his persuasion and then help, I was able to convince Monkhali it would be good for me to continue my studies.

Tutors were brought in and and I worked my way steadily through the matriculation course prescribed by the Punjab University in Lahore, one of the oldest scholastic institutions in the Subcontinent. The biggest problem (as far as Monkhali was concerned) was that I could not sit for my exams at home. After much worrying and changing of minds, I was finally allowed to travel to Lahore, with Jameela and Mahmood accompanying me, to go to Kinnaird College where the exam was being held.

It was the first time I had ever travelled on my own and the thought of such freedom was so exhilarating that my past problems almost melted away. Any place would have seemed wonderful to me but, from the moment I glimpsed Lahore, I was taken aback by the sheer beauty of the place. I don't know whether it was the trees and the greenery or the lovely old buildings or the people themselves or just my own euphoric mood, but the whole city held a special attraction for me.

I stayed in a hostel connected to the college and although

servants were not normally allowed, I was given special permission to keep Jameela with me during the day. Mahmood had to stay in a nearby hotel and wait with the *ghora gari* which I had hired to take me about. When I wasn't sitting in the examination room, I wanted to spend every minute exploring Lahore and enjoying my liberty.

Although Jameela was not meant to stay with me at night, she used to sneak in to my room after 'lights out' and sleep on the floor, next to my bed. I enjoyed the thought of freedom and independence but sometimes the practicalities of it made me feel insecure. As far as I can remember I had always been escorted, so seeing the huge dark shape of Jameela's body during the night was a comfort. In the morning she would bring buckets of water for my ablutions and would help me dress. The other girls in the hostel enjoyed being part of the conspiracy that was needed to keep Jameela hidden from the hostel custodians and teachers.

Because of my constant attendants, Jameela and Mahmood, my fellow students thought I was royalty. "She must be an Arabian princess," they whispered. I have to admit I enjoyed the attention.

Despite, or maybe because of all this attention, I made a number of friends and contrary to most people's experience with examinations, I thoroughly enjoyed myself.

To be in the company of bright young people my own age was exactly the right medicine for me at the time. I learned to laugh and joke again and was almost able to forget my recent dark days for it all seemed far away in a different place. In the world I now found myself inhabiting I was a happy and confident young woman. It was marvellous to know that I could feel like this again for I had pictured myself in a grim, grey world of responsibility and worry forever.

It was hardly surprising that this taste of freedom and happiness should make me hunger for more. Besides I truly felt that I didn't have the strength yet to return to my problems. I needed to stay young a little while longer!

Some of my friends had planned to travel around the country for a few weeks and they suggested I join them. It was a wonderful chance for I had always wanted to explore the beautiful places in India that I had heard so much about but I knew Monkhali would never agree to such an idea. A clever and devious plan was needed yet again!

After consulting both Jameela and Mahmood, I decided to send a telegram to Monkhali saying that the exams would not be considered valid unless I did some practical projects, which would require travelling and, of course, money. Knowing her lack of awareness concerning the outside world, I hoped I could fool her.

She was obviously a little suspicious, for telegrams flew back and forth. Finally however, after much argument and my persistent quoting from the Holy Quran, which explicitly states that both men and women should seek knowledge, I was sent money and grudgingly blessings too. I was ecstatic!

With my friends I travelled by train and then by car to Agra. On a wonderful, silvery moonlit night we cycled to the Taj Mahal. I was enchanted. The beauty and serenity of this monument to love was awe-inspiring. It is a spectacular sight under any conditions but as we stood in that mysterious, magical moonlight I found it particularly moving – a moment that lives with me still.

From there we went to Amritsar and Jullundur and visited many historical and fabulous temples. Not content to be a passive tourist, I remember frightening myself wandering through the maze-like passages of one of these landmarks. Everything mysterious and difficult always attracted my lively imagination; every intoned warning or interdiction I saw as a challenge. No sooner had someone advised "You cannot enter that place; that is forbidden; you cannot climb that mountain, it is dangerous", I had to do it!

We visited many more of India's wonderful, historical and beautiful places whose names I have long forgotten. The whole trip, however, was perfect; I almost felt I was in some sort of enchanted land, where my every wish was being granted.

Finally we reached Delhi, the capital of India since ancient times and an exciting mixture of old and new. We saw the famous Qutub Minar, Jumma Masjid, various elaborate tombs and other quaint sights. While visiting old Delhi, with its fascinating narrow lanes, I saw men carrying what looked like coffins to me. I suddenly stood motionless in respect and started praying. My friends wondered what had gone wrong and why I was acting so strangely.

"Mariam, what is the matter?" they asked.

"Why are these people carrying so many coffins and why are they so small? Do they keep the corpses in a sitting position?"

They all laughed heartily and explained, "No, no no, you silly thing, these are not coffins but *dolis*. Women and children sit in them behind drawn curtains and are transported to their destinations." Tradition dictated that a woman passenger's voice should not even be heard by the *doli* bearers. As a result, if the bearers could not find the address – a common enough occurence – they would turn around and take their passengers home as they were not allowed to communicate with the women.

Of course I had to give it a try and sat in a *doli* but, curious to see how the world outside looked, I pulled the curtain up. The bearers immediately came to a halt and put me down in a busy bazaar area, indignantly shouting, "You don't know how to sit in a *doli*. You shake too much while we move and you have violated tradition by peering out and showing your face!" I must have looked quite a fool.

We also attended a local wedding in Delhi and were allowed to sit with the bride in a large *howda* or palanquin. It was elaborately decorated and several men had to carry it. The music and the procession taking the bride to her husband's house, amid much wailing and weeping of her family, was a scene to remember.

In Delhi, we explored the great mosques and forts, picnicked in the parks and shopped endlessly for the beautiful clothes for which Delhi is renowned. All too soon I realised not only time was running out: my funds were running out too. So I sent another telegram to Monkhali saying I needed more money but even more suddenly reality caught up with me. She gave me an ultimatum – "Return home or I will come and join you." Somewhat reluctantly, I left my friends and fabulous fantasy land and headed for home.

That period of freedom and independence acted like a tonic, and its effects lasted much longer than the pretty things I had bought to wear or the books I had acquired to further my education. Things were different for me now. Although I knew that life could be disappointing and painful, I felt a wonderful sense of well-being as if I had been spiritually transformed. Life seemed to be joyful again.

Especially rewarding on my return home was the waiting envelope from Lahore containing my exam results. I had passed with a first division. I felt nothing short of invincible.

CHAPTER 11

A NEW DIRECTION

Full of purpose, I now only needed some direction. For a short while I thought I might try a secretarial course but I was talked out of that by my good friend and mentor Mr Brohi. "Mariam," he said, "you are not the sort to be dictated to." So I gave up that idea.

He believed that I was cut out for other things in life and he often told me that he wouldn't be surprised if one day I had secretaries of my own. For a woman in my restricted society this prediction seemed a little far-fetched. However, I knew my world was beginning to change, not as rapidly as I wanted it to, but things were definitely different to what they had been 10 years earlier. I dreamt of a time when women like myself would be given the chance to earn responsible positions in the outside world.

My enthusiasm for change and challenge was re-emerging as I regained confidence, and with it returned my love of fun and teasing. People used to say "It's good to see Mariam back to her old self again", but I knew this was a new and stronger Mariam that they were seeing and that the young, innocent girl was gone.

Eagerly I looked around for a place to begin. Opportunities for a young lady of my background seemed to be few but I was optimistic and enthusiastic, believing some door would open for me. Having once overheard my old headmistress say that she thought I had an aptitude for teaching, I decided that this was an avenue I might explore.

It took a great deal of argument and coaxing to persuade Monkhali to agree. "No woman in our family has ever worked," she huffed indignantly. "But teaching is not like real work," I retorted, trying to make a classroom sound like a big family room. Finally, after assuring her I was definitely not going to receive money for the job, I was allowed to become a teacher at my old school, Jufel Hurst.

It was rather a strange feeling returning to the place where I had been a student, especially as many of my old teachers – whom I had teased mercilessly as a student – were now my colleagues. I was thankful that they graciously accepted me into their ranks. One teacher in particular, Mrs D'Souza, my former French teacher, who had often been the butt of my jokes because of her atrocious French accent and her funny walk, became a great friend (and she still walked as if she had swallowed a walking stick!) But as an adult, I had the chance to find out what a charming lady she really was and that she possessed a wonderful sense of humour. She was actually a very good teacher for, even 50 years later, I still remember the French conjugations which she hammered into my head, and during my year at the school, as well as religious studies, I was competent enough to teach French grammar.

Teaching gave me a great deal of satisfaction; all the while I felt I was learning so much from my students. About this time I also joined painting classes, and on the whole my life was happy. Essa was a constant joy but I still wanted more out of life. I was young, energetic and, although a little more wary now, was eager to taste more of what life could offer. I wanted to travel, meet interesting people, do exciting things and learn whatever I could. The chance to get away and, at the same time have fun – at Monkhali's expense – was too much of a temptation so, when the opportunity arose, I took full advantage of it.

For many years Monkhali had been a hypochondriac, complaining constantly about her health to the point where two doctors visited her daily. They would prescribe all sorts of medication which she would never take. Instead she hoarded pills and potions like she did everything else. It seemed such a waste to my sisters, brother and I, especially as our small monthly allowances were never enough. So we set about devising a way to 'divert' the fees that Monkhali wasted for each doctor's visit. We told her that a renowned Iranian doctor who spoke good Farsi had come to Karachi and was very popular because of his skill. She asked to see him immediately.

The 'doctor' duly arrived, a smallish man with a big beard, an impressive bag, and a very strange throaty accent. We were counting on Monkhali's modesty to make the plan work, and she did not let us down. With this stranger at her bedside, Monkhali kept herself well covered from head to foot – her face included. The doctor somehow managed to take her pulse, all the while asking her all sorts of questions about her life and, to her delight, seeming most concerned about all her strange ailments.

"He's a wonderful doctor," Monkhali enthused later. "He seems to understand all my problems and how difficult my life has been having to bring up all you children, who are more of a headache to me now that you are grown up than when you were babies."

The visits continued for a few months and we found it increasingly difficult to control our giggling. Our plan had succeeded beyond all expectations, and moreover Monkhali seemed to have no suspicions, despite the fact that we were all spending much more freely than we should have been able to on our normal allowance.

"Why is Mariam never here when this marvellous doctor visits?" she asked once.

"Mariam met him yesterday," the others assured her. "It's not surprising you didn't see her. You cover yourself up so much it's a wonder you can see anybody."

The deception might have gone on indefinitely had the 'great doctor' not suggested one day that what Monkhali really needed was *taghir hawa* – a change of climate. She readily agreed and, of course, I was the one chosen to accompany her, as there was no one in the household capable of handling all the problems of travelling in those days. "Foul!" cried my sisters and brother, for though we were co-conspirators they thought it most unfair that I should go with Monkhali.

"We will tell her everything," they threatened but I didn't care. The consequence was that the accomplices all fell out and the devious, but until now successful scheme, was revealed. The beard and the bag were brought in as evidence against me. Without needing to be told the finer details, Monkhali picked up the *qalam qalyoon*, which was always handy, and said, "Mariam, we'll see how good you are at healing yourself."

She must have been mellowing in her old age, for although she was angry at having been fooled, she had to admit that the thought of a trip had perked her up, so she stood by her decision. Undoubtedly she would have liked to punish me further, but she knew that I was still the only one able to look after her on a journey, so it wasn't long before we waved good-bye to my envious siblings and my little Essa – who in any case was safe in the care of my sisters Bibiya and Badria – and were on our way to Bombay, happily ensconced in a first-class cabin.

We travelled on a British India Company steamship that plied the Indian Ocean through to the Persian Gulf, the same kind that had transported our family with all our baggage on our earlier epic moves. Being older and not restricted or confined to the cabin as I used to be, I found the sea journey an exhilarating adventure. But Monkhali's attitude towards sea travel had not changed over the years so, surrounded by her personal maids, she took to her bunk and hardly rose during the whole trip. This gave me a marvellous chance to roam freely and it wasn't long before I knew all the other first-class passengers and was having a wonderful time playing cards, chess and draughts and generally being the centre of attenton.

On the ship with us were some of the ruling sheikhs of Bahrain (a few members of this entourage were known to us as they had frequently visited us at our Lingah house and at Great-uncle Farooq's place in Bahrain) and when we arrived at our destination a red carpet was set out for them. Not realising it wasn't for her and remembering past glories, Monkhali sighed as she stepped with great dignity down the carpeted gangway and said to me, "*Moshk boosh nachit* – the fragrance of sandalwood does not disappear with time. Look what they have done for my arrival."

Monkhali's stepson Uncle Abdullah Abbas, who had come to meet us and welcome the sheikhs, did not disillusion her; nor did the rest of our party. Besides, I knew that the retelling would make excellent entertainment for the whole family.

We stayed in Bombay for a few months with Uncle Abdullah Abbas and his family in their century-old family mansion, called Shamrock, which still stands in Byculla. They were wonderful to us. Because my grandfather had married several times there was quite a tangle of relations. I had uncles and aunts whom I did not know and, for that matter, Monkhali had stepchildren she hadn't met either. All those she knew, though, respected and loved her, but it was Uncle Abdullah in particular who she treated as a son. During my short and unhappy marriage, this kind and caring uncle had given Monkhali his full support when she had suggested that I return with her to Karachi.

The trip did both Monkhali and me a lot of good. Best of all, Monkhali was now bitten by the travel bug.

After our return to Karachi she decided that the family needed to visit Bahrain, where Uncle Arshi, who was our trustee, lived. The main reason for the trip was so the grandmothers could look into their finances, and then set a realistic budget that would enable them to live comfortably for the rest of their lives. Along the way we also planned to visit Dubai and Lingah.

We set off, in the spring of 1947, in as grand a style as we could manage with the usual number of boxes, crates and trunks full of Monkhali's valuables and the few servants we had retained. Dignity, however, we had in full measure, and so on arriving in Dubai, Monkhali could not understand why the place was 'bedecked' with black flags, as it didn't seem to be an appropriate sort of welcome. Only later did we tell her that, despite what she thought, the display had not been for us but to mark the sad occasion of the death of Sheikh Rashid's mother, Sheikha Hessa. It was difficult for Monkhali to accept that our importance had slipped since the death of my grandfathers.

Later, forming a delegation of ladies (reminiscent of those grand processions through Lingah in my early years), we paid our respects to the sheikhas and the rest of the ruling family with whom, in those days, my family members were in close contact.

Dubai in the 1940s and '50s was a very different place to

what it is today. There was no electricity, running water or paved roads. The few proper houses all looked like huge fortresses though they seemed to be built like this to keep people (especially women) in rather than out.

It was a very conservative society; even the small amount of freedom we enjoyed in Karachi was not possible in Dubai. One of the main sources of entertainment for the women was peeping through holes in the wall and giving funny names to regular passersby, who were of course mainly men on their way to the mosque or the souq.

At night we sat around and talked about our day. I loved telling stories; any little incident we might have witnessed – and goodness knows, we weren't allowed the freedom to go looking for any real 'inspiration' – was enough to set me going, and it did make the others laugh. We had so much fun that even Uncle Arshi used to join the women's group and insist on hearing all the stories that I and some of the others had to tell.

Although the lifestyle was simple, it was friendly and we welcomed a stream of visitors. For our own outings, we used to cross the creek by *abra* to visit Deira, where other members of the family lived. Crossing the creek could be quite hazardous as we always had to be completely covered and what's more, laden with heavy jewellery, which often hampered our movement and weighed us down. Many a time, because of the awkwardness of the apparel, a dignified, black-clad, bejewelled lady slipped in the mud and fell into the water! Luckily the oarsman was always at hand and the only consequence of this drama was usually gaining a cold and losing a considerable amount of dignity.

We saw the bustling activity of the souks from the *abra* but we never got to the shops there, or any other market or public place for that matter, even though we were veiled. The shopping was left to the men, while women were visited daily by female hawkers and retail distributors who brought with them material, perfumes and the like and took orders for embroidery on personal garments.

Uncle Arshi had remarried and his young wife (whose name was also Mariam) and I soon became good friends. Between us we concocted a plan to add to our fun. I dressed up as a fortune-teller and Bibi Mariam became my interpreter and assistant. We donned long black *chadors* and net veils that covered our faces and in a darkened room, lit only by a candle, complete with pictures of skeletons and burning incense to make it more eerie and mysterious, began to make fabulous 'predictions'.

The mysteries of the unknown had fascinated me since I was a child and I had always been interested in the stars and the art of palmistry. I had met several enlightened people and read books on the subject of ESP. I believed I had a strong sense of intuition; at charitable functions and friendly gatherings I had often made correct predictions, and throughout my life I have sometimes felt the need to warn friends and relations of some imminent danger.

In a short while we became quite famous and women from all over Dubai came to have their fortunes told. I 'forecast' the future by reading coffee cups, by bone counting and palmistry. To make it look even better I had a huge, black leather-bound volume to refer to. It was really just an encyclopaedia, but I used it for special effect. To Monkhali's annoyance, many of our 'clients' brought gifts of food such as home produced vegetables, eggs and yoghurt, to thank me for the things I had predicted.

The strangest thing about this bit of fun was that a few of my 'predictions' turned out to be true, though I suppose a lot of it had to do with the commonsense answers I was able to give to what were often just everyday problems and, of course, to the law of chance.

Although life was simple and nobody knew or cared what was happening in the rest of the world, there was a great feeling of warmth and sincerity about the people of Dubai that made it quite a special place. In those days the ruling family mingled freely with the locals and our family in particular saw a great deal of these generous and honest people. Even today, if any national has a problem he still has the option of speaking with the sheikhs in the *majlis*.

After a few months in this friendly and relaxed place, we

had almost forgotten the original purpose of our trip, but eventually decided that we really should make our way to Bahrain, especially since we had with us Uncle Arshi's daughter-in-law, who was in the last stages of her pregnancy.

Air travel was out of the question as flights were irregular and there could be many months between one flight and the next. There was also very little scheduled shipping from Dubai in those days. The most convenient method of travel was by boat, so we rented a huge barge at an exorbitant fee, and with the usual collection of grandmothers, mothers, children, attendants and nannies, not to mention the crates of food and furnishings, we set off on what should have been only a three or four-day journey.

For the first two days things went well except for Essa getting his hand caught in the helm and causing a huge commotion, which as everybody said, was to be expected as he was "Mariam's son". Uncle Arshi's son, Mohammed Akil, was travelling with us, and we often sang together while I played the harmonium. We also occupied ourselves with all sorts of games and the elders looked upon us quite contentedly. Monkhali Gappi was about 90 then and all she did was pray, half the time forgetting where she was.

It was on the second night that the storm arose. The black skies lit up with thunder and lightning, while strong winds tossed us about on the raging sea. As the situation worsened we prayed aloud in utter panic and promised to be good Muslims if we were saved. All sense of direction and time was lost; fear gripped one and all. In the violence of the storm, the boat's engine packed up. A sail was hoisted but, of course, was soon torn to shreds and we began to drift. The captain ordered all the heavy luggage to be thrown overboard to lighten the load. Everybody panicked. Monkhali clung to us and her jewellery box, which she refused to give up to the sea. Over the side went carpets, iron trunks with clothing, household utensils, samovars, bedding – everything.

It was an incredibly frightening experience and we were lucky to survive. Finally, after what seemed like days of sheer terror, there was calm and miraculously in the distance a small boat appeared from almost nowhere with a single occupant in it waving dramatically to us. Our 'saviour' climbed aboard and alerted the captain to turn the barge around as we were about to hit a rock. Allah be praised, we eventually drifted towards a small island.

From there many of us were rescued by helicopters from Bahrain, which had been looking for us because we were overdue on our expected arrival date by three or four days. The others had to stay on the island until such time as another boat came to help with the repairs. It was wonderful to touch solid ground again. Since then even I have lost my nerve for a sea voyage.

It took us quite a while to recover and begin to enjoy our stay in Bahrain. Once we did though, it wasn't difficult to have a good time in this cultured, progressive place, where people were friendly and exceedingly hospitable. We were invited to many homes and I was impressed by the fact that, in every household we visited, there was always some form of literary entertainment, whether it was reciting poetry, singing verse, or discussing modern books. It was an atmosphere I revelled in. Farsi literature and culture was alive and to this day, Arabic and Persian literature is well-preserved in Bahrain.

The interesting facet about Bahraini culture is that men and women have always been allowed to mix freely with no inhibitions and women were never forced to wear *chadors* or *abayas*. However, many choose to wear a *hijab* and *abaya* today because they believe that it identifies them immediately as Muslim women to the rest of the world – an identification of which they are proud.

During our stay in Bahrain, we received a rare letter from our father, who was living in Abadan. In it he suggested that, because we were nearby, it would be a good opportunity for us to visit him in Iran.

The letter was a complete surprise as, over the years since mother's death, we had had very little to do with our father and truthfully we hardly knew him. This, however, was a chance not only to find out more about this man who after all was an important factor in our lives but also to explore the exciting and newly emancipated Iran. I had to go.

CHAPTER 12

THE REUNION

It was not surprising that I was the only one to accept Father's invitation to visit him in Iran, and I was ever so glad that I had because it gave me the opportunity for the first time to get to know him. He was the type of man who was only able to appreciate and communicate with his offspring when they were grown-up. That works both ways: As an adult, I saw him in a new light and was able to recognise his virtues and weaknesses and respect him for what he was.

Father was a very elegant person. Short and broadly built , he was soft-spoken and gentle in look and mannerism. He was always immaculately dressed. He attached great importance to his environment, insisting on everything looking attractive and orderly. In his circle, he was always known as the best-dressed man, so much so that his friends used to rib him by commenting, "*Aghae* Behnam is never seen wearing the same necktie twice." He had expensive tastes in everything – perhaps a habit from his years in Paris – and wore a large diamond ring, tie pin and expensive pens.

He never shouted, swore or laughed loudly – he despised anything vulgar. But he had a keen sense of humour. When he laughed his whole body shook silently. When angry, he turned crimson, bit his lip and walked away briskly, but he was never rude to anyone, especially his subordinates. Outside the house he smoked cigarettes, but at home, seated on his special cushions, he loved nothing better than a gently bubbling hubble-bubble pipe and his family sitting around him playing cards, draughts and chess. He commanded respect and was extremely dignified in his manners and life style.

Although he had never been particularly close to us, we

always knew him to be a kind man. He was looked upon as a philosopher and scholar for he spoke several languages fluently and not only read classical Persian and Arabic literature but modern English and French books as well. In fact, he had a fascination for words and their meanings and his English vocabulary, in particular, was extensive.

Education was important to him, so he studied law and was the first man in our family to obtain a degree (I was later the first woman to do so). He was also the first man in our family to take up a job, which entailed a reasonable amount of courage. He was appointed a Director of the Anglo Iranian Oil Company at Abadan and, while holding this post, was elected mayor of the town.

By all accounts he was well-respected as a dedicated and successful worker. A popular man, when he had the time he was also a good sportsman and had many trophies to show for his efforts at tennis, cricket, billiards, bridge and chess.

Father was especially kind to oppressed people and would always find time to speak to his lower staff members, while those who considered themselves more important were often left waiting for an interview for hours! "Mariam," he confided, "the more important the person thinks he is, the more of my time he expects to take up over little things. The less important the person, the more urgent the matter will be." I never forgot that insight.

Father worked tirelessly for an average of 14 hours a day. He probably had to, for besides his job with the oil company, he was also in charge of the Water and Power Department of Khuzestan, the province where he lived. He also became a member of the university syndicate of Joondi Shapur and took over the 'Point 4' project in the area, which was a special health and educational scheme being implemented countrywide with the help of the American government. Father could never accept a subordinate position: he liked to be in charge of anything that he was involved in. In that I am certainly his daughter.

He patronised several charitable and welfare organisations, was actively involved in sports clubs and was associated with a range of other societies.

Many years later when I was working in Lahore, Father

came to participate in a three-month management and administrative course and, while he was there, the Shah of Iran paid a brief visit. In my capacity as Cultural Counsellor I had to perform the duty of introducing Iranian dignitaries and students to the Shah. Father, contrary to his usual calm demeanour, got so excited when the Shah approached him, that all he could say was, "She's my daughter, Your Majesty."

You could have heard a pin drop for it was against all rules of protocol to speak before being spoken to by the *Shahenshah*, the king of kings. The Shah, however, only smiled as he recognised my father and stopped to chat with him for a few minutes.

My father's greatest weakness was his vanity. It made him an easy mark for manipulation by those who flattered him. Consequently he was a poor businessman and, at times, acted unkindly and greedily (such as when he took Mother's jewellery) in an effort to appear important to others.

When I arrived, he seemed very pleased to see me and showed a great deal of concern about how I was coping with life in general and asked many questions about my son Essa, whom he always termed as 'Essa-bin-Mariam'.

I stayed with Father for three months and, in that time, we explored Iran. More importantly, we got to know each other. Never having been anywhere but the southern areas of Iran, it was a wonderful and educational experience for me to travel around our rather vast country and learn how much difference there was in the lifestyles of people living in the various regions.

We set out in a north-easterly direction from Abadan, which is near the sea at the top of the Persian Gulf on the Iraq border, travelling in a big car with various members of father's second family on a trip that would take us to Shiraz, Esfahan, Kermanshah, Hamadan and Teheran.

Travelling north, the country becomes steeper and steeper. At these high altitudes the sky seemed so much bluer, the air cleaner and the mountains so sharply peaked and close that it is not surprising the poets of Persia have described such beautiful scenery in an endless number of romantic poems. I was amazed when I saw snow for the first time in my life but it wasn't long before my feelings of awe were overcome and I was learning to ski down some of the magnificent slopes.

Coming from the dry desert area of Iran, I was particularly fascinated by the great rivers and streams that flowed from the Alborz mountains down into the plains and right through the middle of towns. In the Lingah region water, a rare commodity, is mainly underground, so all the beautiful gardens, flowers, fruit, pistachios, almonds and walnuts grown in the north seemed like a vision of Paradise compared with what I had known. Everything was so different. I found it particularly interesting to see that women worked alongside men in the fields and seemed to have more freedom than women from our area.

I was immensely impressed with Teheran, for it is a beautiful city. It has a backdrop of mountains that look so astonishing you can hardly believe they are not a painted scene. I used to find myself looking up and half-expecting them to be taken down one day by a group of busy stage workers!

The city itself is full of exquisite Islamic architecture. The square-shaped, gleaming white or sand-coloured buildings have fine domes and arches, intricately carved wooden doors, windows and balcony rails, and many of them are set in large gardens that feature fountains and small, tiled pools. And everwhere there was greenery and trees in blossom. I especially loved passing between the avenues of trees so tall they met at their tips to form glowing, green tunnels full of fragrant, clear air.

While in Teheran I met yet another branch of the Fikrees who, of course, promptly became known as the 'Teheran Fikrees'. Ismail and his wife Zuleika were good friends of father's and, like other members of their family, they were wonderfully kind and hospitable to me. They took me to the cinema, to the theatre, the zoo and to beach resorts – all exhilarating, first-time experiences for me.

More embarrassing than exhilarating was my first visit to the public baths. For the northern Iranian it is traditional to attend a public (though segregated, of course) *hammam*. It is customary to go at least once a week, and people go in family groups and make a day of it, often taking a packed lunch.

Although private cubicles are available, most women prefer to wash themselves and be massaged, or apply their henna in the open areas, where they can all chat freely. A woman known as a *dalak* performs the massage. The first time I had a massage I got quite a shock: the *dalak* arrived in my private cubicle wrapped in a *chador* but, before she began work with her sponge and special powder, she took this off and underneath she was completely naked and terribly wrinkled. Luckily all the haze and steam hid my embarrassment.

She quickly began to rub every inch of my body with a scratchy loofah and a pumice stone. Pain soon became a greater sensation than embarrassment but slowly the dead and dry cells of the top layer of my skin were rubbbed off and then, while I was still tingling all over, she shampooed and conditoned my hair. After that my body was lathered with soap and just as I was beginning to enjoy the luxurious and velvety feel of the warm, soapy water I was blasted with a jet of icy water until I was completely cleansed. Shivering with cold I was patted dry with a large, fluffy towel, then powdered, and my whole body was moisturised with a fragrant smelling oil. I finally emerged raw and rosy but feeling wonderful.

This whole routine is very much a part of the northern Iranian way of life but, for conservative and extremely modest southerners like myself, the first few visits were still excruciatingly embarrassing. Still, it is a wonderful form of beauty treatment. I believe the exceptionally good complexion of Iranian ladies is due to their habit of taking these baths. Where else could you get the benefits and therapeutic effects of a sauna, a beauty scrub, a visit to the hair dresser and a session of yoga all combined? It is very rejuvenating and I would definitely recommend it.

From Teheran we travelled over the mountains to the Caspian Sea. We were close to Europe and a long way, especially culturally, from my own home area of Bandar Lingah. We then travelled to Tabriz and the Kurdistan area. There the women sometimes wore up to 30 coloured petticoats underneath their skirts – quite a sight. Then we went back down through the centre of the country to Yazd and Kerman.

The variety in the countryside and culture was incredible.

We travelled through deserts and met nomads; through grassy plains, where peasants farmed their land; to cities with sophisticated and cosmopolitan citizens; while high up in the rockiest, barest mountains, we found strange, secretive people, living a bare existence in their harsh homeland. It was difficult to believe that so many diverse and complex communities could combine into one country.

Finally in Kerman we got word that I should make my way to Bandar Abbas and then on to Bandar Lingah to meet up with the rest of the family, who had finished their business in Bahrain. By this time also, Father had to get back to his own work, so we knew the time had come to part company. We went to a local garage to find out what sort of transport was available to make the five to six-day journey through the mountains to the coast. Usually people went by truck or four-wheel-drive as it was a narrow, winding, treacherous road, but there was nothing going that way for some time.

While at the garage, we noticed a tiny lady sitting with a small boy of six or seven, waiting patiently. She spoke our dialect and after introductions she mentioned that she knew of our family, though her husband's name of Pakravan was unfamiliar to me. It turned out she was originally from Lingah, though now living in Bandar Abbas. At the time Bandar Abbas was considered a poor and unhealthy place, full of disease, and consequently populated mainly by fishermen and labourers. The most important people in the town were those who had originally come from Lingah.

The lady told us she was trying to organise a vehicle to get home. There and then Father decided he could leave me in the company of this lady and her son, so he hired a jeep and driver for us to make our journey through the mountains to the coast. It was a strange and coincidental meeting and it took a number of years before I realised how remarkable this chance meeting actually had been.

When we finally arrived in Bandar Abbas after the rather rough and uncomfortable journey, the lady hospitably asked me to her house, where I could freshen up and wait for the family friend who had been contacted by Father to meet me.

The house was far from large or special in any way, but I

*The author (right) aged about five, and her sister Fatma,
dressed for a special occasion. Bandar Lingah, 1927.*

*From the left: Great-grandmother Haji Mariam, called Monkhali Gappi; the author's
mother Hafsa Abbas in her mid-20s; Grandmother, called Monkhali Kingley, who was
'more of a parent to us than our own father and mother.'*

Great-grandfather Haji Mohamad Aqil.

Grandfather Haji Abbas dressed in formal style.

Great-uncle Farooq.

Sheikh Mohammad Ali Sultan-Al-Olema.

Bandar Lingah house where the author was born and lived her early life, photographed on her return in 1991. The house now belongs to Sultan-Al-Olema and is used as an educational institute.

Abdul Karim Farooq (one of Great-uncle Farooq's sons) stands on the right of the late HH Sheikh Rashid bin Saeed Al Maktoum, architect of modern Dubai, in this photo taken in Bombay in the 1940s.

The tomb of Haji Mulla Ahmad Arshi in Bastak.

Father, the family's first graduate. Bombay, 1930

Great-uncle Farooq photographed about 1930 to the left of Mohammad Reza Khan Satwat-ul-Mamalek (seated). To his right is Sheikh Mostafa bin Abdul Latif, and at the back is one of Sheikh Mostafa's sons.

Servants would bring water in these pitchers and bowls for freshening up.

Traditional bridal makeup and jewellery.

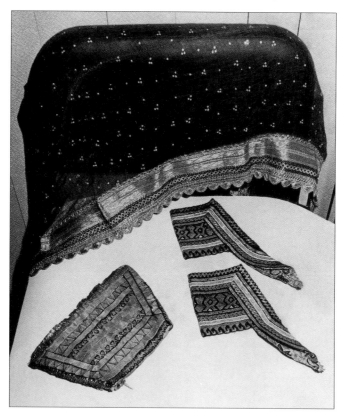

Cuffs and gown edgings, traditional to the Gulf region, embroidered in silver and gold thread (badela), adapted to make an evening bag (left).

Grandfather Haji Abbas, with his Turkish wife Nazmia (right) and Samia Sultan, a daughter of Sultan Abdul Hamid. Paris, early 1930s.

The author's father, Abdul Wahid Behnam, photographed in the 1920s in Bahrain.

Uncle Haji Ahmed Arshi. Karachi, early 1930s.

Schooldays at Jufel Hurst High School. The author's sister Fatma is on the left, the author second from left. Karachi, 1937.

Mother's tomb in Karachi.

*Having a go at rowing.
Karachi, early 1940s.*

*'Young Mariam who liked to take part in every living
activity, having been deprived of old.' Training as a
National Guard volunteer. Karachi, 1940.*

*Pakravan, aged about
17, photographed as
'Chota Baba' during
his days in the
ashram. Mid 1930s.*

The author (centre) with sister Fatma (left) and step-mother in the all-white attire of the young ladies' Progressive Club. Karachi, 1937.

Family photo taken in Karachi in the early 1940s: From left, Fatma, Bibiya, step-mother, Ahmed Noor, Father, Badria and the author.

Essa, aged three, 1947.

'A teenager beset with conflicting emotions'. Karachi, 1941.

With Essa, aged eight. Teheran, 1952.

hardly noticed its lack of grandeur because when she took me inside I found myself in a room which was overflowing with books. I saw copies of *National Geographic*, a big Oxford dictionary, Persian literature and Shakespeare's plays all jostling for shelf space. They all looked well-maintained, and I deduced that the man who owned this library was not the normal Bandar Abbasi businessman.

"My husband is completely mad," my hostess told me. "He cares more for his books than he does for his family." I was intrigued and would have loved to meet this interesting and obviously intellectual man but he was away on business.

Later in Lingah I brought his name up and Monkhali, who knew of him (she seemed to know every *khodmooni's* background), shuddered and was horrified that I had actually gone into Abdullah Pakravan's house. I was further intrigued but all she would say was that he was crazy. The Fikree family, with whom we spent most of our time while in our old home town, were more forthcoming. They explained that Abdullah Pakravan was thought of as being an enlightened but rather private man. He came from quite a good family of Roknis but had been orphaned. At an early age he had built up his own business and now lived in the modest, and, in the eyes of many, austere style of a *dervish*.

What was unusual about him, I learned, was that he had many unorthodox ideas for, in his youth, he had travelled to India in pursuit of knowledge and education and had since then been quite mysterious about his religious beliefs. It was true – his contribution to the social and literary development of Bandar Abbas was considerable; he was respected for this and for his ability to handle the business correspondence of others, because of his fluency in English, Persian and Arabic.

All this made him sound like a fascinating man but, in my joy at being reunited with Essa and the rest of the family as well as the Lingah Fikrees, I soon forgot all about him.

It was strange being back in Lingah after almost 20 years. In many ways it was a sad homecoming. The whole town looked desolate, run-down and neglected, the effect of several earthquakes and famine that had destroyed houses and homes. What struck me in particular were doors, still firmly padlocked, standing proud and mysterious – absolutely by themselves with no support – no roofs or walls.

Lingah was no longer a duty-free port and because of this had lost a great deal of its former importance. The main reason behind the change was Reza Shah's cultural and social revolution. In trying to modernise the country he naturally upset many of the wealthy, conservative families who had profited by the old ways. Also other areas of the country were being developed at a faster pace, so Lingah, with its rough roads and distance from Teheran, had been ignored.

Customs duties also badly affected business. The pearling industry, which was being crippled by the new Japanese market selling cultured pearls, was particularly hard hit. Another factor affecting pearling was that the modern approach to business did not regard a man's word as being enough when making a transaction, so deals were considered legal only when they were written down on an endless number of papers and signed by an endless number of officials. Pearl trading, always a complex business, now it had become expensive as well and more complicated than ever.

On top of all this, the Shah was taking over great tracts of land, which considerably reduced the feudal landowners' power. To people like my family, it seemed that times and values were changing for the worse. Many had abandoned the country and gone to live in Bahrain, Dubai, Kuwait, Qatar or India, where they could still lead a traditional life.

Of our friends and family, there were only the Fikrees, the Wahidis and the Sheikh Sultan-Al-Olema with his large family, left in Lingah. They looked after our interests in our absence and the two main houses and lands were cared for by a few servants and an old guard. Unfortunately, many of our properties there had never been registered, so to this day cannot be accounted for.

We enjoyed our stay in Lingah but in many ways it was a relief to get back to Karachi, where we felt more at home. It was a good feeling to be back, but all our travelling had unsettled me, so, when we received another letter from Father suggestion we undertake some constructive work in Iran rather than waste our time in Karachi, I needed very little encouragement to change the course of my life.

Father had just moved to Teheran after being appointed head of *Sanduq-e-Mushtarak*, a joint American and Iranian Fund project, set up by the Americans to help implement many of the Shah's educational reforms. Father believed there were opportunities open for all of us and that, as Iranians, we should be willing to work for our country.

The encouragement I needed came surprisingly from my brother-in-law Amin Farooq, Dada Fatma's husband. Not normally impulsive, he immediately decided that the opportunity to live and work in Iran was too good to refuse.

It was not an easy decision to make, for we did not speak Farsi fluently; the Bastaki dialect which we did speak is only used in the southern areas. But our English was quite good and we could get by in French as well, so we hoped our problems with communication would not be too much of a stumbling block for us.

However, this was not the only difficulty for, as I had discovered on my trip with Father, the whole culture of northern Iran was different from our own. We realised that we would look out of place in our long *kaftans*, *shalwar-kameez* or Indian trouser suits, and slippers because at that time in Teheran, short dresses, nylon stockings, high-heeled shoes and, in fact, anything Western was in vogue. Having always been willing to try anything new, I wasn't too bothered about this, but Monkhali, when informed, was horrified by the thought!

Another grave problem that stared me full in the face was Essa's identity. As a child he had travelled on my passport, but now he needed a separate one. His father was a Saudi national and up to this point I had not bothered about such things: He was my child and that was all that mattered. Now I had to do something about this and quickly. Somehow, solving other people's problems seemed easier. Not a single piece of paper did I hold to show that I was married to Zakaria Bundakji and that Essa was his son. Back and forth, day in and day out I went to the Saudi Embassy with Essa. Eventually, with Mr Brohi's assistance, the court verdict proclaiming Zakaria's long absence and his sister Aunty Zohra's support, we finally managed to obtain a Saudi passport for Essa.

The hardest thing for Dada Fatma and me about moving to Teheran was to leave Monkhali. We had been with her all our lives and, although she had often stifled us with her traditional and conservative ways, she loved us dearly and was more of a parent to us than our own had ever been.

After Mama's death Monkhali had felt the full sense of responsibility for her grandchildren and she carried out her duty conscientiously to – literally – her very last breath. Towards the end of her life, most of us were scattered and living apart from her, so the one she clung to was my brother Ahmed Noor, who never left her side. She died in Karachi in 1957 on the day that Badria married. This was the last of her responsibilities and, although she had been quite sick for a few days, she was definitely not going to let death take her until her duties had been completed.

After the wedding ceremony, Badria and her husband, Sheikh Abdul Wahed, the youngest son of Sheikh Sultan-Al-Olema, had gone to her bedside where Monkhali gave them her blessings and presented them with a handsome gift of jewellery. She was in such good spirits and seemed better.

After they left, her condition deteriorated rapidly, almost like she had finally run out of steam. She died during the night and as had always been her wish, she was buried next to her beloved daughter. Whenever we are in Karachi the first thing we do is to visit the family graveyard to pray and read the *fateha* for the dear ones who are buried there.

However, all this was in the future. For the present, we had a decision to make. It's strange how, when one is young, difficulties don't seem insurmountable, and separations don't feel permanent. Only the advantages of a situation seem to lure youth and so it was with us. We firmly believed that Iran offered opportunities for a better future. It was therefore not long before we were waving a tearful goodbye to Monkhali and our younger sisters and brother and were on our way to Teheran and real independence.

CHAPTER 13

CHALLENGES IN TEHERAN

Settling down in Teheran was easy; right from the start, people were good and kind to us. Essa and I lived with my sister and her husband as, at that time, it would have been quite unthinkable for us to live on our own. We had always been surrounded by family and, despite our different natures, Dada Fatma and I would have been lonely without each other. We rented a house in a good neighbourhood and quickly began to find our way around. Our neighbours, Colonel Palar and his kind wife, Fatma, helped us adjust and adapt to our new way of life. Then, with Father's influence and help it wasn't difficult for Amin Farooq and me to obtain good jobs. Before long we began to feel quite settled.

For me it was a wonderful lifestyle. Women in Teheran were no longer restricted by many of the old traditions and, for once in my life, I felt relaxed as I no longer had to fight for the freedom that I believed was my right. I grew to love this developing Iran with its air of progress and hope for the future, though there were still many problems – such things as the high degree of illiteracy.

It was around this time that I began to find my niche, to see what I could contribute to society. I became an ardent supporter of many of the reforms that Mohammed Reza Shah (son of Reza Shah) was trying to introduce, for I passionately believed that education could bring about the real progress of our country.

I became involved in an education and health project, the Point Four Plan, which was to be implemented countrywide. Among its objectives were not only to raise the level of awareness about matters of hygiene, but to provide the necessary apparatus. It was an ambitious and well-intentioned programme, but many of the illiterate villagers in outlying parts were confused by it. They couldn't understand how to use the wonderful new objects that they were given to help them live a more hygenic life. In one place shining new toilets were put into each house and although their use was carefully explained there were many who still thought that the 'nice little refrigerator' had been installed in the wrong place.

Another phase of the plan was to train supervisors who would then travel to all the schools and colleges in the provinces, to help teachers there set up special departments in an effort to give as broad an education to Iranian women and children as possible. This was where I fit in.

After an 11-month training course, I became a supervisor in the Home Social Science programme. My area of teaching was mainly child psychology, family relationships and anthropology. I also taught home management and handicrafts, which included making home furnishings and embroidery. All that I had learnt and taught myself in my early years proved useful. Cooking, however – always the bane of my existence – almost proved my undoing. I disliked these sessions and hoped no one would expect me to make any comments in that area.

The whole scheme was excellent for it helped promote hygiene and better living conditions in the outlying villages, while bringing the more important towns well into the 20th century. Until this time social science subjects had been taught in girls' schools and colleges in theory only, out of a book. The new project provided laboratories, equipment and know-how through lectures and practical demonstrations.

In the remotest and poorest villages, we taught girls to use their own locally-made equipment in a cleaner and better organised way. It wasn't just the girls we taught; we showed the villagers how even slight changes could improve their way of life.

In one case that I recall, we pointed out to the older women that instead of wearing layers and layers of petticoats – perhaps 30 or 40 yards of material in all – there would be enough material to provide for other members of the family such as the little children, who often went without proper clothes. It was an obvious thing to an outsider, but hitherto unthinkable to people blinkered by tradition. What a familiar story!

Standards of nutrition and sanitation needed to be improved but, because the villagers were often unwilling to accept new concepts, it was not an easy job. It was rewarding, however, when changes grudgingly accepted proved successful.

My one main problem was that I had trouble with my pronunciation of Farsi. Although I could read, write and understand it quite well, I was not too happy giving lectures in the language so in the beginning I resorted to English and relied on an interpreter. I found this a frustrating way to communicate, for I could understand the translation and felt that I wasn't really getting my message across. I had to take my courage in both hands and try my Farsi.

At first my pronunciation was awkward and this often caused roars of laughter from those listening. One day, for instance, while discussing post natal care, I suggested that the mother and child should be *joonat bergirand*, which in Bastaki means 'massaged'. But in Farsi it sounded as if I had said that 'their lives should be taken'!

My problem was largely due to the fact that Farsi has many words that are similar to those of the Bastaki dialect but with a slightly different pronunciation, such as *tabl* or drum which, in Bastak, is *tobl*.

Traditional Persian is a rich language with a wealth of colloquial vocabulary and elaborate expression. Sometimes a simple greeting can take an eternity with everyone being 'honoured', 'having their lives in others' shadows', and 'the graciousness to the humble self', so it can be quite overwhelming to those unused to this type of speech. But gradually I became confident with it.

I enjoyed this work and rose rapidly in my profession. It was satisfying to help set up several Social Science departments and conduct training courses in schools throughout the provinces.

I knew I wanted to settle in Teheran but I also felt I needed my independence, so finally I made the big decision to rent a flat for Essa and myself. Such a step was yet another 'first' for a woman in our family, but not an easy one to take. It was very difficult living alone with only a maid. Because of my conservative background I was especially careful to observe a strict social etiquette, but I was grateful that here in Teheran it was possible for me to live as an independent woman.

I enjoyed the life I was living and made many wonderful friends. The ones I felt most comfortable with were Ismail and Zuleika Fikree. I admired the women I got to know, for I found that the northern Iranian women in particular were and are extremely practical, competent, gracious and above all, graceful. They are not only well-groomed, but are good home managers and during the changing times were able to blend the old and the new ways successfully without losing the closely-knit family unit, which has always been such an important structure in Iran. I believe the growing emancipation of Irani women at that time was an acknowledgement of the important role they have always played in society.

I was very busy and happy being a working mother but, at times, when I saw warm, loving families, I did regret that I was alone and lacked the support and security of a normal home. Ten years had elapsed since my disastrous marriage and my son was growing into a clever, thoughtful and rather perceptive child. My family had always treated him with some reverence, for Monkhali was convinced he was special, as she had dreamt of his birth.

I always laughed at the way my family treated my son but it was true, he was not like others of his age. Perhaps he was wise beyond his years; perhaps it was just his well-developed and headstrong sense of mischief. I do know that one time in the aftermath of an uprising against the Shah in 1953, Essa nearly got us into serious trouble.

The uprising only lasted a few days, but during that time there was terror and turmoil everywhere. The Shah had had to leave the country for a few days and Dr Mossadeq, whom the Shah had appointed Prime Minister, took charge. He was considered a hero by many Iranians for he had nationalised the oil industry earlier and demanded reforms. He drove through the streets and told cheering crowds that he was going to make life better for the masses. Days of rioting followed. Finally, after a very tense time throughout the country, the army under the command of General Zahedi, a well-known and able officer, restored order. When the Shah returned, there was public rejoicing.

During one of these demonstrations of fervour for the Shah, Essa climbed onto an open truck crowded with people who were cheering and yelling, *"Marg bar Mossadeq"* and *"Javeed Shah"* (death to Mossadeq and long live the Shah).

He was puzzled, for only a few days earlier, he had heard the frenzied crowd cheering and shouting for Mossadeq and condemning the Shah. At the top of his voice he began to shout, "Long live Mossadeq, who nationalised oil and why have you all changed your minds today?"

Although he was only a child of 10, he was apprehended and was missing for quite a few hours. I was frantic with worry and never felt so relieved in all my life as when he was finally brought home by two angry policemen.

I thought they had just discovered that he was missing and had kindly brought him home, so I was shocked when they told me what had happened. They then began to question me about my political allegiance. This was a time when people were extremely careful about what they said, for the very words which might save the situation now, could be used to condemn one later, if the regime changed once again.

Realising that something serious had occurred, Dada Fatma and her husband wanted no part in this and told me not to mention their names or to say that they were related to me at all. In that tense time it was understandable; I did not blame them and rather wished I could get away as well.

It was a delicate situation for a while and Essa did not help, as he continued to call everybody hypocrites for turning against a great leader like Mossadeq. Knowing I needed more solid support than that given me by my family, I called Colonel Palar and asked him to speak to the police. He arrived in his uniform and the police were duly impressed. He told them that Essa's father was away and that I was bringing Essa up on my own.

On hearing this, the police became less aggressive but they insisted on inspecting the house. Fortunately they found three pictures of the Shah on the walls. They then began to realise that they were, after all, dealing with a mere child, who could not possibly understand the complexities of politics and who was completely confused by the fickleness of the adult world. In the end, all they did was advise me to put some sense into his head. I had to keep him inside the house for a few days, but it took quite some time for my sister and her husband to trust him again.

Life couldn't have been easy for Essa either, even though he was a child. It was not surprising, in retrospect, that he began to ask serious questions about his father, Zakaria. In the past I had told him the few things I knew about the man I had only spent three months with and I elaborated these bits of information, for I never wanted my child to think unfavourably of his father. However, it was difficult for Essa to comprehend the situation so when asked his name, he always replied, "Essa bin Mariam"(son of Mariam).

When he first said this, it was thought of as a joke but, as time went on, I felt that it was not good for him to know only a mother. Because his father was a Saudi, he had been fortunate enough to get a Saudi passport but I had been unable to get him Iranian papers. Consequently, a number of problems arose because I was an Iranian citizen and he wasn't. It was difficult even to get him registered in a good Iranian school, so his education was severely disrupted. He felt out of place because, like the rest of us, he had problems communicating in Farsi.

On top of all this, my father and my friends – and even Essa himself – began to put pressure on me to think about remarrying. Society anywhere in the world is not kind to single women so, although I was reasonably happy and respected living on my own, deep down I knew it was necessary to change my status. Besides, I was no longer young and I wanted to have more children. It therefore became important for me to face the facts.

It was rather strange but, after reluctantly accepting the possibility of remarriage, events suddenly assumed a life of their own. Seemingly, out of nowhere, word came that Zakaria had finally returned to Karachi with his wife and children. Although he had never written or asked to see his son, I felt it was important for Essa to meet his father, even if briefly, and get to know each other. I had made up my mind so, without more thought, we immediately took a plane to Karachi.

In those days, the early 1950s, only small Fokker Friendship propellor-driven airplanes flew this route, and tt took us almost 10 hours to reach Karachi. The stop in Zahedan, in a small deserted area, with no form of shelter like an airport, compounded by our emotional upheaval, resulted in an altogether uncomfortable journey. Essa was sick all the way and his plea was, "Mummy, please keep my food; I will eat it when we reach Karachi." But what really took me by surprise was, "Mummy, how many more homes will we leave?"

Amongst all this discomfort, I suddenly spotted a fellow traveller, a lady of about 60, enjoying every moment of her flight. She touched up her make-up several times and at Zahedan she was thrilled to bits when she saw a caravan of camels. She immediately took some photos and was so excited by her experience that she somewhat transferred her joyous spirit to me. I wanted to know what was so exciting in this God-forsaken desert and she wanted to know why we looked so unhappy and what the purpose of our journey was. She had been a teacher and had saved enough to visit the exotic subcontinent. I felt exhausted because the future did not promise much but according to her theory, life had a lot of compensations and blessings. My spirit was lifted. The journey became bearable and the bright side of it was the prospect of seeing Monkhali and some of our dear friends again.

When we reached our destination I worked out a plan on how to introduce son to father and vice versa. According to Islamic tradition, once a woman is divorced from her husband, the man becomes a complete outsider, so there was no question of my meeting Zakaria. Therefore Uncle Abe (the same uncle who was instrumental in the marriage of Zakaria and myself) took Essa and one of his own sons of the same age to Zakaria's home. Although he had never set eyes on his son, Zakaria recognised Essa without hesitation and said, "His eyes are just like Mariam's."

It was an exciting moment for Essa to finally meet his father, who over the years had been a mysterious and heroic figure in the child's mind. Fantasy and fact seemed to blend into one and, quite rapidly, Essa made up his mind that he wanted to live with his father. Zakaria took to Essa as well and was very repentant for being absent from the boy's early life. He promised that he would make up for the past by taking full responsibility for our son's future.

Monkhali was adamantly opposed to the whole idea and I was devastated by the thought of losing my child. It left me in a daze, feeling as if I was being manipulated by everybody. However, in the end I realised that Essa was happy with his new-found family and knew I had to make this sacrifice for my child, so he could grow up with a name and identity. I felt happier knowing that Zakaria's new wife, Kulsum, was a kind, understanding and wise woman, who would give my son the love and care he would need. Also knowing that Monkhali lived close by was a comfort, for she adored Essa and I knew she would make sure he was always happy.

It was a terrible, heart-wrenching time for me. I left Karachi feeling empty and lost – completely drained of life and hoping that I would never live to regret my decision. Sometimes I still wonder whether I made a mistake in letting Essa go, but all I know is that he has grown up to be a good, refined, well-balanced and honest man who is a loving husband and father. His integrity of character, his keen sense of responsibility and his pleasant disposition endears him to everyone he comes in contact with. What more can we ask for in our children?

My own future now loomed even more threateningly before me. I knew in my heart I wanted to remarry but the prospect frightened me, after the experience of my first short-lived marriage. And Monkhali's words rang in my ears. She often said that if I lost my tongue, I would have nothing at all to impress others with. However, there is a saying in Farsi, *"An chenan ra an chenan tar kardan"*, which means "to better something that is already good" so, not being able to change my not-so-flattering points, I worked on my good ones and always kept myself well-groomed and tried hard to be a charming and intelligent conversationalist. Something must have worked for through the years, despite my plain looks, I have never lacked for company. This has taught me one of the nicest things I have learnt about life: No woman is ever totally unattractive.

I was now in my 30s and very fussy about who I might have to spend the rest of my life with, so although I received several proposals of marriage, they were unacceptable to me.

I realised that, because of my age, the only men available would already be married, divorced or widowed. I insisted that I did not want to be a second wife and neither did I think I could ever trust a divorced man, which left me only with widowers or, worst of all, with some one younger than myself. I also expected the man I married to be a *khodmooni* and so one of my own kind. However, I was adamant that I was never going to marry any of my cousins. More than anything though, I knew that no marriage would work for me unless my new husband was an enlightened man with a strong character and an open mind who would respect my attitudes and my belief in the emancipation of women.

On top of the list that had been compiled of likely choices was the name of a man I had heard of only once before and in intriguing circumstances. It was Abdullah Pakravan from Bandar Abbas. I had never given him a second thought but suddenly like a flash, I remembered his house and all those books.

His wife, the woman I had met years before and with whom I had shared a taxi to Bandar Abbas, had died leaving him with two children, the only survivors of eleven she had borne him. He had heard enough about me to believe that a marriage between us would work well. He wrote expressing all this to my good friends Ismail and Zuleika Fikree and they became the mediators.

Jokingly I suggested we write a 'for' and 'against' list of Pakravan's virtues and vices.

"He must be tall," I insisted.

"Yes, yes, he is not only tall but lean," they assured me, so he gained points.

"If he has a high-pitched voice like that of a woman don't go any further."

"No, he has a deep, manly voice." He scored more points.

"If he is a man not involved with the social aspect of local life and has nothing to do with culture but is only interested in dreary business then he is definitely not the one for me."

I found out he was not only the head of the Chamber of Commerce, but also the director of the Red Lion and Sun Society (equivalent of the Red Cross and Red Crescent), and had little love for worldly possessions.

He sounded too good to be true and I was captivated. In fact in all the excitement we forgot to make an 'against' list.

An exchange of intelligent letters followed and I was impressed by his fluency in Persian and English. My friends, the Fikrees and the Palars, encouraged the match as they knew Pakravan to be a man of integrity and an ideal father and they believed that our marriage would be a happy and successful one.

My arrogant and snobbish family, however, were not particularly happy about the whole idea for, as they pointed out, although Pakravan was undoubtedly a good man, he was not from our social background.

There were other disadvantages. The prospect of living in Bandar Abbas, a town which was considered socially backward and restricted, was probably the worst and most difficult barrier to overcome. Hot and unhealthy, Bandar Abbas was used as a place of exile for criminals!

In times not that long past, Bandar Abbas had been ridden with disease. Lack of sanitation, people's ignorance of proper hygiene and the town's stagnant water supply were largely to blame. The most gruesome disease was caused by a worm known as 'peyoog', which grew in the body, especially around the legs and ankles and had to be pulled out carefully, inch by inch. It could grow up to three feet long and if it snapped inside the body the person would suffer immensely and the consequences were usually fatal. Besides this, blindness was common in this area. Hardly anyone reached their mid-30s without their sight being affected, mainly because of dust and heat. Lack of fluoride in the water caused the teeth to turn yellow and decay easily, and old age came to the people who lived in this area much earlier than it did to those living in other regions of Iran.

However, I was told living conditions there had improved since the early days, as there was now a proper supply of water and electricity. Nonetheless, it was still a daunting prospect.

The idea of taking on two children, who were not mine, was another challenging situation I had to face. The choice was not easy but, before I had a chance to think too much about it, the two children along with their nanny, a young relative of Pakravan's, arrived at Father's house where I was then living.

Rokna was 10 and Mariam (Marie) was no more than a baby, about three years old. They were dressed in clothes that looked too large on one and too tight for the other. The children gazed at me with puzzled but hopeful eyes. Marie, whose mother had died giving birth to her and a twin who also died, ran up to me and asked, "Are you my mother? Please don't leave us again."

I was moved to tears and knew I could not resist my fate. In some ways it seemed appropriate that, with my own child being looked after by another, I, in turn, should look after somebody else's children – and these two sorely needed looking after.

The children's obvious neglect appalled me. Haleema, the nanny, told me she was devoted to the children and couldn't bear to lose them, but I soon realised she was insincere and an opportunist for, although she looked well-dressed and well-fed, the children were thin and carelessly clothed.

It upset me to think that a man could allow his children to be so badly taken care of, but the impression I had of Pakravan was that he was such a good person himself that, at times, this obscured his judgement of others. I knew therefore, that if I accepted his proposal of marriage, I would have to do something about this woman, who was obviously taking advantage of the situation.

Finally the time came to meet Pakravan himself. He came to have a meal with the family, so it was not only my inspection he had to pass. When he entered the room, his appearance and personality were exactly as I had expected. He was tall, lean, handsome, slightly grey-haired but not dyed, and seemed a serious sort of person. He spoke little but what he said was to the point and full of common sense. After shaking hands, we sat down to a meal. Naturally, it was not easy for either Pakravan or me to relax and Ismail had to make the most of the conversation to try and lighten the atmosphere.

"You must have had quite an effect on Mariam for when she stops talking we know something serious has happened," he joked, and it was true. For once in my life, I had hardly anything to say.

Pakravan also was very quiet. He seemed to be in awe of my father. Generally it was an uncomfortable meal and I still didn't really know what my decision was going to be. I was impressed by Pakravan but the whole change in lifestyle that I knew I would have to accept made the choice more difficult. It would not be easy for me to change so drastically!

Afterwards Father spoke seriously to me. "Your Pakravan seems a wise and knowledgeable man with a good character. He would keep you safe and secure, but is there nothing else you are looking for? You are used to a high social standing. All your life you have lived in luxurious surroundings, moved in elite circles and you have a sound career. Do you want to give up all this and move to a place that hardly has the basic amenities? What are the compensations for accepting such a challenge? Why are you complicating your life in this way?"

Father's reservations bothered me, especially after I received a letter from Monkhali. In her usual blunt manner, she told me that I had always been a headstrong fool but if I married Pakravan, I was even more of a fool than she had believed.

"You will be lighting your funeral pyre," she warned me.

I was also unnerved by Haleema, the nanny. I realised that this woman could cause trouble, for I knew I could not live with her and she felt that I threatened her position. When I confided my fears to Zuleika she laughed a little and reassured me by saying that she thought I was a strong enough character to tackle and overcome a mere, meddlesome woman.

I took a great deal of notice of my friends' advice for it was apparent that they really did care for me and my well-being. This encouraged me to appreciate the advantages of this proposal and a few days later, after praying to Allah for guidance, I gave up my career, married Pakravan, and moved south to Bandar Abbas.

CHAPTER 14

ACHIEVEMENTS IN BANDAR ABBAS

A marriage where respect rather than love is the prime emotion may seem strange to those with conventional, western ideals but in many ways it is a union that is more likely to succeed, as my marriage to Pakravan did for well over 30 years, despite times of hardship and enforced separation.

As I got to know Pakravan better my admiration and respect for him grew. It seemed a miracle that I had finally met somebody with views so similar to mine. He respected women and believed that they should be given more freedom to help with the building of a new Iranian society. He was a man of integrity, full of love for others, but it was his sense of humility that made him a great human being.

Few people knew just how remarkable he was. While still in his mid-teens, Pakravan had heard he could get free education in India; several children had already gone from Iran, and he got government sponsorship to go too. The educational institution was run as an *ashram* whose head was also the spiritual leader. Over the course of the two or three years he stayed, Pakravan became known as *Chota Baba*, or little leader – in effect the number two in the *ashram*. His family eventually brought him back to Iran. Years later, he was sought out by a documentary film-maker who was researching that *ashram*, and a film was made about Pakravan. Modest to a fault, he would have been the last person to mention such a claim to fame.

Because I was so determined to succeed as the perfect

wife and mother, I refused to be discouraged by my surroundings. Although I was assured life in Bandar Abbas was a lot better than it used to be, when I arrived there it was plain that there was still a great deal of room for improvement. In some ways it was like returning to life in Lingah 30 years ago – minus the legion of slaves, who used to bump into each other anyway for want of something better to do.

All the houses, including our own, still had primitive sanitation arrangements and the kitchen facilities were inadequate. Fortunately the water supply had improved; deep wells had been dug and water was piped to the house through new, clean mains, but I still filtered it as I doubted its purity. Electricity was available but only for a few hours every day so, in the heat of the summer, windtower rooms were a necessity and all my memories of sleeping on the roof flooded back as I returned to this style of life. The open roof space – or any form of large balcony and semi-covered terraces for that matter – have always attracted my imagination. Here the roof-top had great potential and once settled, I organised several roof-top garden parties which became the talk of the town. The house, however, was not comfortable and Pakravan agreed that improvements had to be made.

My 'improvement project' began with the house and the household. The house was reasonably new, so I could see it had potential, but it was not particularly well-designed.

Our block of land was massive, half taken up by the garden area. In traditional houses this usually lies in a central courtyard and the living rooms are built around it. The garden of our house was bigger and located at one end of the compound. It was filled with lemon trees that Pakravan tended with great care.

This orchard gave the whole garden a delightful, tangy fragrance. Besides the lemon trees, there were a few wild rose bushes, a couple of date palm trees and a small vegetable patch. The rest of the area around the house was paved.

The house was built on a high concrete platform. A set of curved steps led to the big, wooden front doors. I liked the raised design of the house but the only real beauty the place could boast of were the steps and the intricately carved doors.

The wooden entrance gates were solid and looked good but the walls surrounding the house were crumbling badly and in need of urgent repair.

Not so easy to repair was our domestic situation. However, I was particularly pleased and relieved when we were able to find a suitor for Haleema and arrange a marriage. Her meddling ways and demands had become frustrating and irritating and the friction between us had increased. Pakravan was also pleased; he had been unwilling to tell her that she was no longer needed, as he didn't want to seem ungrateful for all her past help. This solution was the only convenient way to get rid of her.

Looking after the children and supervising my home was a new and rewarding experience. I even tried to learn how to behave in a kitchen and talk of recipes but there was no use trying to fool myself: I knew that I would not be able to survive in such a place without being intellectually occupied as well.

The first year passed by and life began to settle into a more mundane routine. I was enjoying the simple pleasures of being a housewife, having a comfortable home and a caring husband. For quite some time I had a stream of inquisitive visitors who came to see what sort of a woman Pakravan had married. Those who knew my family background were equally curious to find out how a daughter of Hafsa Abbas (for that was how we were known in the Gulf area in those days) could adjust to such an environment.

Pakravan spent a great deal of time at work and was also busy with the programmes for the Red Lion and Sun Society. He was always helping the less fortunate. When he was home he was busy with his books and his garden.

Although I helped my husband with his welfare work, I knew this was not going to be enough for me. I was young and energetic and confident in my ability to bring about even more spectacular changes.

After the house, the town itself was my next obvious 'project'. It was a dull, dreary-looking place and there wasn't even any greenery around to lend colour and beauty. There was no park, no library, no cinema and no sports facilities – nothing at all for children or the youth of the town or, for that matter, the women. The men had their work but I wondered what else there was to do in this place. More importantly, what were all the women doing?

Certain socialites spoke of various projects in a desultory way but nobody was prepared to see them through. Bandar Abbas was a sleepy, lazy place and the excuse everybody had was that it was too hot to do anything much.It seemed to me that they were unaware, perhaps by choice, of the fresh new beginnings taking shape elsewhere in Iran.

Coming from Teheran where changes were happenng rapidly, and with my own rather energetic enthusiasm, I was frustrated by the general air of apathy and determined to shake some new life into things.

I didn't have too long to wait before an opportunity arose. One day Pakravan came rushing home to change on his way to the school concert. I was surprised when I found out he intended to go alone.

"Why?" I asked.

He looked at me in surprise and explained that women were never invited to public and social engagements. It was my turn to be dumbfounded, for a school concert was after all a performance put on by children, who have a mother as well as a father. I could not understand why mothers who had, like me, put in a lot of work with the costumes and had helped design the sets, should be deprived of the enjoyment of watching their children perform.

We talked seriously about this matter and Pakravan, being broad-minded and clear-sighted, agreed wholeheartedly with my point of view. There and then we decided that a stand had to be taken. Pakravan contacted a few of our friends, who were also important members of the community and, instead of going to the concert, they came around to our house where we spent a stimulating evening discussing the problem of women's social and educational status in this area.

Although the Shah had tried to bring about reforms for women, it was a difficult plan to implement, because of tradition and the selfishness and narrow-mindedness of many men, especially the religious leaders of the area. I heard one such uninformed person lecturing once on the wrongs of educating women. He believed that the only use to which girls would put their new-found literacy would be in writing love letters! When I insisted that this man should be tackled, Pakravan said, "*In ham migozarad* – this will also pass".

In Bandar Abbas women were not being given the opportunity to take advantage of the reforms for, while the men of the family were encouraged to travel abroad to train as doctors, engineers, lawyers and other professions, girls were still only being given elementary education and then were expected to marry these well-educated, cultivated men and keep them happy. It seemed an unfair arrangement for both parties.

Our stand about the concert was one of the first moves to bring about change. The empty seats were noticed and, after discovering that Pakravan and I had been behind it all, the Education chief, Mr Pezeshki, decided to pay me a visit.

He was a charming man and told me that he felt changes to women's status in this area were both necessary and long overdue. He was pleased to find a local lady with enough enthusiasm and energy to help him carry them out. These were qualifications I certainly had and I also possessed a strong belief that women in the area were ready for such a change.

The first cautious steps were taken. I began to attend local functions with Pakravan. For the first few months we sat separately in segregated rows. Soon more wives began to come along and it became acceptable. Eventually the time came when I sat next to my husband in public and after a while even this unheard of behaviour became normal practice. We had, in a reasonably short space of time, changed what had been an established attitude.

I was pleased with our success but I knew it was only a beginning. Women still needed to be given more than a basic education. The town desperately needed a girls' high school before real reform could take place. Up until this time, if girls of good families wanted more education after primary school they had to be sent away to a boarding school as there was no proper schooling in Bandar Abbas. It was more usual for a girl to sit at home and wait for some cousin to return from abroad, so she could marry him.

Mr Pezeshki proved he meant what he said about wanting change for women, for he was very pleased and most willing to help when I approached him with the idea of setting up a high school for girls. With his influence and help the idea began to become a reality.

Setting up the school was an exciting project, one I knew would produce long-term results and would help the whole area. I visited a number of families whose daughters had given up studies in the sixth form; these girls were so thrilled by the idea of further education that their parents soon had to agree.

Plans were drawn up; a budget was sanctioned; a building was appropriated and the school began with girls being taught up to standard 12, which enabled them to go on to university, if they so desired.

Having been trained to teach, I joined the Education Ministry and was in charge of the English department. Also, because of my earlier experience, I was able to set up a Social Science department in the school and helped train girls to be better wives and mothers.

As a wife, mother and teacher, I certainly had no time to worry about whether I had done the right thing in marrying and coming to such a backward place. In fact I think I rather liked the idea that there was still so much to do, for it gave me the sense that there was always something more to achieve – a philosophy that has kept me active and happy all my life.

These years of the mid-Fifties were, indeed, busy and happy times for me and to make me even happier I found I was expecting a child. Twelve years earlier, when my first child was born, I had been young, unhappy and lonely. This time it was different. I had a wonderful husband, who was delighted with the idea of another child and, as a person, I was ready for motherhood.

There were no adequate facilities for delivering babies in Bandar Abbas and, although I didn't expect any problems, I decided to go to Teheran to have my baby in a modern hospital. In Bandar Abbas even in 1956, the situation facing expectant mothers was nothing short of desperate; unqualified midwives attended women in their own homes and cases of infant mortality and the loss of mothers at childbirth were common. Therefore it was not surprising that women were afraid when they went into labour. If the expectant mother was lucky and strong enough to survive the unhealthy conditions under which she gave birth, she was then further 'tortured' by being denied a drink of water – no matter that she was dehydrated from perspiring. Instead a stone was placed on her stomach and hot, oily, peppery food was forced down her throat. These old customs still prevailed in very traditional households.

I'm not really sure what logic was behind this sort of treatment but it seems miraculous that any mother or child survived such an ordeal at all. Naturally recuperation was slow.

Even if all went well, a new mother had to stay in bed for 40 days and only after this period was she allowed up to have a proper bath. But she was still not permitted to go out for several months and, throughout this period, it was also necessary to pretend to be suffering and in great pain to avoid the 'evil eye'.

When I was expecting Essa in Karachi, I had been adamant that I would not have my baby at home. I had seen my sister, Dada Fatma go through the whole gruesome and, at times, melodramatic performance with a number of false alarms; men inept and confused; doctors and nurses being summoned daily; and in the end the child being born in the middle of – and in spite of – a group of screaming, praying old women.

Nobody approved of what I did – especially not Monkhali, who nevertheless insisted on being with me – as nobody else in my family at that time had ever gone to a hospital to give birth, but I felt safer and hoped to be in a slightly less hysterical atmosphere. Essa's delivery had been easy and quick. Though I have to admit there was a reasonable amount of fuss even in the hospital, as Monkhali insisted that we take three extra rooms – one as a prayer room, one where her personal maids could prepare tea and *qalyoon* for her, and another where she could entertain visitors. It was her strong belief that a baby could not possibly be born without any chaos and excitement!

In contrast, my daughter Shahnaz was born with a minimum of fuss – coincidentally on November 18, the same birthday as our children Rokna and Marie – and so I wasn't at all apprehensive when, within the year I was expecting our second child. This time however, I decided that instead of running off to Teheran, which many of the local women seemed to resent, I would stay in Bandar Abbas. It was still far from a traditional home birth, for I made sure our house was turned into a nursing home and that a good doctor and nurse were on standby.

Our second daughter was born quickly and with even less carry-on. It was quite a surprise to have another daughter, because I had been totally prepared for a son, even having the name Jehangir (conqueror) ready. However, another daughter was more than welcome and, because she was such a sweet and adorable little baby, we named her Shirin, meaning 'sweet'.

The night I was due to give birth, Pakravan rang the Electricity Department and asked them to keep the power on at our expense until further notice for, in 1957 it was still not available 24 hours a day. In all the excitement of becoming a father again, Pakravan forgot to ring the Electricity Department after the delivery, so the lights were left on all night – and not without some humorous results. One group of people, whose custom was to play cards every night until the normal 'lights out' time, continued playing right through this "all-night blessing of light" as it came to be called later. The winners of their marathon session were ecstatic; not so the losers who cursed their luck and the circumstances. Khanom Pakravan was blamed!

Although my experience of giving birth at home was quite different from the customary one assisted by a midwife, it underlined for me the need to improve the conditions of the hospitals in the town, so that women would learn to trust them and discover that giving birth there was more hygienic and safer for mother and baby. At that time hospitals were thought of as a place a person went to when there was no hope at all. The worst problem was that people usually left it too late and because of this often died when they were finally taken there.

I knew that giving birth at home was not necessarily dangerous under normal circumstances if there were trained personnel in attendance but, if a woman had an abnormal delivery, there was usually little hope for her survival or the child's.

One of our neighbours, a well-educated woman, who taught at the school and whose husband was also a teacher, had been in labour for three days trying to give birth to her first child. I visited her a few times and was upset to see the unhygienic conditions and the untrained midwife who was attending her. When asked when the baby would arrive, all this hopeless and helpless woman would say was, "Whenever God wills it."

The patient was exhausted and the baby's heartbeat was slow, so even with my little knowledge of these things I knew that both lives were in danger. Although it was completely unheard of, I called the doctor – who, to make matters worse, was a male. He quickly discovered that the baby was a breach and that it was necessary to perform a caesarean section. The family were shocked and outraged by the suggestion, because they were sure the mother-to-be would die; in her present condition, her chances were slim either way. After giving dire warnings, the doctor and I left the house and waited hopefully for the family to change their minds.

Things went from bad to worse and soon, realising it really was a grave situation, the husband – who had very little authority for he and his wife lived with her parents – rushed to our house and begged us to take his wife to the hospital. The Red Lion and Sun Society ambulance had been kept in readiness and it wasn't long before the girl was in good hands.

Reluctantly the rest of the family followed to the hospital and waited expectantly for the poor girl to die, as they felt sure she would in such a place.

I found it difficult to remain calm and spent all my time praying. Much was at stake. I knew that if anything went wrong, my urgings to use modern methods would lose all credibility. This was an important family and the first such in the district to put themselves in the care of a hospital and a male doctor. Eventually, and despite complications, a healthy baby boy was born and he and the mother were pronounced safe and well. The family were astounded.

This was a turning point in the social reform programme. Soon afterwards, pre-natal and ante-natal classes were started at the home-making department of the Girls' High School. Mothers-to-be were invited to attend short courses on child care and family health. These courses were extended to include child physiology, home management, as well as traditional handicrafts. More and more women were shaken out of their lethargic attitudes and joined in and thus began to change their lifestyle.

It was wonderful to see girls participating in sports,

drama and debates – activities which they pursued enthusiastically as soon as the opportunity was there. And once started, there was no stopping them; their enthusiasm knew no bounds. All it had taken was someone like me to show the way, to act as a catalyst.

It was an exciting time, and the more I could see was being accomplished, the more effort and energy I poured into this work. I was elected chairperson of several social and charitable organisations. Still, my spirit was restless; I could see there were other areas which needed improvement. For example, there was a noticeable lack of parks. And cinemas: I had loved going to the cinema in Teheran. "Why should there be no cinemas?" I asked. Pakravan could see no reason why not, so he formed a company of a few interested merchants and between them they financed an inexpensive, open-air cinema – but not without some opposition. There were die-hard elements of the community who thought no good would come of it. So to appease this minority, when it first opened the cinema had special cubicles for women, the idea being that they would enter after the lights went out and then run out during the last scenes of the film before the lights came on again! Gradually of course, the walls and curtains of these cubicles were removed and, eventually, women began to sit with the rest of the family. When I think about it now, it makes me chuckle. And all this in the late 1950s.

Among those who contributed to the cultural and architectural development of the Hormozgan Province was a talented engineer, Jalal Tehranchi, whose constructive and creative ideas placed this once-backward town well on the path to progress. He was actively involved in plans for the construction of roads and highways, schools, hospitals and even the port of Bandar Abbas. His brainchild was the introdction of deep wells in the town. Since those days he and his wife Ziba Shahrava and their families have become closely linked with my family.

Much later Tehranchi formed a vast company called 'Caling' which serviced foreign contractors who implemented development projects in the area. The company was run by him, Pakravan, Mohammad Saleh Shahrava (Tehranchi's father-in-law) and Mohammad Siddick Rokni (his nephew). It was Pakravan's involvement in this vast concern that kept him going after my departure to Pakistan in 1964.

Changes began to occur rapidly, almost too rapidly. Anything that was old or represented old ways was thrown on the scrap heap and all that was new or modern was taken up in the belief that it had to be better. This wasn't the first time I had witnessed how people could get carried away with change and go too far, and later, after the revolution, this euphoric but ill-judged 'spring cleaning' almost cost me my life. Although I wholeheartedly believed in change and the comfort brought about by modernisation, I was aware that our traditions and culture should not be discarded with quite so much abandon.

Beautiful old ceramic ware was being replaced by cheap, plastic goods; old family jewellery was being melted down and cast in modern settings; ill-fitting clothes were being bought readymade; chrome and plastic chairs and tables were being substituted for solid, intricately carved wooden furniture.

In an effort to preserve of our culture before it was completely destroyed and forgotten, I decided to set up a Mooza-e-Moheet Shinasi or an ethnological museum. I hoped it would be a place for all the people of the Hormozgan area. I consulted my friend Mr Pezsheki and Jalal Tehranchi and, with their help, this project was soon under way.

A committee was formed to organise the collection of items and as I was voted chairperson I became very involved. I wrote letters to all the local dignitaries asking for a contribution of things that could be preserved and displayed. Besides this, I and other members of the committee visited houses throughout the province and collected many recently discarded objects, now regarded as junk.

The first articles for the museum came from my family's old Lingah house. I knew that my family would not use these things again and it was sad to see all our lovely old furniture rotting away. I contributed pieces of jewellery, clothes, crystal, pots, our favourite old harmonium, and the gramophone that held so many memories.

To house all these items, an old building was renovated (though not modernised to the point of losing its traditional structure). It took more than a year for us to collect enough objects to be representative, to classify, record, and then display them. When we finished the initial drive, we had everything from huge wooden doors and carved windows to cooking utensils and furnishings; from gold jewellery, musical instruments and manuscripts to seashells, bones of long-dead animals, and preserved insects and reptiles. With all the displays we ensured there was an explanation of how each object was used and how old it was. Mannequins displaying local costumes, customs and activities also inhabited the museum.

This project was very successful – beyond our expectations, in fact – and brought prestige to the region. The Governor General of Hormozgan heard of our efforts and recommended our museum to none other than the Shah and his wife, the Shahbanu, who in particular were interested in local culture and traditions, and we received the ultimate honour, a visit from them.

For me, it was the first of many meetings with the Shah and the Shahbanu. I was very nervous, almost to the point of being paralysed with fear, but I was excited at the prospect of actually talking to this awe-inspiring man and his beautiful wife. The Shah was very regal and, although he was slightly built, he had a stern, commanding manner. It was difficult to relax with him for he rarely showed any human emotions and he seldom joked or smiled. He always spoke in a controlled and often cold way, usually managing to terrify anyone he talked to, despite the fact that what he said was charming and intelligent.

His wife, the Shahbanu Farah, was entirely different, for she was a gentle person and had the talent of making people relax. She was his third wife. His first marriage, at the age of 21 to the beautiful but petulant Egyptian Princess Fouzia, ended in divorce. He also divorced his second wife, the stunningly attractive Soraya Esfandiary, who later became an actress. This was a sadder case, for the two were obviously in love but, because they remained childless for the seven years of their marriage, it became imperative for the Shah to divorce her and remarry someone who could provide him with an heir.

Farah came from a good Iranian family and was an intelligent, well-educated woman. She was some 20 years younger than the Shah and, although possibly not as sensationally beautiful as her predecessors, she was the best consort of the three, for she cared deeply for the people of Iran, for the future of the country and above all for the well-being of her husband.

When they first met she was a student at the Ecole Special d'Architecture in Paris. He was on a private visit and at the time he was a sad man for he had been recently divorced from Soraya. During his stay in the French capital the Iranian Ambassador held a reception for the Shah and at this the best Iranian students in Paris were presented to him.

Amongst the young people there was a tall, attractive 19-year-old girl who stood out as being quite remarkable for she did not seem to show the usual feelings of awe and reverence for the Shah that even his courtiers and members of his household showed for this imperial man who moved many (myself included) to feelings of extreme emotion after any meeting. She, however, seemed undaunted and she stood before him and boldly asked him how Iran could ever progress when grants to study abroad were being cut even though students could not be taught the subjects of their choice in their own universities at home.

Her method of addressing the Shahenshah was completely novel and those present held their breath, unsure of how His Majesty would react. He smiled and everyone relaxed.

A year later when Farah returned to Teheran she was formally introduced to the Shah by Princess Shahnaz (the only child of his first marriage). The Shah claimed that he did not remember their first encounter but it seems difficult to believe that he could forget the young woman who had shown such courage in addressing him so audaciously. They married after several more meetings and 10 months later the heir to the Pahlavi dynasty was born.

On their visit to the museum, I found them both charming and gracious. They were obviously impressed by the fact that, without any financial assistance or guidance from the Government the people of Bandar Abbas had been able to set up a remarkable historical institution for the education of the next generation and the preservation of Iran's cultural heritage. I remember how everyone on the committee of the museum who met the couple was impressed. We talked of nothing but their visit for months and often I commented how they inspired me to do more for the good of our community. As well, of course, I wanted to meet the Shah and Shahbanu again.

Following the success of the museum, a handicrafts centre seemed to be the next inevitable step. A *kargah* or workshop was set up and women from all over the province were soon involved. Girls who had finished school were taught the traditional methods of matting, basketwork, tailoring and hand embroidery of clothes and furnishings by local village women. Classes in modern art and culture were also conducted at the centre and there were many enthusiastic students.

With this renewed interest in local craft work, the centre decided to create something special that represented the work of the region to present to Their Majesties for Nowrooz or New Year.

New Year is an important festive occasion in Iran when people clean their houses, buy new clothes and give each other presents. It was also traditional for each province to send a representative to the Imperial court bearing a *Hadayae Nowroozi* – a gift with a regional theme on the eve of the New Year, March 21.

In 1960 the Crown Prince was born and there was great jubilation throughout the country. Therefore, of course, in that year every gift was to be exceptionally special. Our innovative work in Bandar Abbas was becoming more widely known, so it was not unnatural that as the head of the museum committee I should be selected to represent Hormozgan. After much deliberation among the ladies in the town, we decided on a gift, then we stitched and sewed for weeks to get it ready.

Finally, with my precious cargo, I set off for Teheran. I took a plane as I had to be there that day to register our gift and to receive an entrance permit to the Marble Palace, where I would be presented to the Shah and his family.

Things did not turn out quite that simple. For a start, at the airport a young pregnant woman was entrusted to my care, to be delivered to her husband in Shiraz, through which our route would take us. She was heavily veiled so I did not realise how young she was and how advanced her condition. The plane was a military aircraft with bench seats, small and uncomfortable, and there were no flight attendants: In those days, air hostesses covered international routes and important towns in central Iran. After about an hour, I found my young companion extremely restless. I looked at her face closely for the first time and realised she was hardly 15 years old. She told me with some difficulty that she was going through her first pregnancy, was a full nine months and then some! Good Lord, I thought – what now? It was obvious she was going into labour and was struggling to cope without screaming as she had been advised.

To cap it all, we ran into a storm and the plane was forced to land on Kharg Island, quite a deviation from its normal route. It was a complete wilderness and my chances of reaching Teheran that day were receding by the minute; the plane had been damaged and was unable to fly any further. "How long?" I asked. A few days, came the reply.

There seemed to be no help and I felt quite desperate for, after all the hard work the children and women of the area had put into the gifts, it would be heartbreaking not to be able to present them. Above all, what did we do with Sakina, the little mother-to-be? With the help of one of the crew, we delivered her baby girl and called her Homa, the name of Iran Air.

That crisis over for the moment, the next one was how to get on with our journey. The only chance we had of getting away was in the small, forlorn aeroplane, that was meant to be only for the use of the French engineers who worked on the island. Fortunately this plane belonged to the Red Lion and Sun Society so, after numerous calls to Pakravan, two passengers – Sakina the new mother and an old, sick man – and myself accompanying the crates of gifts with the royal flag attached, were on our way again to Abadan, where Sakina and I parted company, she and her baby in the care of a family member and me on another plane to my destination.

After arriving in Teheran I found that carrying the royal flag certainly made my trip to the place of registration quick and easy, as it attracted a lot of attention and people everywhere made way for me. Nervously I entered the wonderful Marble Palace and marvelled at the extraordinarily large and beautiful Persian carpets it contained and at the general elegance and opulence.

The palace was crowded with people bearing gifts. I felt small and insignificant though the boxes containing my gift were large and heavy, the products of many hours of long and careful work. I was full of apprehension when the big moment finally came. "What a beautiful fish; it looks so real," exclaimed the Shahbanu as she examined the shimmering gift. I explained that it was made in the shape of a hamour, which is the most common type of fish caught by the local fishermen. I showed her where a zip was cunningly concealed and, when she undid this, it opened out into a beautiful bed cover for the Crown Prince's cot. The shimmering effect was produced by the silver wire and intricate sequins worked into pure silk. Weaving gold and silver threads is a special type of needlework known as *khoos doozi*. This type of needlework is only done in the Gulf region but the craft seemed to have originated in India.

Students from our local boys' school had carved a replica of a wooden dhow with oars which, when they came together, formed the imperial crown and the Iranian flag. Inside the dhow we had placed all sorts of local costumes and accessories for the Shahbanu, made by our local women.

In particular there was a beautiful gold embroidered handbag with a belt to match, that had been created out of the embroidered ankle bands of an old traditional *salvaar* or trouser. This type of garment was usually worn by aristocratic ladies – I had often seen my mother in one of them. I loved to improvise and use old things for new purposes.

The gifts impressed everybody not only because they were useful items but because they were unique as well. Our region won the first prize and I was informed that I was to be presented to Their Majesties again as the Shah wished to discuss other projects for the Bandar Abbas area.

Once again I found the Shah an absolutely imposing character and, if I had been nervous when I met him in my familiar surroundings in Bandar Abbas, I was completely dumbstruck by his presence in his own magnificent setting. However, what he had to say was interesting and exciting.

He began by explaining the essence of what was later

to be called his White Revolution, which was a reform plan that was being implemented countrywide. What he wanted was to ensure that there was food, housing, clothing, education and a hygienic environment for everyone. He was particularly keen on an electoral law reform, universal suffrage and votes for women.

The more I spoke with this quiet, unemotional man, the less afraid I became of him. I realised that beneath his calm and haughty exterior he, too, cared deeply for his country.

Because of the reforms I had initiated in Bandar Abbas, the Shah appointed me honorary Mayor and told me I was to be in charge of beautifying the area. I was flattered and pleased by his interest in me and in the town and came away from my audience electrified, full of purpose and direction. This talk with the Shah deepened my resolve to bring about changes that I believed would be for the good of my region in general and women in particular.

An acknowledgement of my contribution came in the form of a letter from the Education Department inviting me to represent the Bandar Abbas area at an international seminar to discuss the problems of youth and education. The conference was held every two years and delegates from most regions, as well as a number of foreign dignitaries participated. It was the first time, however, that Bandar Abbas had been represented.

The conference was held in Abali, a picturesque ski resort in the northern part of Iran near Teheran. When I arrived I was given a badge with my name and province written on it. At first I could not understand why people moved away when I approached them but soon, after a few less ignorant (or maybe braver) people finally spoke to me, I realised what was wrong.

Not many delegates could locate Bandar Abbas on a map and was commonly thought to be "somewhere near Ahwaz," a town hundreds of miles to the south-west, near Abadan,and worse, it was commonly thought to be a place where criminals were sent. Government officials tried to avoid being sent there, for it was considered a complete backwater, where people were conveniently forgotten. There were, in fact, many jokes about officials carrying out their duties, seated in large water tubs to try and keep cool. Worst of all though, it was known as an unhealthy place; people who lived there were best avoided – certainly one did not want to get too close to someone from Bandar Abbas for fear of contracting something dreadful.

Because I was from this area, many of the people at the conference thought I was bound to be contaminated in some way or, at the very least hopelessly stupid, so not worth talking to. Nobody even sat next to me at the inaugural ceremony. I was most upset by their ignorance and their rudeness.

Nevertheless it was interesting being involved and I listened eagerly to all that was said. I was a little surprised that although many male teachers got up to speak, the only woman speaker was a well-known champion of Iranian women's causes, a writer and social worker. Having heard of this lady's reputation I was interested to hear what she had to say, but became more and more disappointed and angered by her negative attitude towards Iranian women. After listening to her speech I knew I couldn't sit back and swallow the slurs she had cast on them.

I stood up, which caused a buzzing around the room. I heard people enquiring about me. I saw the surprise on their faces when they learnt I was from Bandar Abbas – "What? From Bandar Abbas?" Luckily, being a teacher, I had become used to addressing an audience and, in fact, rather enjoyed the experience. Besides, I was angry enough not to let my nerves bother me.

When I began my reply to this eminent lady's unkind speech I spoke in Farsi and firstly affirmed the fact that I was from Bandar Abbas. I expressed concern for our children's future, if teachers had such poor knowledge of their own country that they thought Bandar Abbas was near Ahwaz. Point one to me!

I went on to tell them a little about this so-called terrible place and what developments had occurred there, as well as what it had to offer visitors. The audience was definitely becoming interested. Point two to me!

Point three I really enjoyed gaining. It was a direct reply to Madam F, who I noted was "a most unfortunate lady, as she obviously had few women friends or else she would know many in our country who were not only good mothers, but teachers, social workers, and excellent wives all rolled into one, and who were very involved in the changing face of Iranian society."

"How could she believe that women in Iran were totally inept and indifferent?" I asked, "or that they were self-indulgent and lacked ambition?"

Before I finished I switched to English, to the astonishment of the audience, and spoke to the foreign delegates about the problems of youth around the world. People were stunned that someone from backward Bandar Abbas was so aware of what was happening in the rest of Iran and was also abreast with world affairs. I sat down to warm applause. I became something of an overnight celebrity, and for the rest of the conference was sought out by reporters. This Bandar Abbasi delegate's opinion was asked on quite a few occasions. It was rather satisfying but, more than anything, I was pleased not to be shunned any more.

As a few more years went by the status of the province improved – an oil refinery was set up; factories for fish-canning and ice-making were built; roads were constructed and new methods of farming were introduced.

Although I had had nothing to do with these major changes, I knew my contribution to the educational, social and cultural scene had been important and this gave me a feeling of great contentment.

CHAPTER 15

POSTING IN LAHORE

My life at this stage was busy and truly fulfilling. I felt useful to my family and the community and that is a wonderful feeling of accomplishment.

Our children were growing up and I became obsessed with their education. I didn't want to accept anything less than the best for them. Our son Rokna was in one of the Bandar Abbas boys' high schools but for the girls, I realised that, although the schools in Bandar Abbas was better than no schools at all, their standards were not up to the mark.

Pakravan, having grown up as an orphan and knowing what it was like not to have been loved as a child, did not like the idea of sending such young children away. However, even he could see that the girls' school in our town, with its lack of proper sanitation, no air conditioning and particularly its restrictive curriculum, was not in the best interest of the children. So we decided to send Marie, who was 12, to a school in Esfahan run by French nuns. Then when Shahnaz turned five she joined her sister and they both did well. Meanwhile I tutored Shirin at home.

Apart from the educational side, I knew that if the children stayed with us Pakravan would have thoroughly spoilt them. I lacked his patience and tolerance; although as a child I had railed against the strictness of the household in which I grew up and the complete obedience that was demanded, I did not always agree with his relaxed attitude to the children's upbringing. They all loved their father very much, and in fact spent more time with him than they did with me, almost to the point where our maternal and paternal roles were reversed. Fortunately this generally suited everybody.

Around this time Pakravan was asked to stand for Parliament as the candidate of the Iran Novin Party, of which he was a member. It seemed an excellent idea and he was duly elected – a fitting reward for his many years of work for the area. People seemed pleased to have a true representative of the region. Excitedly we packed up our belongings, Pakravan wound up his business and we moved to Teheran. I was delighted, as I knew it would be better for the children and myself to be in a progressive, cosmopolitan environment.

Eagerly I looked around at all the good schools in Teheran and made plans to bring Marie and Shahnaz back when we were well settled. However, quite soon we realised something was wrong. Accusations of corrupt elections were made and after only a few months Parliament was dissolved.

Although nobody believed Pakravan had rigged his votes, at that time it was not an uncommon practice and influential personalities often monopolised constituencies.

It was many months before new elections took place. We waited in Teheran for some time but this proved expensive, especially as we were getting no income; I had taken leave from the Education Ministry and Pakravan was not working. Finally we went back to Bandar Abbas to wait but unfortunately, when the new elections were held, Pakravan did not gain a seat. So we had to start again from scratch.

After that, things went from bad to worse. Pakravan started a new business, providing heavy machinery and equipment to farmers, but this failed after a locust plague destroyed crops, leaving his customers unable to continue paying their instalments. This left Pakravan on the brink of bankruptcy. Gently he broke the news to me and, although I knew he had been increasingly worried over the months, I had no idea things were that bad. Fortunately friends intervened and offered guarantees, and because of his services to the community, the banks allowed him time to repay his loans.

To save me embarrassment and to give him time to get his affairs in order, Pakravan convinced me it would be a good idea if I got a job with one of the government departments, somewhere abroad, preferably in Pakistan, where most of my family still lived.

At this time I was still affiliated with the Ministry of Education, but in order to obtain a post outside the country I had to transfer to the Ministry of Arts and Culture. This ministry looked after all the aspects of art – museums, archaeological sites, theatres, libraries, cinemas and cultural centres in foreign countries. It was a non-political body and its aims were to foster culture within Iran and to project a positive image of Iran in other countries. It functioned in a similar way to the British Council, Alliance Francais and Germany's Goethe Institute, which have centres around the world.

The head of the ministry was the Shah's brother-in-law, Mehrdad Phalbod, whom I later came to know and respect a great deal. He was a fine man who was forced to leave the country during the early stages of the revolution in late 1978. With my experience it wasn't difficult to get a transfer and soon I was appointed as an instructor of the Persian language in Lahore.

It was not an easy choice to make. In many ways it was an excellent and timely move for Shahnaz and Shirin, for I knew the standard of schooling in Pakistan was good. It meant, too, that my daughters could stay with me, and still receive the kind of education I expected and demanded for them. Also I knew that by going away with the children, I would relieve Pakravan of a great deal of financial burden. So in the end I reluctantly agreed with his plan. Sadly, the children and I left our home and once again I returned to my refuge, Karachi.

By this time, in 1964, Monkhali had died, the houses had been sold and my family's resources had been further reduced. My sister, Dada Fatma, and her family were back in Karachi again and were living with our brother Ahmed Noor and his wife. It was to them that I went. It was not a particularly happy homecoming but I was relieved that Monkhali was not around to worry herself about my affairs and, of course, to nag me with the suggestion that once again I had made a mistake – which of course sometimes seemed so to me too – and that undoubtedly I would remain a fool all my life.

One bright side to all this was that I was able to be close to Essa again and it gave him a chance to get to know his sisters.

All the good friends of my youth welcomed us with open

arms; it was wonderful to see such people as the Ashraf sisters, and my old mentor, Mr Brohi, again. He in particular always seemed to be around during the difficult times in my life and was always there to help me through them. Even if life seemed frustrating and upsetting at times, with all its ups and downs, genuine friends such as this wonderful man enriched any experience.

When I visited my old school principal, Miss D'Abro, she too really motivated me, telling me not to give up, to keep pursuing a goal, to work hard, and to continue learning. At the ripe old age of 86 she was just starting to learn Spanish! She made me realise the truth of the saying that *khoda yak dar banad, sad dar goshayad* – God closes one door and opens hundreds of others.

I had only been to Lahore once before, when I sat for my matriculation exams in 1946. That visit had helped me through a time of crisis in my life and I felt pleased that it was Lahore to which I was returning at another difficult time. And the city did not disappoint me. There is a saying in Punjab *"Lahore Lahore hi hai"* – Lahore is after all Lahore – meaning that there is no place on earth that can compare with Lahore. The people who live there believe that their city holds a fascination for everyone. They could be quite right.

In my teen years I had shared in the fervour of the people struggling for the creation of a free and independent nation –Pakistan. Now I experienced with them a feeling of immense pride and great expectations for the future. Because I spoke Urdu which is the national language of Pakistan and understood and appreciated Punjabi folklore, music and art, the people of this beautiful country made me and my children feel very welcome.

However, for a while things were not easy for me. The director of the Centre where I began work found it difficult to accept me, partly because I was a woman but more because he had not asked for any help and felt threatened by my presence.

Later I discovered that because I used my maiden surname of Behnam, a common practice in Muslim countries, this man, knowing my married name was Pakravan, thought I was a spy for apparently he was convinced I was in some way related to

General Pakravan, the former head of SAVAK, the feared Government Intelligence Agency, and that I had been sent to Lahore to check up on him and his affairs.

It was ironic, but a few years later General Pakravan was assigned to Pakistan as the Iranian Ambassador and I had the opportunity to meet him then and soon became very good friends with him and his family. I found him to be a kind and just man, more a scholar than a politician. It is difficult to believe that this gentle, pipe-smoking man could harm even an ant and that as head of SAVAK, could have condoned torture and other inhumane acts which were said to have been carried out. In fact, it was commonly believed that the General did not last in the post because he was too 'soft'.

General Pakravan loved books and enjoyed a good browse at Ferozesons, a large book shop within walking distance from our Cultural Centre, when visiting Lahore. On one of his many visits he dropped in to Ferozsons as was his habit, and because he and his wife were due to have lunch with me at 1 pm at the Cultural Centre, he told his driver to meet him there at that time. Shops used to close between 1 and 4pm. When the driver arrived with Mrs Pakravan as instructed there was no trace of His Excellency. Panic ensued. Surely the shop would be shut by now. Had he been kidnapped, taken hostage or even worse, killed? Lunch grew cold on the table. Fearing the worst, we hastily made contingency plans. It was imperative that his disappearance be kept secret. Appointments were rescheduled. In desperation we went to the bookshop and it was indeed closed. Finally Mrs Pakravan made a sensible suggestion.

"Find the bookshop owner and get the key to the bookshop," she said. Hurriedly this was done. The flustered owner opened the door. We rushed in and there at the back of the shop we found that, after having been locked in for about two hours, the General was still happily browsing, quite unaware of the fuss he had caused.

My early days in Lahore were made quite unpleasant by the attitude of the director of the Cultural Centre. It did not take long for me to realise that although he was a scholar, writer, poet and professor, he was also a disturbed and insecure man. The main reason seemed to be his unhappy personal life. He had married an American woman and the cultural difference between the two caused terrible arguments. He was also apparently involved in some shady business as well, so scandal surrounded his family and, in turn, affected the Iranian Cultural Centre.

During this early, difficult time for me at the Centre, the Shah and the Shahbanu visited Lahore. As the Shah had a great deal of interest in our cultural and artistic programmes and remembered me from my activities in Bandar Abbas, he invited me to the Governor General's house where he was staying, to discuss the Centre's potential in Lahore and other programmes to be developed in Pakistan.

Needless to say the director was not impressed with my popularity and tried to get me removed from my post. But the reverse actually happened and he received an urgent summons to return to Teheran and was ordered to "turn over the control of the Centre to Behnam." On the day that he left, this unhappy man confessed that he had tried to undermine my influence and asked my forgiveness.

I was not bothered that he had harassed me but felt that, although there have always been strong historical links between Iran and Pakistan, he had tarnished our country's image during his tenure, so my first priority was to rectify this. A fresh beginning was called for, so I moved the Centre to another area of Lahore as quickly as I could, leaving behind the taint of my predecessor. I had some difficulty in renting a place, as people seemed reluctant to let their houses to Iranians. I was shocked and upset by this stigma, so I vowed to turn things around. I like to thnk that in a short while, in my own way, I succeeded.

Once I got myself established in the new place, I felt I could begin the real job I had been given – to promote and encourage Iranian and Islamic culture. Until the time I completed my BA degree in 1967 (from the time I arrived in Lahore I had continued my studies privately and sat for an exam every year), I was officially only acting director. After my graduation, I was promoted to director of the Centre and later to Cultural Counsellor with full diplomatic privileges including a diplomatic passport. It was quite a responsible position for, although there were five other Centres in the country, the one in Lahore was considered the most active and effective. I was extremely grateful for this position because, although Iranian women were being appointed to many top governmental jobs in Iran, it was still unusual for a woman to be granted such a responsible position outside the country and especially in such an important Muslim society as Pakistan.

My role brought me into regular contact with leading Pakistanis, who treated me with the utmost respect. But having to deal with a woman in what they considered was a man's job confused some of them. One old, white-bearded (the longer and whiter the beard the more revered the man) and important Pakistani scholar in particular refused to accept that it was a Madame Behnam he was supposed to see. He kept on insisting that he wanted to speak to Mr Behnam, because he couldn't be convinced that a woman was actually in charge of a Muslim institution. With my head modestly covered and in my most demure voice, I explained to him that I was only in charge until such time as the new director arrived.

This scholar had come to the Centre to read some classic Islamic literature, so as I spoke to him I led the way into the library, which held many rare and antique manuscripts. While we looked through the books, I began to discuss the historical and cultural affinity between our two countries. This led to a discussion about Persian and other Islamic literature. Very soon the man and the woman had disappeared and in their place two seekers of knowledge were communicating.

Suddenly out of the blue he asked: "Would you address a gathering on the subject of *Nozoole Quran*?" (How the Quran was revealed to the Prophet and the significance of the holy book). The request came almost as if on an impulse and before the old scholar had remembered that I was 'merely' a woman.

I accepted though I knew it would be quite an ordeal for me to address an audience of venerable authorities on Islam. I knew that, as men they would be waiting to prove that a woman was incapable of speaking in depth on such a profound subject. Immediately I set to work studying and researching my topic. Many long hours later I felt competent enough to speak on the subject, but I was still extremely nervous when the moment arrived.

Fortunately I was used to speaking in front of crowds and before long the faces all blurred into one. I spoke in Urdu. My talk was based on *ayat-e-Quran* – Quranic verses – and Farsi couplets written by such masters as Saadi and Rumi. It was a simple but effective ploy: By the power of these words, I captured their attention. I felt rather like I had when as a young girl I recited to the elders. The only difference this time was that I shared with my audience an understanding and appreciation of what I was saying.

The talk was a great success and I enjoyed the feeling of being accepted. My elderly visitor became a close friend; he attended many of the functions organised by the Cultural Centre but, best of all, he never again asked when the real director would be arriving!

Toward the end of my tenure in Lahore, one of my fellow countrymen caused an upset. The man in question was my superior, the Iranian Ambassador, the man who had replaced General Pakravan.

The ambassador was a scholar and poet and normally a person I would feel the utmost respect for. Unfortunately his words were often contradictory to his actions, for I discovered he was a devious and cunning character. Although he was a man of around 60, with grown-up children and a most cultured and respectable wife, he had got involved with a 22-year-old Iranian mother of two young children who lived in Lahore. The situation soon became intolerable and extremely embarrassing, especially as it occurred in a country with a very strict moral code of conduct. In deference to our hosts, I always made sure that my daughters and I wore suitably respectable clothes such as long dresses or saris when in public. Even our students never violated any moral codes, yet now the highest representative of our land was blatantly overstepping the mark.

The man became so obsessed that he could not live apart from the woman and, as his official residence was in the capital, Islamabad, he made any excuse to visit Lahore. In the beginning he would ring me and ask me to send a cable to him stating that there were student problems in Lahore, which needed his attention. Of course this was unacceptable to me, and I refused to be drawn in. Despite my misgivings I remained discreet and did not mention his affair in any of my dispatches to Teheran. But the Ambassador knew I was aware of what was going on and realised what a threat I could be to him, which resulted in a cold war between us.

He began to try and undermine my relationship with the people of Pakistan, which had always been warm and harmonious, and was enraged when these efforts failed. After one occasion at which we were both present, the newspaper report mentioned my name before his. He was furious and called a press conference at which he spoke angrily, saying that such violations of protocol would not be tolerated. The reply he got was: "We respect our mothers a great deal and she is treated as one."

My relationship with the Ambassador deteriorated even further. He gave up trying to draw me into his schemes and plans and was openly hostile. At one stage, gloating, he told me that he had stopped the Pakistan Government from conferring one of their highest awards on me, because of my "stubbornness and unfriendly attitude towards my superior officer." I retorted that I had never worked for awards; I was quite content with the love and respect of my friends, and needed no other reward.

It was during the celebrations of the 2,500 years of Persian monarchy that the situation between the Ambassador and myself reached its crisis point. He deliberately set up a situation where he believed he could accuse me of violating protocol, so that he could have me removed from my position.

One of the extremely important functions during these celebrations was held at the Lahore Fort. For security reasons and to ensure law and order, it was decided to allow only two cars, that of the Governor General of West Pakistan and the Iranian Ambassador, to drive all the way up to the stairs of the

Diwan-e-Khas, the special enclosure of bygone Mughal emperors. The rest of the 5,000 odd cars were given different coloured passes for their pre-arranged parking places according to their rank and social status.

The Governor General arrived first and the reception committee, which I headed, greeted him. We then waited for the representative of Iran to arrive as scheduled. We stood and waited while the musicians played.

In the distance we saw the Ambassador walking towards us. This was very odd and I had a premonition that he was up to something. Fortunately his car with the flag flying was driving slowly behind him and I got a photographer to take pictures of him and the car from all angles. I also remarked to the journalists that the Ambassador had obviously decided to walk so he could get a better view of the picturesque surroundings for, indeed, it was a wonderful and colourful sight. Beautiful flowers lined the driveway, peacocks strolled among the glittering decorated trees, and pigeons and balloons were being released from low-flying planes. For good measure photos were taken of the Ambassador being greeted and given all the honour a man in his position deserved. In my heart I knew this man did not deserve even to be spoken to but, because of what he represented, I was cordial towards him as always.

He was then escorted to his special seat and to herald the occasion Pakistan's national anthem was played directly followed by Iran's. As we were the hosts, this order was considered appropriate. The Governor General, the Ambassador, and I spoke and then the entertainment began.

Popular Iranian troupes had been flown in for the occasion and the music and dancing was superb. So, too, was the magnificent banquet that was spread out for the thousands of guests, who wandered around the pools and gardens. Guests were further dazzled by the parade of floats carrying tableaux depicting scenes of Iranian history and emphasising our cultural heritage. These had driven around the main roads of Lahore before ending their journey at the Fort.

I felt pleased but was still suspicious when our Ambassador was so generous with his praise. He assured me that he had never seen such a well-organised function or such a fabulous display. He went on to say he had definitely never enjoyed himself more, but his smile and his words rang false and I was worried.

Rightly so, it turned out, as a week later an investigative team from Teheran arrived in response to a cable sent to His Majesty the Shah by the Ambassador. It read: "Behnam is a traitor. She has humiliated your representative in public and may it please Your Majesty to recall her."

Apparently the Shah had been perplexed by the message and summoned Mr Phalbod, the Minister of Arts and Culture. Mr Phalbod was furious about the accusation and immediately offered to resign if the integrity of any of his staff was questioned, so a team from various ministries was sent to ascertain the truth of this situation.

The charge against me was that I had not respected the Ambassador enough. He said I had sanctioned the playing of Pakistan's national anthem before Iran's. Worst of all, according to him, was that I had ordered his car to be stopped at the third entrance, where he said he had been asked to walk the rest of the way. He claimed that this was done deliberately to embarrass and humiliate him.

It took very little time to disprove the main charges. The Superintendent of Police stated that, when the Iranian flag had been seen, everybody had stood to attention and saluted. They had expected the car to drive through; however they were given to understand that the Ambassador had requested the car be stopped, as he wished to walk. The photos also clearly showed that his car had followed him all the way up the drive. It was also agreed that, out of respect for Pakistan, it was right to have played the Pakistani anthem first.

The investigative team quickly concluded that the whole report was prejudiced and baseless. Subsequently, the Ambassador was recalled and I was able to apply myself fully once more to my proper work.

CHAPTER 16

CITY OF PASSIONS

Life in Lahore was everything I could have wished for. I made many friends and lived a rich, satisfying life, dedicated to promoting art and culture – in my own way contributing to improved understanding, tolerance, respect and acceptance of differences between people.

The Ministry of Arts and Culture supported libraries and research centres around the country and set up cultural exchange programmes. Poetry sessions were conducted where both Urdu and Farsi poets recited their works. It was wonderful to really understand the strong links that bind Pakistani poets to Gulf and Persian literature. One such renowned poet was Allama Iqbal who has penned masterpieces in Farsi and has more literature to his credit in this language than in his own, Urdu. When asked why this is so, he replied: "I can't help it; it comes to me in Farsi!" He was a disciple of the great *sufi* poet Jalaluddin Rumi.

The Urdu language, its prose and poetry, are enriched by Persian vocabulary. I found that no other music or verse has affected me more. The *sufi* music, *qawwalis* and *ghazals* of various Pakistani regions, such as those sung by Allan Fakir and Abida Parveen, have the power to uplift souls. The folklore of Heer-Ranjah, Mast Qalandar, Shah Abdul Latif Bhitai's verses, Bhulle Shah and Saeen Marna have made me realise why music is and should always be such an important part of our lives.

One form of popular music that I have enjoyed for a long time is *qawwali*, a devotional music with roots in the 13th century when it was created by a *sufi* poet. This type of music is often performed at *sufi* shrines, reflecting mysticism's ecstatic nature. Accompaniment is by an eight-man 'party', mostly family members, who play harmonium, *tabla*, drums and provide clapping and chorus vocals. Nusrat Fatah Ali Khan is a leading exponent. The Khan clan has produced distinguished *qawwali* singers for six centuries.

One time we organised a *qawwali* session at the Cultural Centre for some renowned Iranian scholars, professors and poets who were visiting. *Qawwals* like to recite Farsi couplets, specially from the great poet Amir Khosran. Since the Urdu-speaking singers have their own way of pronouncing Farsi, the words are often distorted and difficult to understand. Our particular *qawwal* showed an interest in improving his pronunciation and we helped him for a week.

The big day arrived – five hundred elite lovers of poetry and *qawwali* sat to listen, including our guests of honour from Iran. The performers were in their element, keen to impress and do justice to Farsi poets. They started with Amir Khorrow's Kalam, Allam Iqbal and Ghalib's Farsi poems, intending to continue with Urdu *ghazals*. Things seemed to be going well. I was quite pleased with myself and my organising abilities., to say nothing of teaching the *qawwal* passable Farsi.

But at the intermission, I approached a learned visitor who seemed enthralled. "Ah," he said, "*Khanom* Behnam, the music is beautiful, the *qawwal* has a powerful voice – could they also sing some Farsi *ghazals*, after the break?"

In my capacity as Cultural Attaché, I was not expected to deal with any political situation. It was at times difficult to abide by this, for although not politically active, I was still officially a representative of the Iranian government and, therefore, was often accosted by people who had something to say about Iran and the way it was being run.

In the spring of 1967, the tension between the Arabs and the Israelis was reaching breaking point once again. As usual, invective was flying and many unkind and insulting things were being said. Gamal Abdul Nasser of Egypt had finally had enough of the Israeli propaganda, and stood up against the superpowers to tell the Arab's side of the story. He backed his words with force for, at the same time, he began readying his people for war in an effort to regain the Palestinian land that had been given away to the Israelis by the Western powers years before. National pride swelled, Arab pride swelled and soon the whole Muslim world was united in this cause.

Conflict was inevitable and in 1967 the war between the long-time foes broke out. Everyone was glued to the radio while the announcers told us that "the brave Egyptian soldiers were fighting hard in an effort to teach the Israelis a lesson once and for all".

I was listening to a broadcast when I heard the sound of loud voices outside my office. A man was demanding entrance and my staff could not stop him. He burst into the office, his face red with anger.

"So you, Madame, are calmly sitting here, doing what may I ask?" he shouted at me. "Where is your Shah of Iran?" Before I could utter a word, he answered his own rhetorical question.

"He is skiing in the Alps and busy in Monte Carlo while courageous Arabs are shedding their blood for the glory of Islam. I wish we had more leaders like the noble Nasser!"

While he ranted on, I noticed that he was handling what looked like a weapon in his pocket but I was helpless. I sat and waited for him to either produce the weapon and shoot me or finally calm down; he gave me no chance to tell him that the latest I had heard was that the Shah had announced his support for the Arab cause and, having curtailed his holiday, was on his way home.

Eventually the man paused for breath, which gave me a chance to speak at last. "Please sir, I would request that you return tomorrow, when you are in a calmer frame of mind and we can discuss this rationally."

Obviously all the man had wanted was for me to say something, anything, for he began his tirade again. Out came all his grievances against Iran. When I got my next chance to speak, I reminded him of the true friendship shown by Iran during the war between India and Pakistan. He was not, however, in the mood to listen to reason, but finally, after he had worn himself out, he agreed to leave, though obviously he was still not convinced of Iran's full support for the Arab cause.

This incident, frightening enough in itself, shrank into insignificance when within 24 hours the whole situation changed. The exhilaration and euphoria we had all felt was suddenly destroyed.

The war was not only lost but Jerusalem, the most sacred city for Muslims next to Mecca and Medinah, was under complete Israeli control. The West Bank in Jordan, the Golan Heights in Syria and other lands were also occupied. Thousands of lives had been lost and many people were left not only homeless but stateless. It numbed us to the core, and many months passed before a semblance of normality returned.

While in Pakistan I also became friends with one of the more controversial families in Pakistani politics, the Bhuttos. This came about through an interesting incident. One day a gentleman arrived in my office unannounced. He came to convey a message from Zulfiqar Ali Bhutto, then a dynamic statesman, concerning an award the Shah had conferred upon him. I was told in no uncertain terms that Mr Bhutto wanted to return the *Nishan* award.

I was taken aback, for such a sensitive issue as this should have been dealt with by the Ambassador. As politely as I could, I explained that I was only the cultural representative and had nothing to do with politics.

"Mr Bhutto believes that you are more than a Cultural Attaché and that you have a great deal of power. In fact," he added, "Mr Bhutto would like to meet you."

I had known his wife and her family before she married Mr Bhutto; our families knew each other well in Bombay, but we had not found the time to renew our friendship since my return to Pakistan. However, I was flattered and agreed to meet him. This enabled me to give him my 'motherly' advice not to be too hasty. I found him to be a witty and charming man. Whether it was on my advice or some other's I cannot say, but to my knowledge the *Nishan* awarded by the Shah was never returned.

As a dedicated advocate of women's rights, I felt extremely

proud years later when Bhutto's daughter, Benazir, became the first woman prime minister of Pakistan.

Apart from the cultural and administrative duties I was responsible for, the Centre also looked after any Iranians who lived in or passed through Punjab because there was no Iranian Consulate in Lahore at that time. Most of them were young people, who came to study at the universities, so the affairs of these students became my particular responsibility.

They often visited me in my home and, when homesick, used to come for weekends to get away from their bleak hostel environment for a while. They loved to cook *cholow kabab*, a popular Iranian dish, and just relax. I was often the one who had to sort out any problems they were facing or had caused. Having children of my own helped me know how to deal with most situations.

Rather than report them to the Embassy in Islamabad if they were in trouble, I preferred to deal with the situation myself when possible, as I knew that, if the students were sent back to Iran, their future would be jeopardised. This seemed too big a price to pay for just an over-abundance of youthful exuberance, which was usually the real culprit.

I tried to instill in them the idea that they were ambassadors of their country and what they did would reflect on Iran as well as themselves. When the Shah visited Lahore, I often introduced him to the hundreds of students who were studying at the different universities, and once he asked why he never heard about any of the problems the students created.

"Are they such perfect people? Iran indeed has an excellent future," he smiled (which was rare for him). I had to admit that they weren't always completely exemplary but the problems they created could always be sorted out without too much fuss. I told him that the girls were usually good and that they studied hard but the boys did give me a few more headaches. They tended to be less conscientious about their studies and more inclined to indulge in pranks.

The Shah replied with a smile: "We've always known

women were the real rulers in our society for they've always had more sense than the men."

On the whole the relationship between the students and myself was good and loving. However, some of the problems these young people caused me were very serious indeed. One incident, which was potentially disastrous, occurred during one of the Shah's visits to Lahore.

As usual with his visits, there were many security problems along with the normal organisational problems of keeping royalty entertained for the duration of the stay. Planning for such visits had to begin months ahead.

By the late 1960s and early 1970s, the Shah was becoming increasingly unpopular with his own people, especially the young Iranian intellectuals, who resented the high-handed manners of this 'King of Kings', and the amount of money being spent by him, when there were still thousands of poor and illiterate Iranians. I had heard similar grumblings among students in Pakistan, so when the day of the Shah's visit arrived, I was in agony, expecting the worst. There were around 300 students studying in various universities in Pakistan and I had to get them all lined up to meet him. With the way many of them felt, this required a great deal of careful handling and a lot of tact.

The security people asked me over and over whether I trusted the students. In most ways I did, but I knew that there were some hot-headed young men in the crowd and I was extremely worried that one of them might do something rash.

My worst fears were realised when I spied one young man. His face was ashen, he was sweating and murmuring to himself as if he was feverish, and he fidgeted continuously. But I had no time to act as the Shah had arrived. I greeted him graciously, although all the while I was worrying about that nervous pale-faced youth. Slowly we made our way down the line of students and I introduced him to each one. After every few steps the Shah stopped and asked what that particular student's plans were for the future. As we progressed, I lost sight of the youth for he had moved his position but I knew that each step had to be bringing us closer to him. I had no way of knowing his intentions but I felt afraid and unsure of what to do. I did not want to cause unnecessary trouble for one who might just be nervous about meeting His Majesty. However, my gut feeling was very strong and warning bells were ringing inside me.

Suddenly there was a movement in the crowd and I saw security men whisking away the unfortunate young man. Once these people have a suspicion they certainly don't wait for explanations! Everybody in the area was aghast at the action and all were afraid of what the consequences might be. My knees were shaking and I could not tell which way the situation would swing. The Shah pretended not to notice and walked on. Suddenly another student recited a verse in Persian: "I will turn my hair grey in pursuit of education and knowledge all my life."

I breathed a sigh of relief, for although speaking without prior consent on such a dignified occasion was entirely unprecedented, I realised this young man had saved the situation. All eyes turned his way and suddenly there was a spontaneous burst of laughter, for the unfortunate youth was completely bald! When the Shah also smiled broadly, the tension evaporated.

After the reception I was informed that the nervous young man who had been taken away obviously had sinister intentions, for a loaded revolver had been found in his pocket.

The Shah and Shahbanu visited Lahore many times during my tenure there, and although it was always a great honour, the preparations took a lot out of me. Everything in their programme had to be meticulously researched and readied, down to the last detail. Even then, things could go disastrously wrong, as I found out on a last-minute inspection tour just prior to one of their visits.

I always travelled to the venues along the routes they would use to check personally on preparations and satisfy myself that everything was ready for the Shah and Shahbanu. On this occasion, however, just hours before they were due to arrive, I almost fainted. From every flagpole the Iranian flag was flapping gaily in the breeze – upside-down.

Even now I break into a cold sweat thinking of the repercussions had I not been able to mobilise practically the entire town to rectify the situation. As it was I was a cat's whisker from being late to greet Their Imperial Majesties, and the consequences of that would have been almost as dire.

Riots, demonstrations and strikes were almost a way of life at that time for lively, young, idealistic people who naively believe they have the solutions to right all wrongs. Many Pakistani students were getting caught up in all sorts of social activism. Some of these riots became quite violent and frightening affairs and schools and colleges were usually closed during these disturbances.

In the late 1960s civil rioting and disturbances gained in momentum. After President Ayub Khan fell from grace, the whole place became chaotic. Some of our students returned to Iran but a few stayed and shared the trials and tribulations of our host country.

The atmosphere in Lahore became very tense. Mobs of men began to gather at every street corner – labourers, students, the unemployed. Merchants hastily closed their shops and business came to a standstill. The feeling of tension in the air grew.

One morning during this period, I was in my office when I got a phone call from the school my daughters were attending. "You must come to take your children home." The usually cool and calm Mother Superior of the Convent of Jesus and Mary sounded frantic. "There are mobs of crazy men outside pelting stones and threatening to burn the school down."

"Why?" I asked. I was astounded, for although I had realised the situation in the streets was fragile and dangerous, I never expected fellow human beings could threaten the lives of innocent children.

"They say our school is not complying with other educational institutions, which have remained shut for days, but I believe it is really an uprising against foreigners. You must come and get your girls before something terrible happens." Mother Superior's tone was urgent.

I rang the Governor General of West Pakistan immediately and told him what was happening. He was wonderfully reassuring and promised to send truckloads of guards to protect the children. I tried to wait patiently but sitting and thinking about what could possibly happen was more frightening than actually getting out and trying to do something, so I decided to drive to the school to see what I could do to help the situation.

I sent for my car. My driver, Nazar, was a loyal and brave man though at that time a rather frightened one.

"I need to get to the school," I told him.

"But *memsahib* it is dangerous," he protested.

"I have to get my daughters," I said. He was devoted to me and my family and I knew he would undergo any danger for us no matter how scared he was.

We drove out into the streets. Normally the distance between my office and the school could be covered in a few minutes by car but the crowds had become so thick that we were barely able to crawl. Two hours later we were still only half-way there and we were surrounded by 'lunatics' waving long sticks. They were jumping over the bonnet and roof of the car screaming and yelling in their insane excitement. The noise was deafening. I sat and prayed.

In my haste at leaving the office I had forgotten to take a scarf to cover my head and in my big car I looked like any other *memsahib* or foreign lady. People were peering through the window of the car and I could see their faces made ugly by hate. I wanted to reassure them that I was a Muslim woman and one of them, not a foreigner, so I wound down the window despite Nazar's pleas.

"Children, do you think I am a foreigner? May Allah guide you to the right path." I was truly in Allah's hands and that thought gave me an inner strength which enabled me to feel as calm as my words sounded. The shouting immediately around the car stopped and, for an instant, astonishment showed on the men's faces.

"Who is this person? She speaks chaste Urdu. *Kamal hai* (it's strange). All right if you are one of us, swear at Ayub."

"My dears I was taught as a child not to swear. You say what you like, I will listen." I admired and respected Ayub. We had spent many pleasant occasions together. How could I wish him ill? My feeling of calmness stayed with me. The mobs further away were still yelling furiously and it was difficult to hear all that was being said. I could see the faces of the men surrounding me and I knew they wanted to vent their anger on somebody, anybody.

Suddenly, as if from nowhere, two young men rushed towards the besieged car shouting, "*Pare hatto! Sab pare hatto!* (Move aside). All of you disperse; don't you know you savages, you mad people, whose car this is and who this lady is? She is Madam Behnam and one of us. Make way for her car."

Al hamdu lillah – the tension eased. Like guardian angels, the young men escorted the car through the mobs and the rest of the way to the school, where I found a pathetic sight. All the terrified teachers, students and parents who had been able to get out had locked themselves in the basement. I found them crouched or kneeling, praying and crying. It is a terrible thing to see innocent people victimised.

Fortunately it was not long before the troops arrived and brought the situation under control, though by this time the mood of the violent mob had subsided. But I will never, as long as I live, forget how human love and respect was able to overcome those animalistic emotions of anger and hatred. It gives me some hope that the good in people can be stronger than the evil.

Besides the civil disturbances, Pakistan was jolted by two wars with India – the first in 1965 and the second in 1971. During the first war all foreign diplomats were evacuated, as were all Iranian women and children. However, I chose to stay and the Centre was used to collect clothes and blankets for the army.

I felt by staying I was showing that we Iranians were not *rah gozars* – passersby or opportunists – but were sincere in our wishes to help the country we lived in and with whom we had such close ties. The gesture was appreciated. My house and the Cultural Centre were constantly guarded throughout this dangerous and tense time. I had certainly not been abandoned and felt safe and secure.

On the day the war broke out I gave my cook, Baba, a substantial amount of money to buy supplies, which could be stored for some time. He looked at me but did not say a word and I had to repeat my command.

"I am sorry madam," he finally said, "I would not like to hoard food as it may deprive others and in this war we have to share each other's fate." I felt quite ashamed: How could I have underestimated the selflessness and patriotism of Pakistani society?

Interestingly, the price of food and general commodities decreased instead of inflating as is the general rule.

After this war I was awarded *Nishane Taj* by the Shah of Iran, an award for my bravery in staying behind and being useful. It was a gratifying tribute.

The second war, when East Pakistan broke away and became Bangladesh, was a much more unpleasant experience, for Lahore was bombed day and night and we were subjected to curfews and wailing air raid sirens that warned us of imminent attacks. I was reminded of my childish wish to experience a war for, after hearing reports of the Second World War, I had visions of it being full of thrilling activity and heroic people. I quickly realised the full horror of war and never want to witness such a thing ever again, when man demonstrates how inhumane he can be towards his fellow human being.

At the time we were living in a large mansion which was a part of the Cultural Centre and most of the domestic staff had left to join their families in the villages, where they hoped they would be safer. Soon the whole area became quite deserted at night, which was a frightening feeling for the children and myself, so we left and took rooms at the Inter•Continental Hotel. This felt safer as there were more people around.

Finally on December 18, Shirin's birthday, a cease-fire was declared. By way of celebration we had a small party with the manager and staff and some of the other hotel guests. It was wonderful to feel the calm and peace once again and to know that there were not going to be any more nights of terror, wondering where the next bomb was going to drop.

Although I certainly did not enjoy the experience of war, and there were times when I wondered whether my children and I would live through it, I am glad I stayed, for I wanted my Pakistani friends to understand how much their friendship meant to me. Crossing cultural boundaries between Iran and Pakistan is not so difficult, for the people of the Iranian plateau and those of the Indus valley have, over the centuries, become excellent neighbours and quite often shared common fates, which have brought them even closer to each other.

A Pakistan-Iran Friendship Society was set up soon after I arrived in Lahore, to help foster even better relations between the two countries and because of the respect that has developed between our two cultures, Islamic festivals are not the only celebrations we shared, for the Pakistani people especially loved to help the Iranians observe their old Persian festival of *Nowrooz*.

This is a New Year festival, which is in some ways similar to Christmas, for people clean their houses thoroughly, buy new clothes, exchange gifts and eat lavish feasts at especially laid tables. It is essentially a spring celebration whose origins are lost in time, and is often described as the 'Eid of nature'. It is actually a feast I knew nothing about until I was an adult living in Teheran, for it had not been part of our tradition as Gulf inhabitants. It was a festival however, that I learned to love and, with my friends in Pakistan, it became a very special time, so at the Cultural Centre, it was celebrated in style.

The *haftseen* table is the centre point of this festive time and as a Christmas tree is carefully trimmed and decorated, so is the *haftseen* table decorated. The word *haftseen* means 'seven seens '– the letter of the Farsi alphabet with the sound of 'S'. The letter *seen* is believed to be taken from the word *sepandeh* meaning 'holy' and the figure '7' became important because the Persian prophet Zoroaster, founder of Zoroastrianism, and his archangels were meant to have numbered seven.

The seven traditional items that are used to decorate the table are *serkeh* – vinegar, *sekeh* – coin, *seeb* – apple, *samanu* – mixture of sugar and malt, *sombol* – hyacinth, *sangak* – bread and *sabzi* – greens. Besides these essential things there is always a Holy Quran, one candle for each member of the family, a mirror symbolising light, plus milk, decorated eggs, flowers, cheese, yoghurt and *shirini* – cakes and sweets. A goldfish in a bowl is essential, for it ensures good fortune in the coming year.

The table is usually set a few hours before the vernal equinox. Dressed in new clothes, everyone sits around the table and listens to the head of the family recite verses from the Quran. When the moment of the equinox is announced over the radio and television, messages of goodwill are sent out and celebrations begin.

The festivities last for 13 days and, during this time, there are endless visits to and from friends and relations. This prolonged exchange of visits is obligatory and is conducted according to a time-honoured protocol where younger members of the family visit senior relatives. It is a time for friendships to be renewed, quarrels to be patched up, and resolutions to be made.

Besides these special occasions the Pakistanis also observed events that were important to Iran as a nation. There were countrywide celebrations in Pakistan when Iran celebrated 2,500 years of monarchy and the coronation ceremony of the Shah, which had been delayed by a few years until Crown Prince Reza was old enough to participate.

For Iran this, in particular, was quite an occasion for it was during this celebration in 1967 that Prince Reza was officially named the heir to the throne and his mother, Farah, for the first time in Persian history was not only crowned as Empress but named Regent. The whole affair was meant to mark the continuity of the Pahlavi dynasty but it was also a unique and well-deserved mark of respect for women in general and the Empress Farah in particular.

In Lahore extremely elaborate and lavish ceremonies were organised. Although it was not a national celebration for Pakistan, the Pakistanis wanted to show the depth of their respect and love of sharing.

As a representative of my country I certainly appreciated such friendly gestures. I developed an excellent relationship with these wonderful, hospitable people, who at all times treated me as a personal friend, never an outsider. I was invited to all the local weddings, and was often an 'aunt' to many of the families. Often I was given the honour of inaugurating educational institutions and many a time I returned to distribute the certificates and prizes. I also helped form debate panels. Most of my lectures were on Iqbal and his contribution to Farsi literature. I also delivered talks on other renowned poets of the Subcontinent like Mirza Ghalib and Amir Khusrau.

Among my other commitments, I used to be invited to attend cultural functions as guest of honour, inaugurate exhibitions and art shows and distribute prizes. It was a pleasant duty, not without its moments. One time I was invited to distribute prizes at an annual mango festival, only to find when I arrived that I was expectd to select the winners too. From childhood, I knew five types of mango by their size and shape, but when confronted with so many types and varieties – there are, incidentally, 150-odd – what was I to do? They took me around and then asked to make my judgement.

I started by saying that in God's garden there are beautiful flowers of various sizes, colours and fragrance – all look lovely in their individual rights. When put together they form lovely bouquets. "Now I am faced with a dilemma," I told my audience. "I look at *alphonso* in its glory and turn to *langra*, so sweet and juicy; *anwar ratol*, though small in size is fascinating and beautiful. *Chausa* and *sindri* have other tales to tell..." When I sat down, the organiser turned to me and said: "Khanom Behnam, we are impressed. We didn't think you knew so much about mangoes." I didn't – still don't – but experience had by then taught me a lot about speech-making and diplomacy.

Another time, a seven-member delegation from China arrived in Lahore and the International Ladies Club, of which I was then president, was asked to host a reception for them. In Pakistan speech-making at every function is not only a common feature but a must, so I welcomed the guests, mentioned some of our club's activities, and sat down.

The leader of the visitors' group seemed agitated, and all of a sudden we realised why: She knew no English, we spoke no Chinese, and no interpreter had accompanied them from Islamabad. "*Khanom* Behnam," whispered one of the organisers, "you speak several languages. Why don't you see if you can help?" I hesitated only a moment; they were after all our guests and anyway, what if a little charade entered proceedings? The Chinese ladies were social workers, not politicians, and were involved in community development projects. I knew what they had to say.

Their leader started talking. Fortunately I caught the words "Lahore" and "Shanghai", so I 'translated': "We feel at home in your beautiful city Lahore. In fact the sweet scent of this city reminds us of Shanghai... Women all over the world have the same aspirations... Technology has helped man go to the moon but we are still mothers, we still laugh, still cry, still love... the best values are human relationships and our services to our fellow human beings..." People graciously listened and applauded. Some I must admit looked bemused, others allowed themselves to be carried away by the rhetoric. Face was saved and our Chinese guest sat down smiling.

Many prominent Pakistanis were actively involved in promoting the Pakistan-Iran Friendship Society. The late Syed Zulfiqar Ali Shah, former principal of Atchison College, Lahore, a much respected scholar, will be remembered for his dedication and guidance as a committee member. Syed Babar Ali organised many cultural functions and ordered the printing of books and magazines in Persian and Urdu to generate interest in the culture and national languages of the two countries. Professor Dr Akram Shah who headed the Persian department in the Oriental College of Punjab University, also contributed greatly to the success of the Iran Cultural Centre. An authority on the Farsi language and literature and well-known amongst Iran's literary scholars, his anthology, *Safina-e-Sokhan*, has added a further dimension to the literary work of Iran in Pakistan.

Another member of the committee, who was actively associated with the Centre because of her genuine love for Iran was Mehr Angeez Shirazi. She served as the president of the Society for a long time. Agha Mostafa, Chowdhry Abdul Rahim, Mumtaz Ahmed Khan, Dr Abdulla Chughtai, Dr Ahsan, Mohamed Akram, Chowdhary Mohamed Siddiq and Professor Hamid Ahmed Khan, the vice-chancellor of Punjab University, Profesor Ayesha Akhtar and Afsar Qizilbash were the scholarly team who helped the Centre grow and who gave me strength to serve for almost a decade.

Hakim Mohamed Said Saheb of Sham-e-Hamdard was also an ardent patron of the Society. He is not only a *hakim* but also a scholar and a great human being. His institution, 'Hamdard', besides looking after the medical treatment of the masses in Pakistan, is also concerned with the educational, social, cultural and spiritual aspects and needs of the community at large. I am fortunate to have known him and our Centre to have been patronised by the Hamdard Foundation. He often invited me to various regions of Pakistan to speak on our commonly revered poets, our heritage and culture.

Fostering the friendship between our two countries was a satisfying experience and I felt rewarded when during a visit by Shahbanu Farah, one of our Pakistani students attending Persian classes at the cultural centre spoke on behalf of the class expressing a desire to visit Iran. The Shahbanu was delighted and immediately suggested that a group of 40 girls join their Iranian counterparts at their annual summer camp.

The girls who were finally chosen, after a number of tests that put an emphasis on spoken Farsi, came from the various centres around Pakistan. The excited group was headed by Professor Ayesha Akhter, who spoke fluent Farsi. I joined them later. It was a wonderful and memorable trip, for the girls were an eager and delightful group and grateful that they had been given the chance to travel around Iran and meet so many interesting people. They were even received by Their Majesties which was a particularly thrilling event and was the highlight of the whole trip.

Naturally it made the classes even more popular; other such trips were organised over the years, which certainly helped to bring about an exchange of culture and the chance for lasting friendships.

A great personal honour bestowed on me was the presidency of the International Women's Club of Lahore. Normally a non-Pakistani could only become vice-president. I was touched by the gesture and worked hard trying to ensure that they would not regret their unprecedented decision.

During this time the club was busy and productive and I

helped arrange many cultural and social activities. Generally I was well accepted as the president but one incident occurred which made me realise that in such a position I had to be particularly diplomatic. It was during a visit by 25 members of our club to Iran and Turkey. The ladies represented a wide range of society and had been invited under the CENTO (Central Treaty Organisation) and RCD (Regional Cooperation for Development) pacts.

All went well until we reached Ankara in Turkey. We were met by the Ambassador of Pakistan and an important representative of the Turkish government. Noticeably absent was the ambassador's wife. We were even more puzzled when she did not appear at the numerous official functions held in our honour. One of our delegation knew her so she contacted her to find out what was wrong only to discover that she was affronted by the fact that a group of Pakistani ladies should be led by an Iranian. To mark her displeasure she said that she would not host the reception that had been planned at the end of our visit despite the fact that protocol demanded she be present at this reciprocation of hospitality to our Turkish friends. I realised that the situation was delicate and despite my own rather arrogant and proud nature I decided to visit the lady to try and work things out. Fortunately the awkward situation was resolved.

The greatest compliment, though, was when Ayub Khan, then president of Pakistan, in his official speech at a ceremony welcoming the Shah on one of his many visits, jokingly said: "Your Majesty, we have no differences with you except in one matter – we say *Khanom* Behnam is one of us and you insist she is Iranian."

Although it was a well-meant remark, its effect was not so wonderful. It nearly hastened my departure from Lahore for, after hearing this, the Shah became thoughtful and soon afterwards asked me how long I had been there. When I told him six years, I knew my posting was nearing an end, because it was unusual for diplomats to spend more than three or four years in any one place. Sure enough, within a few months, I received a summons to return to Teheran for other assignments. However, my Pakistani friends intervened by sending a two-member delegation to Teheran with the result that my return was postponed for another two years.

My Pakistani friends were like that – they would observe what was needed and quietly set about doing it. One time, at a reception with some top army and civilian dignitaries, I was asked what I would like to do if I ever had a spare moment for myself. "Well," I replied with a smile, "I wish I would find the time to practice my driving and find a dignified way of getting a driving licence. The sense of freedom and being alone with just myself for company sometimes would be sheer bliss."

Next day in my office, our simple librarian Allauddin came running. "*Khanom, Khanom,* some officer from the traffic department asked me too many questions about you – I told him what I knew."

"What kind of questions," I enquired.

"Your full name, how it is spelt, full address..."

"So what are you so perturbed about?" I asked. But I too became pensive: What was it all about?

A few days later, an army officer was ushered into my office. He saluted politely and put a parcel on my table. "Madam, Major General so and so has sent this for you," he said. Very curious but calm, I opened the mysterious packet to find a driving licence in my name, artistically placed in a silver platter with a note which read: "*Khanom* Behnam, you are very dear to us so please do not drive alone at any time. This officer will be at you commnd for the first few trials. Good luck!"

My eight years of service in Pakistan corresponded to the most enriching, stimulating and possibly happiest period of my life. Although I missed Pakravan, we were able to visit each other often and, through this time, he had slowly straightened out his affairs.

All through our married life, the children were always our first priority. The youngest two had come with me to Lahore and for a few years attended a good school there. I enjoyed having my children around me but after hearing of an excellent boarding school in a hill resort called Murrie near Islamabad, I decided that they should be given the chance to better their education. It was heart-wrenching sending my girls away, especially Shirin for she was a loving child who liked nothing better than to be cuddled and to live in her own world peopled mainly by dolls, but it turned out to be a good decision, for both progressed well.

Shahnaz went on to Moreton Hall, an excellent girls school in England, where we believed her chances of receiving a good education were better than either in Lahore or Iran. Being on her own, Shirin came out of her older sister's shadow, began to develop her own personality and was a real joy to me.

In the meantime Marie had finished her schooling in Esfahan and began university in Lahore. It was wonderful to have her back. While in Esfahan she had met Ebrahim Jamei, a young man whom she later married in Lahore, when he came down as my assistant. Their wedding was the first 'post-war' celebration in the city and in spite of the rationing I still managed to arrange quite a festive ceremony. Rokna, who had completed his university degree in Teheran before I came to Lahore, returned to Bandar Abbas and married his childhood friend. Essa was in Karachi, so was able to visit us often. Although, as a family unit, we did not spend a lot of time together under the same roof, the bonds between us were strong. In the years to come, they would be severely tested time and again.

CHAPTER 17

CULTURE OF BALUCHISTAN

It was in May 1972 that Shirin and I packed up all our possessions and finally left Lahore. Our 'farewells' had taken nearly six months. It was not easy leaving behind close friends in a place where we had been so happy and felt so much at home, but the prospect of being reunited with Pakravan and going back to Teheran was exciting.

Marie and Ebrahim stayed on because they were both still studying, and also looking after the Cultural Centre until a new director was appointed. Later they were asked to open a centre in Multan, where they spent a few years before they eventually returned to Teheran to seek new posts.

That year we were slowly coming back together as a family, for Shahnaz finally completed her schooling in England and returned home. It was wonderful to have her back and we were relieved that she seemed happy to be in Teheran. Because of her love for the theatre, she immediately became involved in the Ministry for Arts and Culture's theatre group and she played important roles in both Persian and English plays. Mr Phalbod had great ambitions for the theatre group and he showed a great deal of interest in Shahnaz's talents. During this time she was spotted by the producer of the film *Caravan*, which was based on the book by James Michener. The film, a joint American-Iranian venture, was to be filmed in Esfahan, and included Anthony Quinn in its cast. I was away on an official visit to Europe at the time but Pakravan gave his full approval when asked if Shahnaz, who was still only a teenager, could play a small part in the film.

Pakravan beamed with delight at the publicity given to his talented daughter but my father was enraged – "All our ancestors were scholars and religious leaders; you people will not let them rest in peace." He did not talk to us for a year at least!

Besides these activities Shahnaz looked after the Sports Club and taught English at the Language Institute. Like me, she enjoyed being busy and even better, being in charge.

Shirin, who was more reserved than her sister, had adjusted well to life in Teheran and registered in one of the top international schools where she excelled in languages and art. She was growing into a very attractive young girl, and was selected for a Teen Princess contest. I was a little worried, for she had always been so quiet and shy. However, she seemed eager to participate and I knew the experience would be wonderful for her confidence. Ultimately she was one of the 20 finalists and the first girl ever to represent Bandar Abbas.

On one of his many visits to Teheran, Pakravan arrived with a handful of our possessions. As we had many beautiful antiques which I had saved from my ancestral home, I asked him when the rest of our things would be arriving but, to my horror, he told me he had given away the lot.

Pakravan liked a simple environment and could never appreciate why the girls and I wanted so many clothes and shoes and liked to be surrounded by possessions. Though I respected his humble nature, I found it difficult to understand, for I believed wholeheartedly in what Monkhali used to say: "People will look at you as you see yourself." To me, this meant that I was never to underestimate myself for then others would as well. Besides, I liked to feel important and be treated as such, while Pakravan didn't care about the opinion of others and was content to be overlooked.

His attitude often irritated me, for I felt he deserved recognition for his selfless work. Never was this more vividly illustrated than when Shams Pahlavi (the Shah's sister and Mr Phalbod's wife), who was the grand patron of the Red Lion and Sun Society, visited Bandar Abbas to inaugurate the new hospital, which had been built mainly by the Society. Pakravan at the time was the regional director of the Society and, as usual, had done more work than anybody else in the planning and construction of the building. However, when she arrived, while every other member of the committee was there to escort her, show her around and to make speeches, my husband was still at the airport arranging accommodation for the pilot and the rest of the entourage! As he said, "Who will look after the real work, if everybody else is in the forefront?"

With us, it was certainly a case of opposites attracting: He was calm, kind, humble and selfless, while I was snobbish, ambitious, aggressive and demanding. I expected first-class treatment and, although Pakravan was quite willing to demand it for me and the children, he would never ask it for himself.

Part of the reason we were so different was because we came from such different backgrounds. I was from an aristocratic family, while his background, though noble, was simple. He was unfortunate to have lost both his parents early in life and had had to struggle on his own. As a teenager he told me he would often stand outside our family home in Bandar Lingah in awe of our palatial mansion and marvel at the elegantly- dressed, well-educated gentleman with the foreign felt hat who emerged from within, never dreaming that this very man who totally ignored him would one day be his father-in-law. However, I think both of us in our own way were well-equipped to get through life together, and the balance we provided for each other was extremely important.

We bought a flat in Teheran but hoped that I would eventually get posted back to what we thought of as our real home in Bandar Abbas.

The only apprehension I had felt when I returned to Teheran was due to the fact that I didn't know where I was going to be placed in the headquarters of the Ministry I worked for. After living a life full of glamour and excitement for so many years and being treated as a VIP in Pakistan, I wondered how and where I would fit in. It is never easy finding an appropriate position for any returning diplomat or attaché, for such people are not used to being *siyahi lashkar* – one of the crowd.

Mr Phalbod obviously had some difficulty finding what he considered the right sort of job for me. Numerous meetings were held and finally I was introduced to a charming young man named Reza Kashefi who was in charge of the audio-visual technical programmes.

He told me that his department was new and had ambitious plans to organise seminars and exhibitions of art in every form. This meant that it was necessary for someone to do a great deal of international travelling in order to meet experts from other countries. Listening to this dynamic young man talk about this new field in the Ministry I was immediately interested and excited by the possibilities it offered.

It did not take long for him to persuade me that he would be pleased to have me join his department. He assured me that I was not to consider him the head of the department for we were all colleagues with the same aspirations. My pride was saved.

It was actually quite an important post and I found it extremely interesting. The use of visual aids had become a popular method of teaching in schools and colleges and I certainly enjoyed the travelling to Europe to attend various audio-visual exhibitions.

While there, I met many well-known artists and lecturers, whom I invited to Iran to display their work and give lectures at conferences – all of which I then had to organise. Life was hectic during the three years that I was in this post but I loved it and it gave me the chance to meet some wonderfully interesting people.

Three years later I was called to the office of the Deputy Minister of Arts and Culture, who informed me that Mr Phalbod wanted to see me. I guessed it was about a new position, and I was right, for when I finally spoke to the minister, I was informed that I had been chosen to be the director general of Arts and Culture in Baluchistan and Sistan province.

The title sounded good but it was not exactly the place where I had hoped to be sent. That part of Iran still lacked many amenities and was less developed than any other province. Apparently each time a representative had been sent there, he had never lasted long, because he found the people of Zahedan, the capital, uncooperative and the problems overwhelming. I was told that I was considered the last hope.

This naturally flattered me and, with my own infinite confidence in my ability to cope, I decided to accept the challenge.

On the flight to Zahedan, I reflected on my situation. Here I was going into the unknown totally alone. I had left Shirin in Teheran to finish her high school; one of our old nannies, her husband and children were there to look after her. Once I was settled I knew she would often visit me, just as I would often be in Teheran. Shahnaz had gone to America for further studies in English literature and theatre art – I knew she would do well. Rokna was married and living in Bandar Abbas while Marie was back in Teheran with her family. Life was good.

I had pause for thought however when I saw the faces of my new staff members who met me at the airport, eying me up rather doubtfully, perhaps not sure what to expect. They had obviously been told I was a formidable, dynamic person who thought she could succeed where men had failed. I don't know if they were disappointed with what they saw but, as I looked around, I knew my job was not going to be easy.

The town was bleak and deserted and reminded me somewhat of the early Bandar Abbas. There was a stagnant, lethargic feeling about the place. The people who were wandering around seemed to have little to do. However, development projects were in progress.

After checking in at the one and only hotel, I decided to go straight to the office rather than rest and think too much about what I was doing alone in this terrible-looking place. I found that my office was tucked away in a corner of the building and the only way I could get to it was by going through lengthy corridors and well away from the offices of the other staff.

That evening I befriended those I was going to be working with, as I knew that I was going to have to rely on them for information about the local conditions and culture. The next day I moved my office from its obscure corner and opened the doors between the administrative rooms, so that access to each office was easy and a feeling of team work could be nurtured.

The head office in Zahedan administered seven far-flung

offices around the province so I invited the heads of these offices to visit me. When they arrived, we spent a few days chatting and getting to know each other. Then I assured them that I would visit each office and examine the cultural and archaeological potential in some of the more remote areas. I found out that there were quite a number of libraries and museums around, but all the facilities needed extending and the workforce to be improved.

I also had to look into the archaeological sites which were being excavated by foreign experts. There had been problems with the supervision of these projects and I discovered that money was not always ending up in the right pockets.

The first problem I tackled was the local attitude towards punctuality. One day I received an invitation to attend a school function, organised by the Ministry of Education which was responsible for Elementary Schools. The Governor General, Mr Manei, was the chief guest and the scheduled time for the function was 6pm.

As is my usual practice, I was punctual and arrived promptly at six o'clock. Nobody was there. The building, in fact, was still being cleaned and aired. I wondered if I had made a mistake but it was a big occasion and I was sure I had the right evening. I sat down and waited. The host, my counterpart in the Ministry of Education, arrived in a flurry, very apologetic. He explained that because nobody ever arrived on time at such occasions, he always gave the time as at least an hour or two earlier.

By 7pm people has begun to drift in and by 7.15pm I asked the host when the programme would start. "When the auditorium is full," he said. "We then ring the Governor General and, after he arrives, the function begins."

I couldn't believe that educated, cultured people, who were mainly from places such as Teheran and who were meant to be improving conditions in this area, could behave in such a way. I was annoyed and frustrated, so I got up and left, telling my host I had another appointment.

The next day Mr Manei rang to say I had been missed at the function. I explained that I had missed him as well – for an hour and a half! We both laughed and he sympathised with my attitude, as he also was not happy with the state of affairs. Between us we worked out a plan. At the next function, which I organised, he arrived, by my request, ten minutes late and then publicly apologised to the hall, which, of course, was empty. The programme then began at the time stated on the invitation, despite the fact that hardly anybody else was present. This seemed to jolt most of the people out of their indifference.

Mr Manei became a good friend and he and his family gave me a lot of support. He always attended our cultural functions and was always on time!

I was pleasantly surprised by the Baluchi culture. Although the people were poor in material possessions, they got a great deal of pleasure from music. Singing and dancing was in their blood and many Baluchis could play at least one instrument. Hardly anyone was formally trained in music but most seemed to have an incredibly good ear for rhythm and harmony.

One of the most rewarding achievements of the centre was the promotion of the musicians and dancers in the area. Their skills were revived and encouraged by the Cultural Centre. The common musical instrument used was known as *qaichuck*, which is a crude stringed instrument shaped like a sitar but smaller in size. Many also played on pots and pans that they called *matkas*, *koozas* and *tashts*. The most sophisticated instruments they used were imported from other countries. These included the harmonium of India, the banjo from Pakistan and the *dhol* or drum from Afghanistan.

I particularly enjoyed the Baluchi dancers, dressed in their vivid costumes. Besides the percussion sound of the pots, they danced to the heady rhythms of the *dholak* and *daira*, which are tambourines they make themselves and decorate with henna. These performances are very colourful.

The musicians and dancers were paid for their skills by the Centre and were trained to perform at special functions. They were all ordinary people who worked at other jobs during the day and then came to the Centre most evenings to play, teach others or learn to play new instruments. The very old people who still played the clay pots often needed special attention, for they were usually undernourished and their bodies bent and distorted from hard work. Sometimes they smoked opium and chewed tobacco, so a lot of help and advice had to be imparted regarding nutrition and hygiene.

I was proud of these music and dance groups and, despite comments that the Baluchis would not know how to behave socially, I suggested that they be sent to America during the celebrations of America's bicentennial to perform at the White House along with the more sophisticated regional cultural groups. They went and were a hit, the Americans thoroughly appreciating the authenticity of the performers and were astounded that such harmony could be produced from such primitive instruments.

Music, however, was not the only area in which the Baluchis excelled for the women were able to create the most beautiful embroidery and crochet work. Yet it seemed that the people gained no inspiration from their own handiwork; washing dishes was done in the same spirit as producing beautiful ceramics or creating artistic embroidery. They quite simply did not realise the importance of their skills.

As a first stop to help overcome this problem of perception, a Fine Arts College was set up in Zahedan and talented girls from all around the province were trained in all sorts of art work, including painting on canvas and silk; pottery; embroidery and weaving. More than this, however, was the need to instill a sense of pride in their work. They sorely needed some recognition.

Because they were poor, they had often been exploited by others. People had come to see their beautiful, intricate work and bought it cheaply, then taken it back to places like Teheran to sell for great sums of money. It seemed unfair that the Baluchis, who needed the money, gained very little from these transactions. So I sought an audience with the Shahbanu, who showed a great deal of concern when I told her of the situation. She promised she would personally visit Baluchistan, so a grand exhibition of arts and crafts of the region was organised near Zahedan.

Potters, painters, weavers and tailors came from near and

far, as did poets, dancers and musicians, until the place was so crammed with culture, that it was difficult to move. Although each artist or performer was able to produce beautiful work or pleasing sound and harmony, none used sophisticated tools or instruments. The weavers wove useful and attractive rugs and saddles out of camel hair and delicate baskets were made from the fronds of date trees. No paint was used on the earth-coloured clay pots but all were beautifully and imaginatively shaped. Even the musicians often only used such things as household utensils – spoons, glasses, pots and pans – to produce lovely melodies.

When the Shahbanu came and visited the exhibition, she was full of praises for the work and talent of the artisans and artistes. The Baluchi style of embroidery particularly appealed to her and she sent many of her clothes to Zahedan or Iranshahr to be embroidered. As these were often the clothes she wore on foreign trips, the potential of this once-neglected area was recognised. By the time the exhibition ended, it was obvious that a handicraft centre in particular would be an excellent source of income for many of the local women. When this was duly set up, it proved to be quite profitable.

Thanks to the Shahbanu's visit, the whole area received a boost and the natives began to look to the future with more enthusiasm and hope than ever before.

CHAPTER 18

RETURN TO BANDAR ABBAS

Far from being a 'hardship' posting, Zahedan proved to be immensely rewarding. I spent two happy and productive years there and had the satisfaction of knowing that, not only had I helped the Baluchi people become aware of their own potential, but I also made other Iranians realise that Baluchistan was not just a place 'far away in the east that nobody ever goes to'.

This latter achievement came about after I persuaded Mr Phalbod, the Minister for Arts and Culture, to grant Zahedan permission to host one of the biannual conferences for regional heads of the ministry. I literally dragged many of my compatriots to the area – unwillingly it is true, for most symposia were held in exotic locations such as Esfahan and Shiraz – and persuaded them to explore the delights of the simple, unsophisticated culture that Baluchistan has to offer.

The Governor General, Mr Manei, gave me full support and the people of the town worked together to make sure that our sophisticated and cultured guests, more used to luxurious surroundings and first-class treatment, would have nothing to complain about on their first visit to this region. It was quite a job organising the event. Private villas were turned into bed-and-breakfast places; caterers flew chicken, fish, mutton, fruit and vegetables in from Teheran by the crate load daily. Huge Baluchi tents were set up and used as dining rooms; 20 minibuses were hired to drive the guests from their accommodation to the seminar venues and entertainment areas. The Baluchi poets, dancers and musicians delighted and captivated even the most aristocratic guests, many of whom revelled in what was to them almost a magical chance to rediscover long-lost and long-forgotten roots of their great Bedouin heritage. It was an experience not many would ever forget.

In the back of my mind all the while I was involved in setting up this conference was the realisation that it could well be my swan song, for although I enjoyed my work, derived a great deal of satisfaction from it and achieved results, I knew my career was nearing its end. I was in my 50s and, more than anything I wanted to spend my last few useful years in my home area.

I had hoped a posting would come up in Bandar Abbas, where in an official capacity I could contribute more towards its social and educational reforms and where all the family could finally get together. It didn't, but something else did. The chance to do something constructive for the region came when I was asked to stand for Parliament in the elections of 1977. Never having been politically oriented, I was not entirely sure how I would cope and hesitated at first. However, I had a long chat with Mr Phalbod, who assured me that I had been nominated by the Ministry under the Shah's programme to encourage able but non-political citizens to participate in government. When he assured me that my post at Zahedan would be kept for me, I was persuaded to stand for the Bandar Abbas district.

I was up against two men and a rather beautiful lady who was not from the area. When she obtained 4,000 votes from a place with a population of only 3,000 people – and only half of those eligible to vote – she withdrew! In the event, I was too complacent. I did very little active campaigning myself, except for a television and radio interview, as I felt it was undignified – and what would I tell them? Besides, the people of the constituency knew me and my background well enough anyway. However, a number of young, energetic people – some former students of mine – actively campaigned on my behalf. It was quite the experience, but despite all their effort, I came second to a young and very capable man from the area.

In retrospect, I am glad I didn't win, but I found the whole experience fun and refreshingly different from anything I had done before. What it did make me realise was how keenly I wanted to return to Bandar Abbas. When I went through Teheran on my way back to Zahedan, Mr Phalbod was worried that I would be frustrated by this failure and showed a great deal of concern. I assured him I was not disappointed at all, but told him I would like to be posted to Bandar Abbas in some official capacity when my term in Baluchistan ended.

Over the years I had come to know the minister quite well and had great respect for him. He had an impressive personality and although he had no royal blood, he seemed more princely than the princes. In his position he could have delegated his work and been merely a figure head, but he took his job very seriously and was personally involved in various projects.

He appreciated my reasons for requesting to be appointed to my own town and, within a short time, I was given the prestigious position of director general for Arts and Culture for my vast home province, Hormozgan, headquartered in Bandar Abbas.

When I returned, I found many changes had taken place in the 11 years I had been away. During that time, outwardly the town had changed a great deal. Electricity was now available 24 hours a day; good roads had been constructed – there was an excellent asphalted road to Kerman; an airport had been built and all amenities had been improved. On the social side, women participated actively in town affairs. However, it was disappointing to find that the general feeling of apathy and laziness, probably brought about by the stifling climate and years of deprivation, still prevailed.

The official house I was given to live in was one of the guest houses of the Sheikh of Qatar. It was an elaborate mansion, beautifully carpeted and fitted with several huge chandeliers. The dining room seated at least 50 people and hundreds of guests could be entertained in the drawing room. I had brought all my hand-carved wooden furniture from Lahore, which added to the opulent atmosphere and gave the place a personal touch.

Having such a large house and grounds, we needed a staff of six to cook, clean, serve and tend the garden. It was not as beautiful as the place I had lived in during my time in Lahore, but it was certainly an improvement on the house Pakravan had brought me to when I first arrived in Bandar Abbas.

From a cultural point of view there was not as much scope as in Baluchistan. My duties, though, were at a more sophisticated level than they had been in Zahedan. I was involved with a variety of charitable organisations; with encouraging tourism in the area and with building and maintaining libraries, theatres, music centres and museums.

It was especially pleasing to be able to relocate and enlarge the museum I had helped found 15 years earlier, but which over the intervening years had been neglected and become quite run-down. As soon as it became known that the museum had now become a government project and not just a community one, people's enthusiasm was rekindled and donations of objects picked up, for they knew everything was going to be well looked after

My position helped me realise another pet project – doing something constructive with the old *berkahs*, the tanks once used for collecting and storing rain water. I was keen to save these structures for, besides looking impressive (they are huge with an almost egg-shape appearance and made entirely out of mud brick), they were an important part of our heritage. It was something I had long wanted to do.

As there was now a good underground water supply, the disused *berkahs* were becoming dilapidated. I believed they had to be retained. It seemed a waste to allow such interesting buildings to crumble away for want of care and use. Of the several ideas I had on how to turn them once more into useful and important to the community, the folkloric theatre was the one that caught the imagination.

With the approval of the Shahbanu, I was allowed a large budget and architects and builders were employed to make all the necessary alterations. To convert one of the *berkhas* into a theatre, first the bottom was scraped and layers of cement were put down to prevent water seepage. The inside was then tiled and a central stage was constructed. Seating was arranged around the walls and dressing rooms were set up underneath. It was such a large building that even a small restaurant was incorporated. As the Shahbanu had been interested in this

Newly married with Pakravan. Bandar Abbas, 1954.

Two views of the garden of Pakravan's house in Bandar Abbas: Left, with Rokna and Marie in 1954; right, with Shahnaz in 1957.

Demonstrating needlework in the crafts workshop.
Bandar Abbas, 1955.

Marie, Shahnaz and Shirin in costume for a school play. Bandar Abbas, 1961.

Presenting Bandar Abbas people's New Year's gift to the Shah and Shahbanu. Teheran, 1960.

With VIP visitor Mrs Mesbahzadeh of Keyhan Publications in the Bandar Abbas museum. 1963.

Newly-appointed Cultural Counsellor and Director of Iranian Students' Affairs (East and West Pakistan). Lahore, 1964.

Official residence for eight happy years: Iran Cultural Centre, Lahore. 1964-1972.

On the occasion of receiving the 'Nishane Taj' medal. Lahore, 1965.

With Amir Mohammad Khan, then West Pakistan's Governor General, on his visit to the Iran Cultural Centre. Lahore, 1965.

With Iranian scientist Dr Syed Hussein Nasr (left), and Dr Javed Iqbal, scholar and son of Allama Iqbal, national poet of Pakistan. Lahore, 1965.

The author delivering a lecture on the contribution of Allama Iqbal to Farsi literature. 'Allama Iqbal Day', Lahore, 1965.

The author reciting her own poetry at a gathering in Iran Cultural Centre. Lahore, 1966.

Officers and executive members of the Pakistan Iran Friendship Society and other dignitaries photographed with the Shah and Shahbanu. Seated, from left: the author, President Ayub Khan, the Shah, Society president Chowdhry Abdul Rahim, the Shahbanu, Governor General Musa of West Pakistan. As director of Iran Cultural Centre, the author held the post of vice-president of the Society. Lahore, 1969.

Greeted by children of the Muslim High School in Multan, West Pakistan on arrival to inaugurate the school's new wing. Multan, 1969.

*With Mehrdad Phalbod, Minister
of Art and Culture. Zahedan, 1974.*

*With then-President of Pakistan, General Yahya
Khan, at a banquet in Lahore. 1970.*

*With Mr and Mrs Manei,
Governor General of
Sistan and Baluchistan
Province, at the opening
of a painting exhibition
at the Cultural Centre.
Zahedan, 1974.*

*Ceremony presided
over by Governor
General Razaki of
Hormozgan
Province. The
author wears the
ceremonial
'uniform' designed
for high-ranking
ladies. 1977.*

With daughter Marie and son-in-law Ebrahim Jamei.

Greeting the Shahbanu on one of her visits. Bandar Abbas, 1976.

Faiqa Farooq with the author's grand-daughter Rasha. Dubai, 1983.

Triple celebration every November 18: Shahnaz, Rokna and Marie share a common birthday and cake. Dubai, 1984.

An historical berkah in Bandar Abbas renovated under the guidance of the Art and Culture Ministry, for use as a theatre. Inaugurated in 1977.

With Essa and his family. Jeddah. From left: Zahra, Essa, Shameem, Faisal, 'Grandma' and Mohammad.

Noora and her cat Molesworth.

With Shahnaz and her family. London. From left, 'Grandma', Ayesha, David, Shahnaz and Aliya.

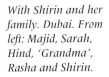

With Shirin and her family. Dubai. From left: Majid, Sarah, Hind, 'Grandma', Rasha and Shirin.

*Cousins across the Gulf: The author and some of her family
with the Tehranchi family. Bandar Abbas, 1993.*

*The author's nephew Sultan
and children Yasmin and
Soraya. Dubai, 1990.*

Revisiting Berkah-e-Abbas in Bandar Lingah, 1991.

project from its inception, she was invited for the grand opening. She was especially pleased to see that despite substantial alterations within, very little was done to change the outside appearance, so it still looked authentic.

The most popular sort of performance for this type of theatre is the traditional entertainment that is rather like a special gymnastic exercise done to music. The round pit or stage area is called a *zoorkhooneh* or house of power. The musicians seated around this arena beat a rhythm on drums and chant epics from Firdausi's *Shahnama* – Book of Kings – while the performers in the *zoorkhooneh* move their bodies energetically and gracefully in an aerobic-type exercise. They also wrestle and do weightlifting exercises. It is a spectacular and unique form of entertainment.

A second *berkah* was later converted into a handicraft centre while a third was too run-down to be converted. I was extremely happy to find many years later that these restored relics of the past continue to be used and appreciated by the people of the area.

In my capacity as director general, I visited Lingah while doing some research for a book about dhow making. While there I went to see our old houses. I wasn't prepared for what I saw; it was a painful experience, for both were in a terribly dilapidated state. Ahmad, the old guard, who was by this time totally blind, still occupied a tiny portion of the huge sprawling mansion we had called *khoone bara*. Every morning he still dressed himself immaculately and dutifully stood on guard, exactly as he had done when my grandfathers were alive. It was a pitiful sight. Inside conditions were even worse, for the poor old man had been quite unable to cope with looking after everything.

A number of houses had been left abandoned in the town; no doubt their owners had every intention of returning after a year or two abroad, as they had done in earlier times, but with changing circumstances and times, never did.

Poorer townspeople had been removing much of value from abandoned houses in order to survive. The furniture that was left in our house was in a terrible state. Carpets had turned to powder, wooden chests were riddled with pests, and the house was full of pigeons. I salvaged what I could from *khoone bara* and then spread the rest of the things, which included marble table tops, Omani chests, huge mirrored beds, mats, crockery and cutlery outside and told the people of the town to come and take their pick.

Eventually the house itself was sold to Sheikh Mohammad Ali, the Sultan-Al-Olema, and he converted it into a theosophical school which he runs to this day.

The older house called *khoone zeer* had squatters living in it. I was introduced by one of my staff as the director of the Ministry of Arts and Culture but my actual name was not mentioned. The family of squatters were not keen on the idea of our group looking through the house and, when asked, they told us the family that owned the place were all dead and gone! They were finally persuaded to let us enter.

It was an emotional experience and, as I moved slowly through each room, I felt I could almost see and hear the shadows and whispers of my elders. With tears in my eyes, I ran my hands over the forbidden glass-fronted cabinet that I had so longed to open all those years ago. It was bare now of all its beautiful and delightful objects and it looked forlorn and forgotten and so much smaller than in my memory. The house was so old that, although it stood erect, some parts had become dangerously weak. I was worried for the safety of the people who lived in it but they assured me that they were quite happy living in the portion that was still intact.

As I lingered with my memories, it was obvious that these people were becoming impatient with me as, of course, they could not understand why a person in my position should be so interested in a run-down old house. Finally one of the members of our group told them who I was. Their attitude changed immediately when they realised what a threat I could be.

It was true: I could easily have evicted them, as I had been planning to donate the house to the Red Lion and Sun Society to be used as an orphanage. However, the squatters promised to carry out repairs and to look after the place so, in the end, I decided to leave it in their hands for it was still after all a home, providing a haven for these misplaced people. We had given so much away and lost so much more that I really had no other choice. To renovate either of the houses would have cost millions.

There seemed little I could do for our family's immediate past, but one project that I began during my tenure that made me feel I was honouring the memory of my ancestors was the setting up of a beautiful new library in Bastak. I still had not visited this place that had always been spoken of with pride and reverence by my family. We all spoke the Bastaki dialect and had always been referred to as Bastakis. We were more than proud of this heritage. However, it bothered me that, although I had travelled widely, I had never set eyes on this place, even though we all thought of as our spiritual home.

The library that was proposed for Bastak was to be a massive undertaking and was to include an audio-visual section, a language laboratory, a large reading room, handicrafts centre and a restaurant. It was to have a games room to promote chess and a sports ground

The people of Bastak did not expect everything to be handed to them on a silver platter by the government, for when they requested assistance, they proudly informed me that the land did not have to be bought as a large piece of ground had already been donated. They also insisted that the appointment of the staff and the running of the facility would be their responsibility. I was pleased and happy to be able to help and went personally to Mr Phalbod to seek governmental approval. The Shahbanu was present at the meeting and, always perceptive and direct, asked me: "Why are you so keen on this particular project? Do you have personal reasons for making sure the permission is granted?"

I explained that, although my family were Bastakis and proud of the connection, this was not the reason I was making sure the project was approved. "I am anxious that it is built," I told her, "firstly because the Bastaki people are scholarly and secondly because they have never asked for anything before, not even a cinema or a music centre. Over the past 10 years the only thing they had ever asked for was a library."

The Shahbanu was most interested when I told her that there was not one illiterate person in Bastak, so it didn't take long for the ministry to agree that this was one place that certainly was deserving of government help.

When the building began, I was impatient to visit the town to view progress, but was persuaded to wait until the library was completed. It was planned that I would inaugurate it; I was told that the people of Bastak wanted to receive me in a style befitting my official position and my family background. I looked forward to the day, but unfortunately it was not to be. The 1979 revolution quashed this among many other dreams. Later I learned that the whole project, though initially set aside, was completed at a later date on a more modest scale.

CHAPTER 19

WINDS OF CHANGE

Although I had worked for the Iranian government for many years, I had never been particularly interested in politics, but, during the 1970s, it was difficult to ignore the events that were taking place.

The head of our constitutional government was a monarch known by the title of *Shahenshah*, the King of Kings. However, the Pahlavi dynasty, of which our reigning Shah was a descendant, did not have its roots way back in any ancient past, as it had only been established in 1925.

Reza Shah, the father of the late Shah, was born during the 19th century into a relatively ordinary family, who lived somewhere near the Caspian Sea. He grew into a well-built, athletic boy and chose soldiering as his profession.

At that time the Russians were the dominant force in Persia and so the army was run by the Cossacks. Because of his sharp mind and air of authority, young Reza rose rapidly through the ranks and, by the time the Communist Revolution took place in Russia, he was known as Reza Khan and was the most senior Persian officer serving under the Cossacks.

When the revolution began all the Russian officers left and Reza Khan took command of the brigade. Around this time the English realised that, with the collapse of Russia, there was a chance for them to step into strategically placed Persia, so Reza Khan with his armed forces was persuaded to help put pressure on the reigning Ahmad Shah to accept English protectorate. Reza Khan took his brigade down to Teheran, where they sat outside the gates, making the last Shah of the Qajar dynasty tremble in his silken slippers.

However, the Persian commander's plans were not quite

those of the English, for what he wanted was to force Ahmad
Shah to turn Persia into a republic. In this ambition he was
following the same course as that of his neighbour in Turkey.
Kemal Ataturk, after the collapse of the Ottoman Empire, had
done just this in an attempt to propel his ancient Islamic
nation into the 20th century.

It was obvious that if Persia was ever going to be great again,
it would have to modernise itself. Reza Shah saw a definite
role for himself as the person most able to force the necessary
changes. Because of his strength of character and powerful
physical attributes – he was over six feet tall with a
commanding presence and piercing eyes – he gained not only
the respect of the English, during the next few years, but also
the rich and powerful *bazaris*, the merchants who lived in the
bazaars and, most importantly, the religious leaders.

He was soon in a position from where he was able to
overthrow the crumbling, corrupt 150-year-old Qajar dynasty
and, on the insistence of senior religious leaders, accepted the
title of *Shahenshah – Zill-el-Lah* (the Shadow of God). A new
constitution was drawn up, the outcome of which was that the
religious faction was given official power of veto. This meant
that a council of *mullahs* reviewed all the actions taken by
Parliament and discussed whether they conformed to the
teachings of the Quran. If it was found that they did not, then
those actions were declared null and void.

The state that Reza Shah 'inherited' was in shambles, so he
did not have a great deal of time or energy to spend on
worrying about what the clergy did or did not approve of.
During the 15 years of his reign, he worked and fought
tirelessly to consolidate his control over the country and bring
back authority to Teheran. He instituted land reforms, which
meant that he moved against the aristocracy and feudal land
lords. He took much of their land away and limited their
control to one village per family. Most of the land he took
formed the basis for the future Pahlavi fortune although, later,
some of this was given to the peasants to gain their support.

During this time he also worked on his plan to modernise
and secularise the country. He began to install a basic
infrastructure of roads, railways and modern buildings and

introduced education and rights for women. The religious leaders were not happy with all his changes, but he had military might for, above all, he had strengthened his army, knowing this to be his real source of power. Although he was a despot he was an enlightened one and his attempts to rid his country of ignorance and disease show his concern for the people.

The confrontations between the Shah and the religious faction became increasingly bitter during the 1930s. As this decade came to a close, internal struggles became overshadowed by foreign matters. The Second World War loomed.

In a futile attempt to cause even more problems between the English and the Russians, who had been aggressively imperialistic as far as Persia was concerned, Reza Shah became seemingly pro-German. He even changed the name of Persia to Iran to emphasise the Aryan nature of the people and the regime, making the English and the Russians very unhappy.

In 1941 the Russians moved in and took control of the northern areas of Iran and the English did the same in the south. Reza Shah was subsequently arrested and sent into exile and his 21-year-old son Mohammed Reza was placed on the throne. Bandar Abbas was the last stop in Iran for the deposed monarch. This sad and dejected man stayed there as a guest of Mohammed Khan Galadari on his way to exile in South Africa. He died within a few years on the island of Mauritius.

Like his father, Mohammed Reza Shah realised that his strength lay in the army and looked after it well, lavishing it with material possessions and land.

After the Second World War the Americans became a major power in the world and, because of the oil finds in Iran, they took a special interest in our country. Consequently, we found ourselves being dominated by yet another aggressive world power and the young Shah seemed to allow them to dictate to him, which many of our countrymen resented bitterly. Through it all, however, the Shah continued the reforms of his father but, unfortunately, did not have the same charisma.

Reza Shah had been a man to whom nobody dared lie. He wanted to hear the truth and people trembled when he looked at them with his piercing eyes. His son was different; people were frightened to tell him the truth and so, in the end, they told him only what he wanted to hear. When he visited any area, especially in the latter years of his reign, people were forcibly brought out on to the streets in large numbers to cheer him.

Although the Shah's popularity waned over the years, his wife, Farah, was loved and respected. The Shahbanu was particularly interested in social welfare and cultural activities and made frequent visits to all the regions. Her visits were always constructive and people loved to meet her. Wherever she went, there was always a spontaneous response and a feeling of goodwill towards her.

On one particular visit to a district of Bandar Abbas the Shahbanu decided to visit the *Parvareshgah-e-Farah Pahlavi* Orphanage, which had been named after her. There were several similar institutions throughout the country and she took a special interest in them, always making sure that ample money was available to be spent on the children's welfare. On this occasion she was to have lunch at the orphanage and insisted that she be served the same food the children were normally given. The meal was tasty and nutritious and she seemed pleased but, as she was about to leave a small, mischievous child called out, "*Khanom, khanom*, will you come and have lunch with us every day?"

"That would be nice," the Shahbanu smiled at the little girl, "But why do you wish it?"

"Because we had such nice food today, and we would like to have it every day," was the reply.

The staff looked stunned and shame-faced but the Shahbanu only smiled gravely and continued chatting. She discovered that the children were usually fed only an orange and a biscuit. She finished talking with the children, and giving no indication that she was angry, maintained her composure and carried on with her tour, which then took her to the Girls' High School next.

There she was shown around the school that had been built three years earlier. In the laboratory, which was full of gleaming, modern equipment, she commented on how shiny and bright everything looked and how well kept it was. She then went to one of the sinks and turned on a tap. Nothing happened, which was not surprising, as the water wasn't connected. In fact, nothing in the laboratory had ever been used.

The Education Minister trembled in his shoes and the rest of us almost stopped breathing in our embarrassment, but the Shahbanu said nothing and continued chatting and smiling and putting people at ease. Outside, as we crossed a patch of garden, she lingered to look at it, exclaiming with pleasure, "In spite of water shortages you have done wonders. Even out of season, flowers grow well here." She left the group and walked up to the pretty garden and bent down to pick one of the flowers. The whole bush came out of the ground. It wasn't only the flowers that began to look wilted.

As the next part of the programme was in my department, I felt a little nervous. Still as if nothing was wrong, the Shahbanu walked to the cultural section, where the children's art was being displayed. I knew her well enough to realise that she was genuinely interested in original rustic works rather than glamorous presentations, so we had deliberately placed two pieces of art, done by our star pupils, in prominent positions for her to see. Both these children came from poor homes but one was very good at *khattati,* or calligraphy while the other was a talented painter.

The Shahbanu inspected the work of some women, who were weaving baskets in plain and dyed straw and also of those doing embroidery. She chatted with the ladies and then moved on to the children's corner. Immediately she noticed the two particularly good pieces of artwork and inspected these closely. After what she had experienced so far, she had every right to doubt everyone's performance, so she asked to see the two children. They were immediately brought forward and the Shahbanu spoke kindly and gently to them. She asked both of them to do a little piece for her. Quickly and confidently our little artist drew a very good rural scene featuring goats and the calligrapher wrote a couplet from the great Iranian poet Hafiz Shirazi. The Shahbanu looked sincerely pleased and I breathed a sigh of relief.

That night on the radio the Shahbanu spoke about her deep concern about having been given false impressions of the work and achievements of some, as she much preferred to be presented with the facts. It came as little surprise that a short while later the chief of education and the director of the orphanage were both recalled to Teheran.

If the Shah had been less concerned with his image abroad and more able to relate to his people, like his wife who so obviously cared for Iran and its citizens, I believe he would have had a chance of surviving longer. However, as time went on, the chasm between the Shah and the masses only grew wider. Government officials were expected to praise him endlessly as though we owed him our very existence. Having met the Shah often, I did have great respect for him, but like most people I was irritated by the superfluous show of pomp and ceremony that accompanied him everywhere. I knew his ideas were good but I felt the man behind them was losing his way. He did introduce useful reforms such as free food in schools, a programme known as *Taghzia Rayegan*, but we began to worry that he was demanding praise all the time.

In addition, the excesses of his court did not endear him to anyone. He took over a small island called Kish, in the Strait of Hormuz, and converted it into a weekend retreat. He built a huge palace there and spent a great deal of time on the island. Millions of dollars were poured into private villas and luxury hotels and the island even became a free port to encourage rich foreigners. We heard tales of Kish becoming the Monte Carlo of the Middle East. The general public in Iran did not like this at all.

Our country was supposed to be reaching the wondrous gates of modern civilisation, *darwaza tamadun*, but many people seemed to be getting left behind on the journey. It was true that huge skyscrapers were being built, but only the rich would live in them and the poor, who built them, were crammed into slums in the south of Teheran.

Increasingly out of touch with reality, in 1975 the Shah eliminated the token opposition party and introduced a one-party system. He was of course the head of this one and only party, which was known as *Rastakhiz* (National Resurgent). He often said that those who did not support the *Rastakhiz* party and become part of this great new civilisation would either go to prison or be exiled. "We shall take them by the tail and throw them out like mice," he emphasised.

In 1976, to celebrate the 50th anniversary of the Pahlavi dynasty, the Shah even went so far as to change Iran's calender and, from then on our country was to set its dates according to the reign of Cyrus the Great. The reason he did this was to emphasise the point that Iranians are descended from the ancient Persians and that it was Cyrus the Great 2,500 years ago who created the first mighty Persian Empire, which, at the time, stretched from the southern part of the Soviet Union right down to Egypt. However, since then a series of invasions by the Greeks, the Romans, the Turks, the Mughals, the Arabs, the British, the Russians, and the Americans resulted in the land being conquered repeatedly and the people being controlled by aliens. The Persians have had to serve each successive conqueror as administrators of their own country. Throughout the centuries the Persians have been allowed to retain their monarchy but the Shahs have only lasted as long as it suited the conquerors, as Reza Shah and subsequently his son discovered.

As a nation, Iranians have always taken great pride in a glorious past and hoped for some sort of renaissance. I thnk the Shah seriously believed he was bringing this about after so many years of being manipulated by foreigners; during one speech he even sent a message to Cyrus the Great: "You can rest in peace now. We are awake." Far from having the desired effect, however, many saw this as simply arrogant and worse, as blasphemous, so he ended up upsetting people even more.

The oil boom had brought money pouring into the country and his dream was to turn Iran into an industrial power by the year 2000 AD. He had huge hopes and ambitions but, unfortunately, he overlooked the human factor. Adjusting to modern Western ways and ideas was difficult for people brought up in an orthodox Islamic tradition.

It was the 'White Revolution' that included land reforms and the emancipation of women that brought about the most bitter confrontations with the rich land owners and the religious leaders. The groundwork for this had been implemented by his father but he gave the reforms a proper structure. People did not like being taxed on land that had been in some families for centuries. Many of the aristocracy – like our family – left the country to live in places such as Bahrain, Kuwait, Dubai and India.

It was difficult to believe that trouble would not follow, for the changes were too radical and too rapid. Beneath the modern appearance of many people there beat a profoundly traditional Iranian heart. It was not wise to abandon carelessly the moral codes of conduct.

Religion and politics in Iran have always been closely intertwined, because religious authorities such as the *mullahs* and the Ayatollahs in past times were also often chieftains of local tribes, so in a way always had greater power than any Shah. They were the real policy-makers whom people trusted and believed. Religious leaders have never tried to abolish the monarchy; however, over the years many Shahs have either tried to suppress or bribe these powerful men, sometimes successfully.

As the whole world remembers, it was Ayatollah Ruhollah Khomeini who, bitterly detesting the Pahlavi dynasty, and campaigning against it from exile, was the catalyst for the Shah's downfall.

The country was ready and ripe for such an event. Corruption was at its peak and the Shah had begun to look more and more like a puppet of the United States and increasingly seemed to be losing all credibility and dignity.

Despite the fact that he was a supreme religious leader, the Ayatollah had been arrested, though not harmed, and exiled by the Shah. It was a shocking act, but it helped the Ayatollah's cause as it upset all Muslims and so, from afar, he was able to sow seeds of hatred and disturbance among an already unhappy and restless people.

Riots and demonstrations began. Things became more and more violent. A fire in a theatre in Abadan, where more than 300 people were burned alive, shook the country. It was rumoured that this fire had been deliberately started in order to trap certain dissidents that SAVAK, the Government

Intelligence Agency, wanted to eliminate. Anger rather than fear spread. Soon there was an angry atmosphere even at Friday prayers.

On September 6, 1978, at the end of the month of Ramadan, a huge procession of *Olemas* and thousands of their followers marched through the streets of Teheran. Though peaceful and uneventful, it was a powerful and unprecedented display of political opposition.

Meanwhile tape-recorded messages from Ayatollah Khomeini were being smuggled into Iran and listened to countrywide. He exhorted the people again and again to crush and terminate the Pahlavi dynasty, until finally the common citizens began to believe that despite the fact that the Shah was the 'King of Kings' and had a great army and powerful friends, this could be done and, when it was finally achieved, life would be good.

Through the months of September and October, things in Iran got worse. Thousands of rioters were slaughtered in Zhaleh Square. Sharif Emmami remained prime minister because of his links with the clergy, but he appeared weak. Nothing was expected of him, though he did give freedom to the press, released some political prisoners and spoke about human rights.

By November, people had taken to climbing onto rooftops and shouting, *"Khomeini Rahbar"* – Khomeini the leader. Nobody now said, *"Javeed Shah"* – Long live the Shah. The wind was definitely blowing from a different direction.

Violent riots and clashes between demonstrators and the army weakened Sharif Emmami's administration. Teheran began to look like a battleground – buildings were in flames, cars were bombed and burned in the streets.

An attempt was made to begin negotiations between the Shah and the Opposition. A military government under General Azhari was formed and the Shah agreed to a democratic election with freedom for parliament to select their own prime minister, although he would stay as constitutional head of the government. As events progressed, he ate a great deal of humble pie and admitted he had made mistakes.

Meanwhile the Ayatollah had been sent out of Iraq, because

of complaints that he was causing disturbances there. He moved to Paris and, even though he was farther away, his influence increased. Since Iranians did not need a visa to go to France, he was soon surrounded by political activists. Many of his supporters were Western-educated, enlightened and idealistic young men, who sincerely believed that good would come out of a revolution.

However, when I was in France visiting Shirin, who at that time was continuing her studies there, I heard Ayatollah Khomeini speak and I felt frightened for the future of our country. I rang Pakravan that night and said that I thought things were worse than most of us realised and he should think of sending some of our possessions out of the country. He laughed at me and said that he thought the French food must have given me indigestion, as it was not usual for me to be so pessimistic.

"Come back," he said. "It is all nonsense."

The tension increased through the latter part of December, 1978. The pressure on the Shah became so great that there was talk that he would leave the country for an extended period. He even suggested that he would go to live in Bandar Abbas in a Navy compound. In this way he would, for all intents and purposes, be exiled from his country, but would still physically be living on its soil. For a while it looked as if Bandar Abbas, true to its reputation of being a place of exile for criminals and political dissidents, was also to be the last resort for ex-kings.

Meanwhile, strikes in the oil fields, power plants, airlines and public services continued. The Shah, on the advice of the United States, left the country and sat waiting in Morocco, hoping that he would be called home.

On February 1, 1979 Ayatollah Khomeini stepped down from an Air France Boeing 747, on to Iranian soil again and was met by an ecstatic crowd. It was *Dasht-e-Mahshar*, the Day of Destiny.

CHAPTER 20

FAREWELL IRAN

It would be an understatement to say that this was an incredibly tense time. Those of us not caught up in the revolutionary fervour watched the situation warily and attempted to go about our business as usual.

Imam Khomeini's every movement was televised and every word he uttered was reported in all the newspapers. Bakhtiar, a social democrat, was the man left in charge of the government and he believed that, with his middle-of-the-road policies, he could calm the situation down. Unfortunately, being very 'French' and urbane, he contrasted sharply with the simple style of the Ayatollah, who was content with a corner to sleep in, a blanket and a prayer mat.

All the poor people who followed Imam Khomeini about could see he was a God-fearing man who would not squander the country's riches on glamour and frivolity but would distribute the wealth evenly. They also trusted him as a religious mentor. It was little wonder therefore, that in many ways people virtually worshipped the Ayatollah and followed him blindly, believing that he could miraculously bring about the changes they had so long waited for. What really happened was that the country descended into a state of confusion and total disarray. In their zeal to root out the "evil" they seemed to have forgotten that machines don't run without a hand on the controls.

Our life in Bandar Abbas continued quietly, though commodities such as electricity, fuel and water were being restricted, which made day-to-day living more difficult. I knew that nobody was going to bother me, for I believed that the people of Bandar Abbas were too conservative or possibly too apathetic to join wholeheartedly in this violent movement.

I also realised I wasn't having any serious problems, mainly because I was a well-respected local woman and because I beieved I had always shown myself to be neutral as far as politics was concerned. Unfortunately I was not aware of the true situation – until one night, when one of my neighbours came running to tell me what was happening.

A few years earlier I had helped these neighbours retain their rights to live on unattended property, on which they had been squatting for years. Most of them were fishermen or workers in the fish canning factory that was one of the major industries of Bandar Abbas, but they were very poor and therefore powerless. Previously I had fought on their behalf with quite a few officials who wanted to destroy their *kapars* or shacks, arguing that these people had no right to live on the land they occupied and that their shacks made the area unsightly and unhealthy. The latter was certainly true, but they had nowhere else to live. After I had won the case, I made sure that new and better housing was built for them. It was these neighbours who now became my saviours.

"Khanom! Khanom!" There is terrible danger." One of the men I knew quite well stood at my door. He was frightened and upset and, when he eventually calmed down, reported all the news. The revolutionaries had begun to come to the outlying places like Bandar Abbas and were trying to stir up the local people against those they called the *taqootis* meaning people of the Shah's regime, who lived in palatial houses in high style and lorded it over the commonfolk. In their eyes I was a *taqooti* – the oppressor.

Unknown to me, these good neighbours had patrolled my house each night and so far had managed to keep intruders away, but that night they had found tyres spread around the high walls. Somebody had plans to burn down our house and wipe the country clean of one more *taqooti* – me.

I telephoned the Governor General in the hope that he would send me some guards and arrange to move us to our villa, which at the time was still being built. It was too late – he had no guards to spare and had his hands full with problems all around the town. I then tried the Sheikh of Qatar's representative to warn him of the potential danger, but he had already left town, being no doubt fully aware of the dangerous situation that was developing.

Pakravan then told me that he had received a number of anonymous phone calls telling him in no uncertain terms that people like us had no right to be living in such luxury, especially as we were not joining in with the demonstrations or indicating that we were revolutionary supporters. He said that the callers had threatened to burn down our house and punish us. Being the type of person he was, Pakravan could not believe in the evil of others and had treated the calls as a crazy sort of joke. Now it seemed that although they might be crazy, they were very serious about their intentions.

Hurriedly, we abandoned the house, taking very little with us, and fled to our unfinished villa some distance away. We were only just in time for, a short while later, mobs of screaming men arrived at the house. Finding it without occupants they looted it but, as it was still standing the next day, they had apparently postponed the idea of burning it down.

The demonstrations and strikes continued – shops were closed and the food we had stored was beginning to run out. Having lived through two wars during my tenure in Lahore, and civil riots in Pakistan and Teheran, I was not too shocked or frightened by the happenings, but I'm sure no one ever gets used to the horrors of such times.

By the month of March 1979 life had become a nightmare. Everything was rationed and little was available. There was looting and burning everywhere and bodies of dead soldiers and dissidents lay in the streets. Clashes were frequent and devastating. Soldiers and hooligans entered houses without passes and people were asked to surrender all sorts of things, ranging from important documents to electric toasters.

Women had to observe strict *purdah* and if they were seen unveiled they were lashed and taken to prison. It was as though the clocks had been sent spinning backwards 50 years overnight. Iran had come a long way in that time: Women had become a part of life in many fields – there were women judges, politicians and teachers – but, with the coming of the new regime, it seemed as if we were meant to give it all up and go back in time and once again be imprisoned in our homes.

There was fear everywhere but most frightening of all were the puppet courts that were being set up around the country. Peculiar trials took place, and even worse, sometimes people were condemned without even a trial. There were executions daily and the bodies of the victims were displayed on television. Many of them I knew and had associated with over the years.

Central government seemed to disintegrate. The ministers had all left or were being killed. Bakhtiar had also somehow spirited himself away. The revolutionaries were definitely taking control and, to show their power, in November 1979 they overpowered the American Embassy and so started the hostage crisis that had repercussions halfway around the world in helping lose Jimmy Carter the American presidency.

At this time my daughter Shahnaz was studying in New York. I had been unable to send her any money for a few months as there was no means of communication with the outside world. I was desperately worried that, being an Iranian, she would be in danger. We had no way of knowing how she was coping.

Meanwhile Shirin had finished college in Paris and had come home amid all this turbulence and tension. My children too had been through the horrors of war; Shirin had been with me in Lahore and again in Teheran during violent disturbances, so they knew what it was like to live in a chaotic and frightening environment. For her age, Shirin was well experienced and I knew she could cope in times of crisis. All the same I wanted to send her to New York to join her sister but with the US Embassy under siege, it was impossible to get a visa.

Disappointed, Shirin started work with the Swiss Peace Corps. This group was doing a wonderful job bringing some relief to the families of those who had been taken away and incarcerated with no one knowing of their whereabouts. In fact, in many of these cases, families were informed only after their relatives had been executed.

It worried me that my daughter should be exposed to so

much unhappiness and ugliness, but she felt she wanted to do something useful in these awful times and she proved to be an asset to the organisation because she could speak Farsi, French and English. But soon I managed to get her away from all this horror, to London.

I was still officially 'working' but salaries had not been paid for months and at this time nobody was particularly interested in culture and the arts. My office was sealed but I attended punctually every day, sometimes with only chairs and tables for company.

Although no slogans had been written on my office walls and no windows had been smashed, I knew my position was precarious, so I decided the best thing to do would be to retire. I wrote several times to the ministry asking for release of service and got the rather odd reply (I suppose bureaucratic impetus kept things going) that I had to complete my four years of service in Hormozgan before my retirement could be considered.

Finally, after yet another urgent letter, I got the reply that much as the ministry would like to release me it was impossible, for the minister and his deputy along with everybody else had left. Even so, I rushed to Teheran and managed to get the papers signed by one of the few people still working; these I have kept in my possession to this day.

The release was all I got for, although I had been a high-ranking civil servant with many years of service and so entitled to a good pension, I was now regarded as *paksazi shodeh* – dirt and litter that had to be cleansed. As far as anybody was concerned, my life's work was not worth anything and for it I would receive exactly that – nothing.

Ironically, I was now free to travel within the country and live my own life, but the future did not look particularly promising. I was desperately worried about all the family and how and where we would live. Finally I got word from Shahnaz, through our good friends the Brohis in London, and found out that she was being well looked after by her American friends and was about to graduate. Having an official invitation to her graduation, I was allowed to visit America though I still couldn't get a visa for Shirin.

It was wonderful to see Shahnaz again and know that she was safe, but I was even more pleased to see that the Americans we met held no bitter feelings towards my daughter or myself, although the hostage situation was still dragging on.

More than ever I wanted to get Shirin to America where at least she and Shahnaz could be together. Suddenly as if by inspiration I remembered my cousin Sultana, who at the time lived in Toronto, Canada. I knew it would be easy for Shirin to get a Canadian visa. I had no idea of Sultana's address or telephone number, but with the help of a kind telephone operator it wasn't long before I made contact with her. It was difficult to talk to her, for she was alternately laughing and crying with relief, as listening to the news reports, she had been convinced that all of us had been killed by the revolutionaries.

Arrangements were made and in no time at all Shirin, Shahnaz and I and even the dog Kocholoo (who travelled everywhere with Shahnaz) were finally reunited in Sultana's house.

This reprieve in Canada with my beautiful and fun-loving cousin Sultana stands out in my memory, for it was like an oasis of peace and joy between periods of madness and fear. However, I knew I had to get back to Iran to make final plans to get all the family out. Marie and Ebrahim and Rokna and his family were in Teheran, but none of them were working, and Pakravan was still in Bandar Abbas. When I left, Shahnaz returned to New York with Kocholoo and Shirin stayed on with Sultana, who took her to Trinidad where she was eventually able to get her visa to join her sister in America.

It was risky returning to Iran, especially as so many of my associates were being imprisoned and executed; women who had been part of the old regime were being punished along with the men.

In the Ministry of Arts and Culture there had been only three women at my level: One had been assassinated immediately after the revolution, the other was missing and I was still a target. As the plane came in to land at Teheran Airport, I wondered what sort of reception I would get. I need not have worried unduly because the place was still in a chaotic state, so I managed to slip through immigration in my black *abaya*, right into the waiting arms of my step-children without anybody looking twice at me.

As we drove back to the flat I felt like crying when I saw the state of the beautiful city. Buildings were destroyed, shops were shuttered and there were very few people on the streets except for soldiers with guns. There was an air of fear and, despite the millions who still lived in the city, a sense of desolation pervaded the place. So many people had fled. Foreigners were a rare species, women even rarer and those I saw were covered completely in black and looked like dark ghosts from the past. The tree-lined avenues now looked even more like tunnels but there didn't seem to be any light at the end of them. Why had I returned?

In my heart I believed that I would somehow be safe, for I was innocent of any political activity. I reasoned that I had only worked for the good of Iran and promoted the arts and culture – what had I to fear? Quite a lot, according to Pakravan, when I told him I was coming to Bandar Abbas to pack up our belongings.

"You are well-known here," he said. "It is not safe; people will connect you to the old regime and you will be put in prison."

I tried to explain to him that I was an innocent person and nothing would happen to me.

"There has been more than one innocent person executed in times of revolutions," Pakravan warned.

"But I can't just go and leave everything and everybody behind. What is going to happen to Rokna? Marie? Our flat? All my beautiful antiques and ? Our house in Bandar Abbas? I must organise it all." I insisted and Pakravan knew me well enough to realise that any more argument was futile.

Meanwhile my noble-hearted sister, Bibiya, was also begging me to leave and come and live with her in Dubai. I had always intended to live in Dubai after my retirement, for my family's association with this Emirate has been a long and warm one. Now it seemed the perfect haven for me.

Bibiya's son Sultan was wonderful, making all the necessary arrangements, and was finally able to get my family resident visas. All that was left for me to do was to pack my possessions and get myself safely out of the country, before I was recognised by some petty official or person with a grudge and ended up sharing the fate of so many of my former colleagues. Each day added to the risk.

"*Jahannam-e-male donya* – to hell with worldly goods," Bibiya urged me to save myself. Pakravan and the children became more and more frightened for me. However, I had spent years collecting my precious belongings, most of which held great sentimental value for me. I felt I just couldn't leave everything and go.

Packing my furniture and books was not an easy task. The whole of Bandar Abbas was at a standstill. There were no shops open at all and, of course, no packers available. Everything also had to be done secretively. I did not want too many people finding out that I was leaving because this would draw unnecessary attention to myself.

During one long, dark night I went around to a few local stores. The owners secretly opened them for me and I was able to buy enough styrofoam sheets which I brought in to the house through the back door. A couple of friends, some of the very few I could trust, helped me pack up whatever I could by candlelight. It was a difficult job deciding what I would take and what I would leave, for I knew that the chances of ever again seeing those things I left behind were slim. However, I hardly had the opportunity to feel any sadness, for I was too scared and nervous.

A decree stipulated at this time that no antiques, carpets or valuables were allowed to leave Iran but, because of the chaotic state of affairs, there was nobody around who could properly assess the value of any antiques anyway, so I packed up all I could.

When I approached the Customs officers I was pleased to find out that it was still my old department's job to sign the documents for the release of my packages. Only one staff member, the librarian, had survived and he was brought over to inspect my goods. He bowed and apologised to me and after a cursory glance, signed the necessary papers. With these vital documents clutched in my hands, I was able to hire a launch and have my goods shipped to Dubai, where Bibiya and her husband Sheikh Abdullah received and stored them for me.

It was now only a matter of getting myself safely out of Iran. Bandar Abbas was becoming more and more dangerous. Riots and bitter fights between religious sects continued and there were disturbances in schools as well. Even young girls who demonstrated against the new restrictions were being locked up. The former Governor General and other high officials, though they had pledged allegiance to the new regime and had taken part in several demonstrations, were arrested and humiliated by being made to do menial jobs such as cleaning toilets and bathrooms. The world as I knew it was being turned upside down and I knew that it really was time to try and get out.

In order to leave the country it was necessary to give a week's notice by delivering one's passport to the appropriate ministry. Nervously I handed this valuable document to the officer concerned and wondered whether I would ever see it again. Would my name and face be remembered?

The week dragged by and I became increasingly anxious as I packed a few remaining bits and pieces which I planned to take with me on the aeroplane. Despite the terrible risk, I decided I had to take all my jewellery for, like my poor unfortunate aunt of so many years before, my gold was now my only security as all our assets were in Iran and my long-dreamed-of pension was nothing but a burst bubble.

I wrapped the entire collection first in separate nylon packets and then in plastic bags and placed them all in a cheap-looking hold-all. On top I put some jars of jam, a ripped bag of henna and a sewing kit with the needles exposed in the hope that one would prick any probing hand. The bag had no fastenings, so I tied it up with an old belt.

With a faint heart I arrived at the airport. As a red herring, in one of my suitcases I had put some brass crockery and glittering gold-like cutlery, that was set with stones resembling rubies and sapphires. The plan seemed to work and the Customs official who went through my cases stopped short when he found these items.

"They are not real," I insisted and, to my glee, he didn't

believe me and there was a great deal of running around looking for an expert to assess the authenticity of these goods. Soon I was surrounded by people and all the attention was focused on the suitcase.

"They are of no value to me; I insist that you keep all these things yourself." I handed over the collection to them.

This put the officials in a dilemma. How could they confiscate goods that were possibly worthless but then again, how could they accept goods that were more than likely worth a great deal? Was this bribery? Meanwhile a lady officer had put her hand inside the 'important' bag and just as quickly took it out again. She screamed at me in anger.

"Look at my finger, it is bleeding! There is a broken bottle in this bag. You should be more careful with your packing. You had better not be trying to hide something."

My heart lurched. The punishment for smuggling was severe. I apologised as humbly as I could and explained that the last-minute packing of bottles for a friend's children in Dubai must have caused the mess. With trembling fingers I retied the bag and, as it disappeared on the luggage trolley, prayed that despite its dilapidated state, it would reach its destination intact.

With my luggage now all in the hands of the airport staff, I made my way to the long queue of people waiting to pick up their passports. I looked around and wondered if my face registered the same worry, fear and sadness that I saw on everybody else's. So many of us would be leaving our country forever.

At last, after an hour of waiting that seemed never-ending, I arrived at the front of the queue and faced yet another official. I went clammy with fear that this could be the man who would pronounce my fate. He asked me many questions and I squeaked rather incoherent answers. I was almost past caring when finally, miraculously, he handed me my passport.

I was almost tottering when I reached the plane. All emotion seemed to have been drained from me. Even when I had one of the rings I was wearing confiscated I hardly cared. I collapsed into my seat shaking uncontrollably.

"Mariam Behnam, report to a flight attendant."

This was it: "They have discovered who I am! They've found the gold! I will be imprisoned and most likely shot! What will the children do without me? How will Pakravan cope?" Wild thoughts flew through my head as I made my way down the steps of the plane. My worst fears seemed to be realised when I was confronted with my old bag.

"This bag is open." An official looked accusingly at me. "Is it yours?"

The belt had loosened and, although none of the precious objects inside could be seen, to me the whole bag seemed to glow. As calmly as I could, I told the man that the bag was of no real consequence but made sure it was tied up more securely this time. I hoped he would not think it too incongruous that a smartly-dressed woman would have such a shabby-looking bag. Apparently he didn't and I was allowed to reboard. The door of the aeroplane closed with a thump.

I wept as I left Iran.

The short flight to Dubai was soon over and I was safe, my jewellery was safe, even my furniture and most of my antiques were safe. But I had lost my country.

A week later I found out my name had just been placed on an official list that would have prevented me from leaving the country. I was *mamnoo-el-khorooj* – blacklisted. The charges against me were that I had helped and supported the past regime.

CHAPTER **21**

DUBAI, THE HAVEN

In 1979, after the revolution in Iran, many unfortunate and unhappy people were forced into exile; some fled to Europe, Canada and America; others, like the Shah himself, moved constantly, unable to find a safe haven. Many flooded the Gulf region, especially the United Arab Emirates, which is known for its neutrality and stability. In fact it was one of the very few doors that remained open in the Gulf area for Iranians during the eight-year war between Iran and Iraq later in the '80s.

For me to say that I am exiled in Dubai, is strictly speaking correct concerning my state of affairs but, in reality, it is a contradiction in terms. How can one be exiled in a place one considers to be home? I have always had more relatives in Dubai (including my sister Bibiya) than anywhere else in the world for it was this wonderful place that became a haven for many of my family when social and economic changes were taking place in the Lingah area decades ago. They lived and traded here; I too had visited Dubai on many an occasion.

There is some sort of strong and inexplicable bond with the place one first comes to know and becomes familiar with on this earth. My trip back to Iran 12 years after my forced departure proved this. However, I have always believed that it is the people who make a place special and the bonds between southern Iranians, especially the Bastakis, like myself, and the people of Dubai, have been forged over generations by trade and marriage. Our culture is shared to the point where it is difficult to differentiate what particular aspect comes from which source. Although Iran is the country in which I was born, Dubai is now my home.

Since the 1960s, after the discovery of oil, the friendly town of Dubai, the second largest of the seven emirates that make up the UAE, has grown rapidly into an ultra-modern city with an enviable infrastructure and progressive social planning. Lush parks give a welcome relief of greenery, so even the desert looks less harsh.

To me, the most interesting aspect of Dubai's development is that despite all the progress, the traditional ways have not been foresaken.

If you look hard enough, you will still find some of the the old, rectangular, coral-stone houses with their elegant *badgirs* or windtowers and beautifully carved wooden doors, now overshadowed on all sides by the modern skyscrapers built to accommodate the huge influx of business and technical people and their families, who have come from all around the world to help put Dubai prominently on the map.

Although the face of Dubai has changed so dramatically, fortunately the character of this commercially-oriented city has not changed at all. It is still a friendly and pleasant place where people are able to conduct their business in a hospitable, courteous and honest environment. The moral values have not changed and the men and women still proudly wear their traditional garments. It is encouraging to know that progress doesn't always have to mean that old ways must be discarded.

The rulers of the Emirates come from noble tribes and have always had the welfare of their people at heart. Dubai will forever cherish the memory of its late ruler Sheikh Rashid bin Saeed Al Maktoum. The great wisdom and vision of this man, which led to the phenomenal progress and multi-faceted development of Dubai in such a short time, is being carried on by his sons, who continue to enhance the image of Dubai.

Understandably, arriving as I did during tense and troubled times, my first few months in Dubai were not easy. I had never envisaged such a drastic turn of events; suddenly, after having believed that I could retire on a high-grade pension which together with Pakravan's business would enable us to live comfortably the rest of our lives, I found myself in a very difficult situation.

Pakravan was still in Bandar Abbas, though his business, a clearing and forwarding firm, had stopped functioning, like so many others. He could not assist us financially and we had never made any arrangements with foreign banks as so many other people had. I needed to work and be independent.

They say that when one door shuts, another opens. Sultan, my sister Bibiya's son, gave me wonderful support and helped in every way that he could during this particularly difficult time. So somehow I managed to survive.

In April 1980 my daughters Shahnaz and Shirin arrived from New York after an arduous journey that tested their mettle. It had not been easy to get visas for Dubai in Washington. In the end Sultan came to the rescue. He sent visas and we settled down to wait. But that wasn't the end of it. Breaking their journey in Paris created another hurdle. With Kocholoo, our little Yorkshire terrier, in their arms, these two 'unwanted Iranians' as we were called at the time were barred from entering France although their connecting flight to Dubai was not available for several days. "Mummy, what do we do now?" came the plaintive cry from Charles de Gaulle Airport. Finally, through the intervention of the French Consul-General in Dubai, my daughters were allowed into the city to await their flight. It was a tearful reunion on their arrival in Dubai some days later, after which we put the whole episode behind us. and got on with the job at hand – getting settled and finding work.

Shahnaz joined Dubai television as a newscaster, making a name for herself over the years before moving to London to further her broadcasting career. It was a curious experience being eclipsed by my own children; even now, although I have never used my married name of Pakravan, I get smiles of recognition for being "Mrs Pakravan, Shahnaz's mom." Years before, my father had commented on the same thing, so I guess it happens to us all.

Shirin, having studied design and clothing in Paris, took over the family fashion business, and much later opened her own specialist design house. She introduced the concept of local fashion shows which she choreographed and supervised.

Soon I was also earning an income as a journalist for a local newspaper owned by Abdul Wahab Galadari, whose family has been closely associated with the development of Dubai.

With steady income, we were finally able to establish ourselves in a home of our own and once we did this, Shahnaz boldly took a trip to Teheran and brought her father to Dubai. It was a shock to see him, for the effect of the revolution and his diabetic condition had turned him into a frail and sad man. He was in his 70s.

Old family friends such as the Fikrees, Mohammad Hashem Khoory, Mohamad Sharif Fereidooni, the Behroozians, the Faqihis, and the Mir Shahabuddin Riyahi family of Qatar were especially sympathetic and helped us settle into our new home. *'Az har cheh begzari sokhane doost khoshtrust'* – there is nothing to replace genuine friendship.

However, more than anything, we wanted all our family to be together during this difficult time. We were ecstatic when Marie and Ebrahim and their children came to live with us in Dubai. All our girls were now with us and Essa, married and the father of three, was not far away in Jeddah. Our one worry was that Rokna and his family were still in Iran.

Pakravan and I were delighted when Shirin met her future husband Majid, a handsome and hard-working young man from a respectable family in Dubai – the Abdul Razaks. Soon we were approached by his family for her hand in marriage – a nice traditional touch to a modern engagement.

Some marriages in this part of the world are still arranged but because both young men and women now have the opportunity to study and work outside the home they are able to meet and get to know their peers and possible future partners, even if only briefly. They now have the chance to make their own choice which, if acceptable to both families – as it certainly was in this case – leads to a union.

Having so much experience in organising grand functions I wanted to make my daughter's wedding a never-to-be-forgotten affair. Months of preparation went into making the festivities a very happy occasion, not least for the mother of the bride.

Shahnaz, on the other hand, married her husband David (now Khalid) in a quieter but no less joyful ceremony in London. I was concerned about the marriage for the two came from such different backgrounds, he English and she Iranian, but Pakravan wasn't. Many wellwishers from Dubai attended the wedding, a successful mixture of Eastern and Western traditions complete with traditional music and dancing, thanks to our dear friends the Wahidis who generously provided their home as a venue. When I was invited to join in the dancing, I hesitated. "How could I? I'm the bride's mother." Old habits die hard!

The wedding luncheon was attended by relatives and dignitaries, but the person dearest to Shahnaz, her father, was missing. Pakravan had lived long enough to see Shirin's first daughter, Rasha, born but not long enough to see his beloved daughter Shahnaz marry.

In 1983, in declining health, he suffered a stroke and was admitted to hospital. Every day he asked when we would take him home where our little dog, Kocholoo, sat sadly outside, waiting for his master to return. Although he disliked being in hospital, Pakravan never complained. He had daily visits from the whole family, except Rokna who was unable to leave Iran. Pakravan missed his son and prayed that he would be able to come. After 10 days he seemed to be improving and the doctor said that he could go home the next day, which was *Nowrooz*, Iranian New Year. However, while we were visiting him, he seemed to become slightly disoriented. Suddenly he looked up and said: "That is Rokna with his wife and children. I prayed to see them and after all they did come. How wonderful!" We looked to where he was pointing but saw no one. Later that evening I told him we would take him home the next day to celebrate Nowrooz. "Which home are you talking about, Mariam?" he asked "There are two types of home. One is our temporary home and the other is our permanent one."

We were astounded and wondered why he was being so philosophical. We had thought he would be delighted at the prospect of going back to familiar surroundings. We left the hospital at 8pm. All the way home Shahnaz kept insisting that she wanted to return. As we reached the house the telephone rang: Pakravan had had another stroke. By the time we reached the hospital, our beloved husband, father and friend was gone.

A month after Pakravan died, Rokna and his family finally managed to get out of Iran. He lived for a few years in Dubai; then he and his sister Marie and their families all migrated to Sweden. Tragically, five years later in 1988 Rokna died after a massive heart attack.

In 1987, at an age when my involvement with children should have been nothing more than as the kind and loving grandmother, my own family was extended once more with the addition of a sweet young girl named Noora, meaning 'light'. The child was in a pitiable state for her mother had died years earlier and her father was unable to look after her. She was seven and needed a home. Unfortunately her father had also lost all the relevant documents, and it was with great difficulty that we were actually able to find her birth certificate. Up until that time the child had not even known the date of her birthday.

As her plight became known a local school magnanimously took over all the costs of her elementary education. I became her guardian, and with the security and love of three new 'sisters' (as Shirin's girls quickly became to her) she changed from a frightened, unkempt being into a bright student and cheerful child with every hope for a happy future. She is still stateless, but I have learned over the years that providence works in mysterious ways. She is after all a child of this soil.

My sisters Fatma and Bibiya live in Dubai and we see each other often. Our youngest sister, Badria, lives with her family in Kuwait. Sadly our brother Ahmad Noor died in 1992 during a visit to Dubai.

For a few years I continued to work for the newspaper but when it changed hands I finally decided it was time to retire completely. I planned to sit back and contemplate; something I had never had the chance to do during the previous 70 years.

Thinking, however, to a restless spirit like me is akin to fanning the glowing embers of a charcoal fire: Sooner or later they burst into life again. The same thing happened to me, and the result was my first tentative trip back to Iran 12 years after fleeing in terror.

It wasn't a hasty decision – anything but! The idea grew slowly, nudged along by things like the sight of the old windtower houses of Dubai in which I saw the reflection of my birthplace in Lingah. A chance strain of music would remind me of my mother's harmonium. More than anything it was my grandchildren's endless curiousity about the strange faces peering from countless cracked and faded photos on my walls. The more I explained, the more I remembered ... and wondered. My dreams haunted me.

The catalyst in my decision to return was the death of my father in spring 1991 in Teheran. Although I had seen him since my departure from the country as he had been to Dubai to visit, it was the finality of his death that started me actively considering a visit, weighing up the risks against the need to go back until finally the scales tipped.

From what others had said, I felt reasonably confident that provided I kept a low profile, nothing untoward would happen to me. Anyway, my one brush with politics, in running for Parliament, had been of no consequence. So I went – and every door I knocked on opened, every bend in the highway revealed something new.

Most wonderful of all was the unexpected meeting with my life-long friend Zuleikha Fikree, who incredibly had also chosen the holy month of Ramadan to visit Bastak for the first time in her life. We were reunited in Bandar Lingah where we made plans to be together – to visit Teheran, where I would pay my homage to my father, and we would see what the capital looked like after all the changes.

And that is what we did. Thinking the worst, we were pleasantly surprised to find that, apart from the outer garments that women now wore everywhere, everything in Teheran seemed to us to have settled back to normal. The city looked busy and purposeful. Our visits to museums, especially the carpet museum, was awe-inspiring. Re-united with family and friends was just what we needed. But all this came later: For now we were both excited and single-mindedly obsessed with our pilgrimage to the place of our ancestral roots, Bastak.

This visit was everything I could have hoped it would be – and more. The town of Bastak is small, word carries as swiftly as the wind and Bastakis love guests. Being Ramadan, sleep was not part of the agenda.

Women in Bastak normally stay with the womenfolk inside the house and men remain outside in the separate *majlis*. But in my case it was different. Such was the occasion of my long overdue visit that to honour me, the women and the men all joined together in the *majlis* for *Iftar*, the breaking of the fast

Years earlier, I had set the ball rolling on a library in Bastak, and this visit allowed me finally to see the finished product. It was not what I had bargained for. An air of lethargy and indifference hanging about the modest structure was disappointing. In an impromptu gathering in the reading room, I was asked to say a few words – in Bastaki, not Farsi. Did they think I had forgotten my own dialect? This got my hackles up.

"The people of Bastak," I told them, "should not for a moment believe that this sacred town is forgotten or abandoned. You have ample proof that the Bastakis all over the Gulf – in Dubai, Bahrain, Kuwait, Qatar, wherever they are – have you constantly in their thoughts. The town has received generous donations time and again for its development, especially for drinking water which is your main problem.

"However I am disappointed to see the state of disrepair you have allowed your library to fall into. Where is your civic pride? To mend the lighting, paint or repair the gate is not a major problem – you young people don't have to wait for government or the well-wishers outside Bastak to help you.

"I remember your enthusiasm and the promise of self-sufficiency before the library project in Bastak was sanctioned. You are all promising young men who love your region; I hope you will help towards its development as much as you can."

People graciously listened to my 'motherly' advice, knowing how deeply I was attached to the area. Many spoke to me of their gratitude for my involvement and interest in the overall development of that area in the past.

Later, an old friend of Mahmood's, who knew my family in Bombay, dropped in and entertained us with all the old Bastaki folk songs as well as the hits of Bombay in the 1920s and '30s. Even at 83, Haji Mohammad Ali Vatan Parast still had a powerful command of his voice and memory, and kept us enthralled for hours until we broke up for *Sohour* and the return journey to Lingah. It had been a truly memorable day.

I had gone to Bastak looking for meaning among the tombs and monuments of my ancestors. What I found was peace of mind, serenity and a sense of fulfilment and achievement, particularly in furthering the cause of women's rights.

As I look back at all I have done, what sticks in my mind is the joy on the faces of women, once confined – like I was – within four walls, who siezed the chance to shed their shackles and inhibitions, emerging to participate usefully in a vibrant pulsating world. In doing so, they and countless others who followed through the newly-opened door of opportunity managed to acquire and hone skills, become more productive, make new friends and discover that they had something special and constructive to offer our rapidly changing society.

Throughout my life I have tenaciously fought to open doors that were unjustly shut on me. Some I have managed to break down even when so many more have closed in my face. Nothing ventured, nothing gained. By believing in and living by the thought that struggle is the most wholesome food for eternal life – that life itself is movement – I have also learnt a most important truth: Even an unsuccessful struggle is an achievement.

Derakht agar moteharrek bodi ze joy be joy,
Na joore arreh kesheedi na jafaye tabar.

If the tree could move hither and thither,
It would not fall victim to the saw and ax.
– Saadi

ACKNOWLEDGEMENTS

I take this space to indulge in personal words of thanks to the many people who have helped in making my dream – this book – come true.

Reminiscing into a lifeless machine day after day can become tedious. Once my ramblings had been transcribed, I soon realised I needed an audience, someone to react to my memories, stimulate me to conjure up my past more clearly. Fate brought Prue Mason to me. With infinite patience, she worked with me for months, put up with my continuous changing, rewriting and revising of the manuscript, until we felt we could do no more. Her mother Pam O'Connor read the manuscript and was very encouraging.

Thanks are also in order to many members of my family who also read the manuscript. My daughter Shirin, son Essa and nephew Sultan encouraged, criticised, discussed and advised with tireless care. My son-in-law Majid made valuable comments. From a distance my children Shahnaz and David have been supportive and helpful, with constant encouragement and interest that helped keep the project alive. My daughter Marie, after going through the manuscript, said: "Mama, now I feel I know you better and have come closer to you." This was all I needed to hear.

My grateful thanks to Jean Smith and her daughter Carol who took time to go through the manuscript in its initial stages. Their generous and encouraging comments gave me hope for the book's future. I am also indebted to Farida Abdullah Qamber for her valuable support.

Thanks are due to my *Ustad* Prof Dr Mohammad Akram Shah of Punjab University, Lahore, whose wise and apt comments opened fresh avenues in my mind. It was he who wrote the couplet reproduced on the cover. Prof Aisha Akhtar, my very dear and close friend of Lahore, who has always inspired me, made useful suggestions.

I am grateful for the inspiration and encouragement of my late brother-in-law Sheikh Abdullah Sharifi whose tragic death shortly before the book's publication saddened us all. He was a walking encyclopaedia, always ready to answer my queries from the depths of his vast knowledge of Arabic and Farsi literature, history, geography and world affairs. A modest man, he was a *Bahre bi Kiran* – an ocean without shore or boundary. He is sorely missed.

Thanks to Uncle Ahmed Bayegan for supplying copies of some old photos and to Dariush Zandi for shooting some of the recent photos; to Malik Omer for his sound and wise advice and valuable guidance; to my dear friends of long standing, Phil Brohi and Barbara Kulesza from London who have shown considerable interest and encouragement.

My young and talented friend Tina Ahmed has been a constant source of support and inspiration; thanks are especially due for her work in creating the cover artwork.

My thanks to all at Motivate Publishing, especially Jan and Ian Fairservice, Roohi Ali Khan, Catherine Demangeot and Chuck Grieve, who some years back as the first person besides my children to see the original manuscript offered encouragement, and now as my editor has finally put the book 'to bed'.

My appreciation and warm thanks to Samia Mango, a noble friend who has asked me sincerely and with keen anticipation: "Aunty, when will we see your book in print?" Samia, here it is; to you and all the friends too numerous to mention who asked me the same question, I hope the wait was worth it.

Last but not least, hugs and love for my little grandchildren whose pranks and laughter are a constant joy, a mirror of my memory and the greatest inspiration of all.

GLOSSARY

abaya — long robe worn over the clothes
abra — ferry
aftaba lagan — large pitcher and basin for washing hands after a meal
"Al hamdu lillah" — "Thank God"
"Allah-o-Akbar" — "God is Great"
Alphonso — types of mango
ami — paternal uncle
angoshtar — ring
ashram — Indian school with religious overtones
Anwar ratol — type of mango
asr — afternoon
attar — an oily perfume
Ayat-e-Quran — Quranic verses
"Az har cheh begzari sokhane Doost khoshtrust" — "There is nothing to replace genuine friendship"

bad-e-Nowrooz — New Year breeze
badela bafi — gold and silver braiding
badgirs — windtowers
bast — closed, to take shelter
batoola — Black mask worn by women of Arab Gulf Region.
bazaris — rich and powerful merchants
behdoona — herbal glue
berkahs — brick-domed traditional water reservoirs
bibi — miss

bilalit — vermicelli sweet dish
biryani — rice dish with meat
bokhnak — child's long bonnet
Bombay berr — a fruit, locally known as *konar*
booms — large traditional wooden boats
bukhoor — aromatic incense

chadernomaz — large one-piece overall covering of women
chadors — womens' outer covering
chash benaki — hide-and-seek
Chausa — type of mango
chelgees — hair styled into forty plaits
cholow kabab — Rice and kebab - a popular Iranian dish.
chombor, morasokh — bangles decorating the wrists
chota baba — "little leader"

daira — tambourine
dalal, setani, morsia, mansoori, mortasha, gardanband. — Necklaces of different length and design placed around a brides neck.
dallak — masseur
darwaza-e-tamadun — threshold of modern civilisation
darzis — tailors
Dasht-e-Mahshar — The Day of Destiny; a din, commotion.
"Dastut soboken" — "Your hand is light"; healing hand.

dervish — æsthete
dhobis — launderers
dholak — drum
dishdasha — Full-length white shirt worn by men of the Gulf region.
doli — a small palaquin
"Domboreeda" — "Monkey with cut tail" - term of ridicule.
doorgoosh — earring
doroshkah — carriage
dozd — thief

Eidis — gifts given by elders on festive days

fajr — dawn
fala — brunch
faqir — spiritually-elevated person
Fateha — Last Rites
"Fiamanallah" — "With God's protection"
fitakh — ring for the large toe
galazangi — legendary ugly black men with horns
ghazals — love poem
gholooms — slaves
ghora gari — horse-drawn cart

Hadayae Nowroozi — New Year gift
Hadis Paighombar — sayings of the Prophet
Hafiz-e-Quran — one who has memorised the entire Quran
haftseen — Seven S's - traditional Iranian New Year table
hajams — local barbers
hakims — local doctors following 'unani' (greek) system
halwa — sweet dish
hammam — public baths
hijamat — cauterization
hijla — bridal-room
howda — A palanquin; ornate Indian wedding dolis.

iblis — the devil
iftar — open fast period

"In ham migozarad" — "This will also pass"
isha — night

"Jahanamot!" — "To hell with you!"
"Jahannam-e-male donya" — "To hell with worldly goods"
janamaz — prayer mat
"Javeed Shah" — "Long live the Shah"
jinns — evil spirits
jollowi va shekhap — Band stretched across a bride's chin and pinned to her cap.
"Joonat bergirand" — "Get your body massaged"; "Your life should be terminated."

kabkabs — bath slippers
kaftans — long flowing dresses
kaling — seashell, anything useless or worthless
"kamal hai" — "it's strange"
kandar — The wooden rod used for joining a bride's many necklaces; a yoke for carrying anything heavy like water tins from Berkahs.
kandooras — day clothes
kaneezes — women slaves
kargah — workshop
kashfe-hijab — New reform in 1930s ordering women to discard the veil.
katchacha-va-mahak — Coined cap with pendant hanging from it designed to sit on the forehead.
"Khair nabenesh" — "May you gain nothing"
khalkhal — gold anklet band
khanjar — dagger
khanom — madam
khattati — calligraphy
"Khoda yak dar banad, sad dar goshayad" — "God closes one door and opens hundreds of others"
khodmooni — same community

"Khomeini Rahbar" — "Khomeini the leader"

khongoy — small sister (term of endearment)

khoone bara — upper house

khoone zeer — lower house

koozas — clay urns

kumduzi — embroidery using a frame

"Lahore Lahore hi hai" — "Lahore is after all Lahore"

Langra — type of mango

lowz — almond (triangular shape)

maghreb — evening

majlis — traditional drawing room for visitors

maktab — school

maleka — queen

mamnoo-el-khorooj — blacklisted, forbidden to leave the country

manhoos — person of ill omen, a curse

manqal — hearth

"Marg bar Mossadeq" — "Death to Mossadeq"

mashata — Woman who does a bride's hair and make-up.

mashk — goatskin bag used for carrying water, milk or yoghurt

Masnavi — couplet poems attributed to Maulana Rumi

matkas, koozas, tashts — pots and pans sometimes used as musical instruments

mawa — Dark paste of sardines, herbs and special spices — spread on bread.

meel, champali — ankle ornaments

memsahib — foreign lady

mokhadas — large cushions

mosanni — courtyard

"Moshk boosh nachit" — "The aroma of incense does not go"; Good reputation sticks.

Moulood-e-Noori — History of the Prophet's life

mubasher — adviser and overall manager of the family

muezzin — man who calls the faithful to prayer

mullah — respected religious man

nihangboon — instrument made out of a goat's stomach, not unlike Scottish bagpipes

nimtas — trousers (in Bustaki dialect)

Nishan — award

noql — round sweets

Nozoole Quran — How the Quran was revealed to the Prophet and its significance.

Olemas — religious scholars

ood — incense

paksazi shodeh — ethnic cleansing

"Pare hatto! Sab pare hatto!" — "Move aside!"; all disperse.

patri and poozi — nose button and round ring attached to the nostril

purdah — drape, screen, covering for women

pushtis — large cushions

qaichuck — Stringed instrument shaped like a sitar but smaller — used in Baluchistan and made locally.

qalam qalyoon — hollow wooden "hubble-bubble" stem

qalyoon — "hubble bubble" water pipe

qawwalis — religious songs from the sub-continent

rah gozars — passerbys, opportunists

rakhtkan — changing room

raml — fortune-telling stones

rangina — sweet dish with dates

sablas — covered platforms, raised above the ground as protection from insects and reptiles

sabzi — green vegetable
salvaar — traditional trouser
samanu — mixture of sugar and malt
samovar — water container and boiler
sandooge surati — ornate dowry chests
sangak — bread
sayyed — direct descendant of the Prophet
seeb — apple
sekeh — coin
serkeh — vinegar
Shahenshah — King of Kings
shalwar-kameez — ensemble of women from the sub-continent
sharshan — gypsy woman
shirini — sweets
Sindri — type of mango
siyahi lashkar — one of the crowd
sofra — table cloth usually spread on the ground
sohour — food taken before dawn during Ramadan
solh — peace
sombol — hyacinth
"Sorot bachenen" — "May your hair be cut": May you be ridiculed and humiliated.

sufis — saints and religious scholars
suras — verses from the Quran
surma — mascara of Mughal origin

taghir hawa — change of climate
tahamada — celebration when a child has completed reading of the Quran
tanoori — common bread
taqooti — oppressor
tee-zulf — ornaments decorating the ends of hair plaits
thobe — dress
tobl — drum

yakol chakol — child's game with pebbles

zaar — a form of exorcism
zar-kharids — to purchase with money, slave
zelzelah — earthquake
Zill-e-Lah — The Shadow of God
zohr — noon
zoorkhooneh — Traditional pit where athletes perform historical feats accompanied by verses from Shahnameh Ferdowsi.